THE GOD APPROACHED

The God Approached

A Commentary on the Poems of
William Empson

By

PHILIP GARDNER
Professor of English,
Memorial University of Newfoundland

AVERIL GARDNER
Associate Professor of English,
Memorial University of Newfoundland

ROWMAN AND LITTLEFIELD
TOTOWA, NEW JERSEY

For our parents
and
for our son

First published in the United States 1978
by Rowman and Littlefield, Totowa, N.J.

Library of Congress Cataloging in Publication Data
Gardner, Philip.
    The God approached.

    Bibliography: p.
    1. Empson, William, 1906 -   —Criticism
and interpretation. I. Gardner, Averil, joint
author. II. Title.
PR6009.M7Z67   821'.9'12   78-1397
ISBN 0-8476-6059-1

Printed in Great Britain

CONTENTS

PREFACE

The commentaries which follow are not intended to abet what F.R. Leavis once called 'the common propensity to arrive without having travelled'. Our teasing-out of difficulties will increase, we hope, the understanding and enjoyment of Empson's poetry, but we offer no substitute for the experience of reading it. Nor indeed could we do such a thing; as our title from 'Doctrinal Point' suggests, much of Empson's poetry – like that of any good poet – eludes analysis and 'explanation'.

The text on which our commentaries are based (and the order in which they are presented) is that of Empson's poems as published in the first British edition of *Collected Poems* (1955). Earlier readings have however been taken into account where this has seemed likely to be illuminating; and the date and place of each poem's first publication have been indicated at the head of the commentary on it. No commentaries have been provided for Empson's four translations, 'The Fool', 'The Shadow', 'The Small Bird to the Big' and 'Chinese Ballad', or for the collaborative masque 'The Birth of Steel'.

We gratefully acknowledge the generous research support furnished by The Canada Council and the Memorial University of Newfoundland, together with the help given by the staff of the Inter-library Loan Division of the Memorial University Library and by the staffs of the Periodicals Room and the Rare Books Room of Cambridge University Library. We are also grateful to the following: Professor Ariyoshi Midzunoe; Mr. M.D. McLeod, Keeper of the Ethnography Department of the British Museum; our colleagues Professor Eric Bullock and Professor Ernest Deutsch, for information on matters of science; Mr. Ian Parsons, for his invaluable recollections of Empson as a poet at Cambridge; Dr. George Rylands, for his constant encouragement; and Mr. Charles C. Empson, for allowing us to visit Yokefleet Hall and for all his kindness on that occasion. Finally, we are grateful to the subject of this study, Professor William Empson, for his benevolent interest in our work.

Philip and Averil Gardner.
St. John's, Newfoundland,
August, 1977.

INTRODUCTION

In 1961, his eminence among literary critics soundly established on three major volumes, William Empson made clear in the fourth his view of his position as a poet: 'Milton certainly has often been a bad influence on minor poets, but speaking as one myself, I do not think that nursemaiding us on such matters does much good'.[1]

To the extent that productivity is a yardstick of stature, one must agree that Empson is a minor poet. The total number of his poems is only sixty-three, of which fifty-six constitute the slim *Collected Poems* which appeared in England in 1955. But even this by no means recent date is misleading. Empson's active poetic career, which began in 1927, virtually ended in 1940, with the publication of his second volume, *The Gathering Storm*: only four published poems and the short and uneven masque 'The Birth of Steel' were written later. Thus Empson's output is not simply small, but mostly derives from the experiences and pressures of a limited, if important, section of his life. And what is particularly striking is that almost half Empson's output belongs to the three academic years, from 1926 to 1929, when he was reading English at Cambridge. Seven of Empson's twenty-eight undergraduate poems were never reprinted; even so, rarely if ever can early work have accounted for so large a part of the reputation of a poet in his seventies.

Minor status may also be inferred from the sales of Empson's various collections, which have never been large. One thousand copies were printed of *Poems* (1935); by 1942 six hundred of these had been sold, at which point the remainder were destroyed in an air raid. *The Gathering Storm* was published in 1940, also in an edition of one thousand copies; nearly four hundred were sold within the first twelve months, but the rest over ten years. An upsurge of interest in Empson's poetry in the nineteen-fifties – prompted partly by John Wain's article 'Ambiguous Gifts' in *Penguin New Writing* (1950), partly by the publication of *The Structure of Complex Words*, partly by the return of Empson himself from China to the Chair of English Literature at Sheffield in 1953 – led to the issue in 1955 of his *Collected Poems*, in an edition of 2370 copies. The sales of this were sufficiently rapid to warrant a new impression in 1956 of 1250 copies; a further printing, of 1100 copies, followed in 1962. Nevertheless, total sales from 1955 to the end of 1975 averaged out at little more than 200 copies a year. One is clearly not dealing with a popular reputation comparable to that of Dylan Thomas, say, or John Betjeman.

But sales tell only part of the story, whether of a poet's stature (popular is not necessarily major) or of his readership. Far more people are likely to have read some Empson poems than have bought collections of them, since there is hardly an anthology of twentieth century verse in which his work does not appear. One may attach diminishing importance to continued appearance, as the choice of poets for inclusion tends to perpetuate itself; but the start of the process may be allowed greater weight, as indicating more reliably the good opinion of the anthologist, whether an established poet, a near-contemporary fellow practitioner, or one's university peers, the latter as likely to be ruthless as to be cliquish. With Empson the process began early, when six of his poems were included in *Cambridge Poetry* (1929) and singled out for high praise by F.R. Leavis, then in his thirties, in the *Cambridge Review*. Five more poems appeared in Michael Roberts's anthology *New Signatures* in 1932, and hardly had Empson achieved his first volume than a poem of his was chosen by W.B. Yeats for *The Oxford Book of Modern Verse* (1936). That same year he was firmly placed among the significant twentieth century poets when six of his poems were chosen, again by Michael Roberts, for *The Faber Book of Modern Verse*, which influenced the tastes of a generation of readers.[2] Roberts's guiding principle in his anthology, none of whose younger poets failed to achieve a lasting reputation, was stated in his Introduction: 'I have included only poems which seem to me to add to the resources of poetry, to be likely to influence the future development of poetry and language'.

Though it is cause for regret that Empson's poetic energy so soon ran down, and that only one new volume followed the publication of these words, they make it easy to understand how the poems he did write have continued to live, and have not faded into the silence that stretches between them and the present. If Empson is a minor poet, he is one of great power, distinction and originality; and despite the difficulties his poems offer to detailed interpretation (difficulties which made John Lehmann, Empson's contemporary at Cambridge, say that 'I looked with a suspicious and unbelieving eye on those of my friends who said they understood them'),[3] the vitality and interest of their manner has convinced many that such an effort would be worthwhile, even though that effort has not often been made. The American poet Richard Eberhart, another Cambridge contemporary, recalled how 'in Cambridge everyone talked about Empson's poetry', but also noted that 'one had the tendency . . . to enjoy single successful lines, savouring them as they were, out of context with their grammatical relation to previous or succeeding lines.'[4]

Such lines, striking and memorable, abound throughout Empson's work; not only the easily detachable refrains of 'Aubade' and 'Missing Dates', but the ominous mutter of 'We do not know what skeleton endures' ('The Ants'); the brisk impudence of 'Thorns burn to a consistent ash, like man' ('This Last Pain'); the sonorous opacity of 'Stars less monogamously deified' ('Letter IV'). Empson's flair for what he has called the 'singing line' (though he is equally successful with the off-hand colloquial) combines with a forward thrust of argument to embody a distinctive voice, whose air of authority and conviction imposes itself on the reader well before the meaning of a whole poem begins to emerge. If anyone's poetry exemplifies Eliot's famous dictum, 'True poetry can communicate before it is understood', Empson's does.

II

Unlike most English poets, including those who, like W.H. Auden, were his poetic counterparts at Oxford, William Empson was born into the landed gentry:[5] into an old Yorkshire family whose earliest recorded members lived at Goole Hall when Andrew Marvell was Member of Parliament for Hull, twenty miles away. At some point in the eighteenth century the Empsons established themselves at Yokefleet Hall, which faces the River Ouse just before the Trent joins it and both become the Humber, and it was here (or rather in the high-gabled ivy-covered Victorian house which replaced it) that William Empson was born, six generations later, on 27 September 1906. He was the youngest of the five children of Arthur Reginald Empson, then aged 53, and his wife Laura; striking and handsome, and celebrated in her son's poem 'To an Old Lady', she was one of the Micklethwaits of Ardsley House, Barnsley, who traced their descent back to 1600. William Empson was not the first poet in the family. His father wrote at least one poem (which is mentioned in the commentary on 'Flighting for Duck'), and his great-grandfather, the Rev. John Empson, known as 'the Hunting Parson', had a redoubtable local reputation as a writer of satirical verse.

Yokefleet feels remote: the village is tiny, without church or shop; at the bottom of the Hall garden, beyond a high bank, the wide Ouse flows slowly past. The still atmosphere, well conveyed in 'Flighting for Duck', is not without charm, but it must have been a lonely place in which to grow up. Empson's nearest sibling was his sister, four years older (he recalls, in *Milton's God*, reading her *Girls' Own Paper*);[6] his nearest brother was eight years his senior, and the other two already in their teens and away at public school. When Empson was seven his eldest brother John, a lieutenant in the Royal Fusiliers who had joined the Royal Flying Corps, was killed in a flying accident in May, 1914, at the age of 23. He was buried in the small churchyard at Blacktoft two miles away; his father sombrely led the funeral procession on foot, and soldiers fired a volley over his grave. Two years later Arthur Empson died, aged 63. In 1919, his second son, also Arthur, who had won the Military Cross and the Belgian Croix de Guerre in the First World War, left the army with the rank of Major and returned to administer the 4,000 acres of arable land that made up the Yokefleet estate. After her husband's death Laura Empson moved to Fulford near York, and in 1920 William Empson left his preparatory school at Folkestone and entered Winchester College as a Scholar, coming tenth on an election roll of 27. (No. 13 was the future Labour politician Richard Crossman.) There he learnt to 'think the traditional God of Christianity very wicked'.[7]

From Autumn 1920 to the end of 1922, no activities by Empson are chronicled in the Winchester school magazine, *The Wykehamist*, and in 1923 only his brief participation in a couple of debates, in one of which he 'demanded a substitute for corporal punishment.'[8] From 1924 onwards he took part in debates more frequently and fully, and continued this characteristic note of ebullient and dissenting open-mindedness: Britain should recognise the Soviet government; industrial disputes should be submitted to compulsory arbitration; education, not a strong British Empire, was the only hope of world peace; no such thing existed as a 'golden age of English Literature'. Empson's most sparkling oration, 'full of brilliant humour and shrewd criticism' though 'delivered too fast', appears to have been made at a debate on the relevance of public schools to 'the best interests of the nation'. In it Empson strongly criticised 'the everlasting spirit of competition', objected to wasting his time on games, 'especially upon cricket, where nothing ever happened',[9] warned against complacency, and hoped that Public Schools would be opened up to the 'lower classes'; there is a nicely ironic touch in his patronising passing reference to 'country gentlemen' as 'a class no doubt delightful but one which the country could no longer afford to support'.

Meanwhile Empson had clearly been working hard. By the end of 1924 he had won the Richardson prize for mathematics and a scholarship in mathematics to Magdalene College, Cambridge. He had also appeared in *Doctor Faustus*, playing the parts of Sloth and 'A Clown' (the latter's scene with Wagner, Faustus's servant, was 'well acted'). In May 1925 he was runner-up (to Richard Crossman) for the Warden and Fellows' English Essay prize; the subject of his essay is not recorded.

What Empson does not appear to have done at Winchester is publish any poems, though he did write some there, which have not survived,[10] and 'was intoxicated by Swinburne'.[11] The orientation of a number of his Cambridge poems, however, may well have been suggested by various lectures which were given at Winchester in 1924 and 1925. An Oxford professor spoke, technically but lucidly, on 'The Size of a Star', making a number of references to the work of Eddington; in a debate two weeks later Empson declared that 'Science had a distinctly ennobling effect in teaching us the greatness of the universe.' A Fellow of the Royal Geographical Society who had explored Tibet as far as the border with Turkestan gave a lecture entitled 'The Roof of the World', and not long afterwards the same general area was described in detail in an illustrated lecture on the 1924 Everest expedition on which Mallory and Irvine died. Perhaps the most distinguished visitor to Winchester was Dr. Julian Huxley, whose lecture on 'The Control of Growth' touched on such topics as the life cycles of animals and the prolongation of life by operations on the ductless glands. But if Empson's germination at Winchester as a poet can only be guessed at, his recorded performance there reveals the lively and wide-ranging mind of his later work, and something of its individual tone of voice. One late remark, made during a close-run debate on the future of the House of Lords, has an amusingly accurate premonitory ring. To a speaker who suggested that Referenda be substituted for an Upper House, Empson replied that he 'could not see why the people should be consulted about abstruse questions which even he could not understand'.

III

Empson went up to Cambridge in October, 1925. With its strong scientific bent (Ernest Rutherford was Director of the Cavendish Laboratory, Sir Arthur Eddington Professor of Astronomy), it was an exceptionally congenial place for an intense, rational and innovative mind like Empson's. Yet it equally encouraged his literary inclinations. At Cambridge the gap between science and 'life', and between science and literature, was not a wide one. I.A. Richards brought the two together in *Science and Poetry* (1926), having already re-examined literature and art, in his *Principles of Literary Criticism* (1924), with a rigour learnt from science and insights drawn from psychology. Conversely, it is worth noting that Eddington's *Space Time and Gravitation* (1920) has an epigraph from *Paradise Lost*, serving to remind the modern reader of Milton's earlier evocations of the size and majesty of the universe.

Empson's career at Cambridge, academically and artistically, was nothing short of brilliant. His first academic year was quiet enough, marked only by his participation in three Union debates ('Mr. Empson is always interesting', commented the *Cambridge Review* in its report on the third);[12] but it ended in Summer, 1926 with his obtaining a First in Part I of the Mathematics Tripos.[13] It is at this point that he appears to have switched to reading for the English Tripos, and from then until 1929, when he obtained the rare distinction of a starred First in Part I,[14] his life was more and more crowded with literary activity of all kinds. What prompted the change of subject is not clear – partly, perhaps, the charismatic lectures of I.A. Richards, who happened to be a Fellow of Empson's college, Magdalene. But distinguished visitors to Cambridge early in 1926 may have had something to do with it: Gertrude Stein, who lectured in her own remarkable style on 'Composition as Explanation', and T.S. Eliot, who gave the Clark Lectures at Trinity College on the Metaphysical Poets. As if to signalise his new affiliation, Empson (who read Aldous Huxley as an undergraduate) spoke first for the 'Noes' in a Union debate (9 Nov. 1926) on the motion 'That this House deplores the prominence given to questions of sex in the post-war novel'. In Empson's view, 'it was ridiculous to suppose that the novelist could omit from his theme one of the primary topics which the public were discussing.'[15] Unfortunately, Empson's 'clever things' were said 'sotto voce', which did not help much with an audience of over 500, attracted by the subject and by the presence as second speaker for the 'Noes' of Compton Mackenzie, author of *Sinister Street*. The motion was lost, but it is an interesting sidelight on the 'Gay Twenties' that 210 people still voted in favour of it. (Gilbert Harding spoke in its support.) Almost a year later, with a smaller audience, things were different: a motion 'That this House sees only degeneration in Modern Literature' was lost by a resounding 185 votes to 54. Empson's contribution was an 'entertaining' speech to the effect that 'modern literature is trying all the time; even if it fails, that is no reason for condemning it.'[16]

By that point Empson had become one of those who were trying, and for more and more of the time. In February, 1927 his play *Three Stories* (now lost) was performed at the A.D.C. Empson was praised for 'experimenting with a complicated technique' and (an amusing sign of the times) his 'almost complete mastery of the Oedipus complex.' The review (*Granta*, 11 Feb. 1927) is worth quoting at some length, since it suggests not simply Empson's lively talent but a characteristic blending of science and ethical concerns in its expression:

> A theme of the rebellion of an idealist young man led from excellent Shavian comedy to plain, honest melodrama, and was framed within romantic scenes in heroic couplets and contrasted with a scientific disquisition fathered on to Dracula. It sounds very complicated, but, if we interpret it rightly, it amounted to something like this: that the ethical problems of life differ from the scientific problems only if one conceives them romantically, and even then, the apparent romanticism achieved, they become scientific again. The last line of the play, in which the hero, having slain his business-like ogre, is compelled to proclaim himself a 'managing young man', we thought a triumph.

In June Empson's earliest published poem, the delightful rhythmic fantasy 'Poem about a Ball in the Nineteenth Century', appeared anonymously in his college magazine, and the new academic year (1927-28) found him as Literary Editor (or 'Skipper', as the post was called) of the undergraduate journal *Granta*, regularly producing reviews of books and films. (The issue of 16 November 1928 contained a parody section entitled 'Pomegranta'; in his unreprinted contribution, 'Laus Melpomines' — a spoof on Swinburne and the *Rubáiyát* — Empson ruefully commented: 'I know the laboured number of their plays./Have counted all their countless matinees'.) Empson also contributed, as author or collaborator, to a continuing saga of humorous pieces, which lasted into 1929, concerning one Montague Slumberbottom, a modern young reprobate; and published in the 'Military Number' (2 Nov. 1928) a pseudo-Blimpish military parody curtly entitled 'Major Gives Men Meat'.

The direction in which the more serious side of Empson's creative mind was moving is suggested by two of his *Granta* reviews late in 1927. One is of E.M. Forster's Clark Lectures, given at Trinity earlier in the year and published as *Aspects of the Novel*. Empson was not greatly pleased, least of all by Forster's aversion from *Ulysses*, and his reaction expressed a decided touch of contempt: 'An attempt, successful or not, to include all possible attitudes, to turn upon a given situation every tool, however irrelevant or disconnected, of the contemporary mind, would be far too strenuous and metaphysical an exertion' for him. (28 Oct. 1927.) The use of 'metaphysical' is telling, and the general idea owes more than a little to I.A. Richards's essay on Eliot, published as Appendix B in the 1926 edition of *Principles of Literary Criticism*. A recollection by M.C. Bradbrook illuminates Empson's approach as typical of 'Cambridge English': 'There was a general feeling that a student ought to have his wits stretched. We tended to prefer the difficult poets — Donne, or Marvell, or Eliot. "Strenuous" was a word of praise.'[17] The other review (4 Nov. 1927) was of a translation of Maeterlinck's *The Life of the White Ant*, and makes its point positively: 'M. Maeterlinck has taken upon himself one of the artist's new, important, and honourable functions, that of digesting the discoveries of the scientist into an emotionally available form.' In moving from the science to the arts side Empson had left none of his scientific interests behind; rather, in the poetry soon to come, he was to employ 'every tool . . . of the contemporary mind.'

1928 was Empson's *annus mirabilis*. Far more of his poems were published in that year than in any other — a total of twenty, fifteen of which ended up in *Collected Poems*. Half, including 'To an Old Lady', 'Invitation to Juno', 'Arachne' and 'Letter II', appeared in the *Cambridge Review* between April and June, during the editorship of Ian Parsons, who had acted in *Three Stories* and been a contemporary of Empson's at Winchester. (Later he became a Director of Chatto & Windus, Empson's publishers.) The poems exhibited great technical skill and a crisp sense of structure, and gave their traditional metres a modern inflection: Shakespeare, Milton and Donne were crossed with entomology, biology and astronomy; on the one hand words like 'superannuate', 'eringo', 'appanage', 'conclave', 'hydroptic'; on the other,

19

'asynchronous', 'differential', 'toxin', 'sector' and 'molecule'.
The voice, though, was a distinct original, more than the sum
of its echoes. Seven weeks after 'To an Old Lady', a poem in
the same stanza form appeared in the *Cambridge Review* (6
June 1928). Written by Empson's colleague Harold Cooper,
Editor of *Granta*, and entitled 'To an Old Man', it was clearly
not parody but the flattering response of imitation. Its performance only emphasises the superiority of the model:

> *Yonder assemble on the peaks of morning*
> *The scorching vanguard of the younger day.*
> *Ask for no treaty, think of no returning,*
> *Shoot, like a falling planet, on your way.*

Other of Empson's 1928 poems (and more in 1929 and 1930)
appeared in a new Cambridge magazine, *Experiment*, whose
first issue was published in November. According to John
Lehmann the magazine represented the 'extreme left' of
Cambridge literary opinion; its attitudes derived from I.A.
Richards's lectures, and its three active editors were Empson
himself, Jacob Bronowski and Hugh Sykes Davies. Empson's
reputation for difficulty was enhanced by publication in it of
such poems as 'Dissatisfaction with Metaphysics', 'Letter I'
and 'Camping Out', the latter particularly Donne-ian in its
progression from a strikingly mundane opening ('And now
she cleans her teeth into the lake') to a splendidly imaginative
climax ('See, where they blur, and die, and are outsoared.').

The atmosphere of *Experiment*, and the power of Empson's
poetry for his contemporaries, has perhaps been best described by Kathleen Raine in her second volume of autobiography;[18] her admiration for such intense intellectuality was
compelled against the grain of a natural romanticism which
the Cambridge of that time seemed to her not to welcome.
Less ambivalently, Julian Trevelyan recalled that 'by far the
most brilliant member of the *Experiment* group was William
Empson whom we all, to some degree, worshipped',[19] and
Richard Eberhart summed up his kind of appeal to Cambridge
readers thus:

> . . . Empson was considered a startling poet by the
> learned . . . His poems challenged the mind, seemed to

defy the understanding; they amused and they enchanted; and even then they afforded a kind of parlor game, whiling away lively hours of puzzlement at many a dinner party. The shock and impact of this new kind of poetry were so considerable that people at that time had no way to measure its contemporary or its timeless value. They were amazed by it.[20]

Unlike contemporary Oxford, where W.H. Auden was *primus inter pares* among Day Lewis, MacNeice, Spender and Betjeman, Cambridge – though it had in *The Venture* a magazine of the literary 'centre' to rival *Experiment*[21] – had no other poet of Empson's calibre. The publication by the Hogarth Press of *Cambridge Poetry, 1929* (Empson's final year) set the seal on his pre-eminence: his group of six poems was the largest, most striking, and most original in the volume. Reviewing it, F.R. Leavis pointed to a fruitful awareness in Empson of Eliot's critical ideas and the poetry of Donne which was in no way 'parasitic' or 'derivative': 'He is an original poet who has studied the right poets (the right ones for him) in the right way. His poems have a tough intellectual content (his interest in ideas and the sciences, and his way of using his erudition, remind us of Donne – safely), and they evince an intense preoccupation with technique.'[22] Singling out 'To an Old Lady', 'Villanelle' and 'Arachne', Leavis concluded that 'Mr. Empson commands respect.'

IV

Clearly enough, Empson's early poetry and reputation owed much to their time and place: the Cambridge of the mid-twenties, excited by the expanding horizons of science, by literary innovation, and by the rediscovery of the Metaphysical poets, whose work seemed to fuse intellect and emotion. The atmosphere of post-Einsteinian physics and astronomy, with its combined pride in human achievement and possibility and humility before the size of the universe and the extent of the unknown, is marvellously captured in Sir James Jeans's *The Universe Around Us* (1929) and Sir Arthur Eddington's *The Nature of the Physical World* (1928). Both books invaluably bring to life for the present-day reader of Empson's poems the world in which his imagination moved freely; as does also a wide-ranging collection of essays on scientific discoveries in fields from astronomy to entomology, entitled *Possible Worlds* (1927), by the Reader in Biochemistry at Cambridge, J.B.S. Haldane. Such a plurality of awareness could not but have reinforced for Empson the contention expressed by T.S. Eliot in his famous essay of 1921 on the Metaphysical poets: '. . . it appears likely that poets in our civilization, as it exists at present, must be *difficult*. Our civilisation comprehends great variety and complexity, and this variety and complexity, playing upon a refined sensibility, must produce various and complex results.' This was the view of poetry pressed on undergraduate Cambridge by Mansfield Forbes, Leavis and Richards, and if science gave many of Empson's early poems their imaginative framework and taste in metaphors, it was this new critical emphasis (one naturally sympathetic to his enquiring mind) which determined the density of their detailed operation. In this connection the opening paragraphs of an essay by Richards on Hopkins, published in the *Cambridge Review* six months before Empson's poems started to appear in force there, may have been especially influential, since by now Richards was Empson's tutor in English:

Modern verse is perhaps more often too lucid than too obscure. It passes through the mind (or the mind passes over it) with too little friction and too swiftly for the development of the response. Poets who can compel slow reading have thus an initial advantage. The effort, the heightened attention, may brace the reader, and that peculiar intellectual thrill which celebrates the step-by-step conquest of understanding may irradiate and awaken other mental activities more essential to poetry. It is a good thing to make the light-footed reader work for what he gets . . . These are arguments for some slight obscurity in its own right. No one would pretend that the obscurity may not be excessive. It may be distracting, for example. But what is a distraction in a first reading may be non-existent in a second. We should be clear (both as readers and writers) whether a given poem is to

INTRODUCTION

be judged at its first reading or at its nth:

Nevertheless, even in Cambridge there were some dissenting voices, unwilling to give a difficult poet the amount of rope implied here. F.L. Lucas, Richards's contemporary at King's, approved neither of him nor of Eliot, and in 1930 published a derisive squib called 'Chorus of Neo-Metaphysical Poets' which contained the lines:

> We twist the riddle of things terrene
> Into such a riddle as never was seen,
> And nobody knows what on earth we mean,
> So nobody contradicts us . . .[24]

Two months earlier Virginia Woolf's nephew Julian Bell, recently a King's undergraduate, had spoken in similar terms (but naming names) in an essay on the state of poetry in Cambridge: 'After Pope's parodies of Cowley, to say nothing of the works of the later metaphysicals themselves, one would have thought that anyone wishing to write in this manner would have exercised a certain discretion. Mr. Empson, on the contrary, is more extravagant than one would have believed possible.'[25] Like Lucas, Bell did not go quite so far as to declare Empson's poetry fraudulent (though he felt obscurity to be an all-purpose camouflage), but he concluded dismissively enough: 'Another use for obscurity, Mr. Empson's, is setting ingenious puzzles for old maids to solve in the *Spectator*.' (This seems to be the first use of the word 'puzzle' in connection with Empson's poetry.)

Whatever the merits of the different views, Empson himself became progressively more uncomfortable about the 'difficulty' of his poetry as he passed from the largely encouraging atmosphere of his Cambridge audience to the wider literary world, dominated by the 'social poets' of Oxford, and from the metaphysical, intellectual concerns of the 'twenties to the darkening social and political problems of the 'thirties, about which they wrote. During the decade he published in national magazines more sporadically than he had in Cambridge ones; at the same time his verbal texture and allusiveness grew less dense (though the extent and consistency of the alteration has been exaggerated) and his subject-matter rather more 'public'. And when his first collection of poems appeared, in

1935, not only were the poems furnished with individual notes (their matey though variable helpfulness counteracting their reminder of Eliot) but these notes were preceded by an apology, of evident sincerity, which ended: '. . . it seems to me that there has been an unfortunate suggestion of writing for a clique about a good deal of recent poetry, and that much of it might be avoided by a mere willingness to explain incidental difficulties.'[26]

Of the reviews of *Poems* (1935), that by Michael Roberts was the most sympathetic, and the most perceptive, pointing out their memorableness of rhythm and language and their ability to express 'the attitude and the sensation of thinking as well as the idea itself.'[27] For Roberts, Empson's difficulties hardly existed, and his attempt to encompass the world of science was both valuable and relatively successful. *Scrutiny*, however, saw little advance in Empson's work beyond what Leavis had praised in 1932 in *New Bearings in English Poetry*, and noted as a 'fault' Empson's 'pleasure in subtlety for its own sake.'[28] George Every's brief review in Eliot's *The Criterion* (Oct. 1935) talked of Empson's 'limited range of material' and, while praising 'This Last Pain' highly, justified Richards's concern about 'doctrinal adhesions' by misunderstanding its drift. And despite the fact that a new poem by Empson appeared in the very same issue, Louis MacNeice expressed a frank dislike of his kind of poetry in *New Verse*; at any rate, his reluctant admiration for the volume's cleverness and 'some nice lines' was outweighed by his sense (unsurprising in an Oxford poet who valued the plain reporting of the 'homme moyen sensuel') of the volume's inappropriateness to the times:

> On the whole I admire his tricks; he is a great hand at words, his syntax arrests, and he can manage the significant pun. What I complain of is that he is merely inhuman. To put it sentimentally, there is not enough blood and sweat in him. Inhuman poetry has its place but today is not its day . . . In poetry we want a spareness and clarity.[29]

Since, despite his later willingness to reduce their difficulties by notes, the poems in Empson's first volume essentially represent his work up to 1930, its publication in 1935 was not ideal. For all the book's absolute merits, times had changed and attitudes had shifted. One reason for the volume's delay may have been Empson's absence from England from 1931 to 1934 – his poem in *New Verse*, 'Travel Note' (later entitled 'Four Legs, Three Legs, Two Legs'), had been prompted by his journey back; but that very absence distanced Empson from the developing events in Europe, including the coming to power of Hitler in 1933, which were preoccupying his contemporaries, just as his later absence from 1937 to 1939 was to remove him from the direct pressures exerted on them by the Spanish Civil War and the German occupation of Czechoslovakia. However Empson's pattern of activities during the decade was for the young writers of the nineteen-fifties a demonstration of his independence and individuality, it only made him out of step with those of his own generation, for all his concern with the 'gathering storm' of world crisis.[30] And even while this concern simplified the surface of some of his mid-thirties poems, his devotion to 'Bacchus', his most complex poem, sustained itself from 1933 to 1939.

Having completed *Seven Types of Ambiguity* (1930) and done a certain amount of reviewing for London journals, Empson was recommended by I.A. Richards (himself at Tsinghua University in Peking during 1929-30) for the post of Professor of English Literature at the Tokyo University of Literature and Science (Bunrika Daigaku), which had fallen vacant due to the return to England, after only one year, of its incumbent Peter Quennell. Empson travelled out via the Trans-Siberian railway in August, 1931, staying for the full contract term of three years and lecturing also at the Tokyo Imperial University where the poets Robert Nichols and Edmund Blunden had taught in the 1920s.[31] In his first term Empson chose to use A.E. Housman's *A Shropshire Lad* for detailed reading with his students. (His enthusiasm for Housman was underlined when he reviewed the posthumous volume, *More Poems*, early in 1937.)[32] Only one poem by Empson, but that the greatly-admired 'Aubade', resulted from his time in Japan, though he also began 'Bacchus' and later published three translations of work by a contemporary Japanese poet, Miss C. Hatakeyama.

Empson returned to England by ship in 1934. Three years later, at the end of summer, 1937, having seen the publication of *Poems, Some Versions of Pastoral*, and half-a-dozen new poems in magazines, he was on his way back to the Far East. This time his destination was China, where he was to be Professor at Peking National University. Travelling through Siberia and Manchuria (occupied since 1931 by the Japanese), he found himself arriving in Peking by Japanese troop train: the Sino-Japanese war had begun, and Peking had fallen at the end of July. Luckily the two Peking universities, Pei-ta and Tsinghua, together with Nankai University in Tientsin, had been able to evacuate in time and to instruct their students, then on summer vacation, to re-assemble at Changsha, 1000 miles to the south-west.[33] Somehow (the bizarre and adventurous story has never been told) Empson managed to catch them up, and spent his first term teaching largely from memory in the mountain village of Nan-Yueh 80 miles further on. At the end of 1937 the combined universities moved on again, to establish themselves at Kunming, at the end of the Burma Road in Yunnan, and at Mengtzu, 100 miles further south-east along the French-owned railway that ran from Hanoi into China. Empson's fascinating description, published in 1940,[34] of his time with the wartime 'National Southwest University', conveys a resilient response to adverse conditions (he returned from a trip to Singapore to find the dining-hall at Kunming bombed) and intense pride in the intellectual calibre of Chinese colleagues who were fully informed about Eddington's recent calculation of 'the exact number of protons in the universe.'

While in China, Empson at last completed 'Bacchus' and in addition wrote four poems prompted by his Chinese experiences. He returned to England in 1939 on 'indefinite wartime leave'. His state of mind at the time was recalled in 1961, with the understatement of retrospect, in *Milton's God*: landing at Los Angeles and finding a hill in a city park, 'I went to the top of it and screamed; this was in 1939, so my feelings need not all be blamed on Los Angeles.' (p.67.) Back in England, Empson joined in 1940 the Monitoring Department of the B.B.C., and in 1941 transferred to the

Far Eastern Section where, in the words of his colleague and friend George Orwell, 'he wore himself out for two years', as Chinese Editor, 'trying to get them to broadcast intelligent stuff to China.'[35] Also in 1941, Empson married. His wife, Hester Henrietta Crouse, a South African, broadcast in Afrikaans at the B.B.C.

Empson's second collection, topically entitled *The Gathering Storm* (Churchill's title copied Empson's, not the other way about), was published in the autumn of 1940. Its poems, like those of the 1935 volume, were accompanied by explanatory notes, but the longish 'Note on Notes' which preceded them was un uneasy mixture of apology and defence: 'No doubt the notes are partly needed through my incompetence in writing; they had better have been worked into the text. I do the best I can. But partly they are meant to be like answers to a crossword puzzle; a sort of puzzle interest is part of the pleasure you are meant to get from the verse, and that I get myself when I go back to it.' A few of the poems in the volume (like 'Ignorance of Death', 'The Beautiful Train' and 'Manchouli') are open and relatively simple; others (like 'Courage Means Running', 'Reflection from Rochester' and 'Autumn on Nan-Yueh) are turned towards the tensions and challenges of the decade. Yet the greater accessibility is often only a matter of appearance, and despite a colloquial and engagingly quirky idiom, the elliptical rapidity of thought creates problems for the reader, different though these problems may be from those set by the dense ambiguities and unfamiliar references of *Poems* (1935). Both the tortuous and multi-layered 'Bacchus' and the frank, chatty 'Autumn on Nan-Yueh' are later poems; but each poem, in its different way, is a virtuoso piece. More recent views that *The Gathering Storm* is a generally easier volume than its predecessor were not anticipated by the *T.L.S.* reviewer of 1940: '. . .although the wrapper of his new book of poems informs us that they reveal a remarkable development towards clarity and simplicity and the expression, at times, of intense feeling, the prevailing impression they still leave is one of intricate obscurity.'[36] And for the reviewer in *Scrutiny*, who seemed unable to respond favourably to any poems by Empson not already given the imprimatur of Leavis in 1929 and

1932, any simplicity attained was merely the 'looser . . . emotionally flabbier rhythms' of 'prattle', and no less essentially obscure for that.[37]

The Gathering Storm contained only 21 poems, ten of which were being published for the first time. In view of the collection's small size, one may feel that its epigraph, from 'Satire V' by Edward Young (an eighteenth-century Wykehamist), was as much a comment on the decreasing frequency of the poetic impulse as on the deepening darkness of the 1930s:

> *Like cats in airpumps, to subsist we strive*
> *On joys too thin to keep the soul alive.*

Between 1940 and 1947, when he returned to his university post in Peking, Empson published only three poems; and from his five years in Peking he brought back only one, his translation 'Chinese Ballad', published in 1952. His last piece, written shortly after he became Professor of English Literature at Sheffield University, was a contribution to a Masque, 'The Birth of Steel', 'a co-operative affair' on an appropriate subject, performed during the visit of Queen Elizabeth II to Sheffield in 1954. In 1955 Empson's *Collected Poems* were published,[38] and they have not been added to.

V

Up to the end of the 'forties, most responses to Empson's poetry took the form of reviews – that is, they were rarely of any great length. All, however, whether more or less short, and whether favourable or otherwise, possess the particular interest and value that attach to the opinions of a poet's contemporaries and seniors: though one may not always agree with them, they indicate something of the live climate that shaped, not only them, but the work to which they respond. Thus, though Louis MacNeice may now sound crass for calling Empson an 'inhuman' poet, the view may be forgiven someone writing in 1935, when Empson's concern for 'Man in the Universe' seemed remote enough from the problems of 'the man in the street', or on the dole. Conversely, if some contemporaries (far from stupid) were dazzled by Empson's complexities, rather than repelled, and if another such (Michael Roberts) could take them in his stride, perhaps more recent critics should hesitate before writing them off, as Ian Hamilton did in 1963, as 'pointless dexterity' and 'sterile naughtiness.'[39]

Since 1950 there have not only been reviews (of *Collected Poems*) but articles on Empson and chapters about his poetry in critical books. With the exception of some essays by old friends in the Festschrift volume *William Empson: The Man and His Work* (1974), this increased quantity represents the response to Empson of poets and critics younger than himself: a larger scope for assessment, and a freshness of post-war reaction, have thus tended on occasion to be distorted by a hazy sense of history and the polemical purposes for which a new generation of poets adapts some of its elders. The former tendency is demonstrated by Ian Hamilton's totally incorrect statement that 'some of the poems in [*The Gathering Storm*] appeared in the anthology *New Signatures*';[40] the latter by the slant of John Wain's otherwise admirable article 'Ambiguous Gifts', published in 1950. This, though helpfully informing potential new readers about Empson's use of science and his affinities with the Metaphysicals, and bravely attempting an exegesis of 'The Teasers', was also a ranging shot aimed at unspecified 'reputations which today occupy the poetic limelight' — presumably the surviving 'Neo-Apocalyptics' (one of whom, G.S. Fraser, has been an equally keen admirer of Empson) and the many disciples of Dylan Thomas, if not Thomas himself (on whose 'A Refusal to Mourn the Death, by Fire, of a Child in London' Empson had published an excellent critique in 1947).[41] Against such 'poets of the 'forties', the 'passion, logic, and formal beauty' of Empson were conscripted by the emerging 'poets of the 'fifties' who wished to displace them: 'If the day ever comes when poems like *This Last Pain, To an Old Lady, Manchouli, Note on Local Flora*, are read and pondered, and their lessons heeded, it will be a sad day for many of our punch-drunk random "romantic" scribblers.' Seven years later, Anthony Thwaite indicated a different characteristic of Empson which he judged attractive to 'the young literary generation . . ., tired of slogans and dogma': his 'moral honesty.'[42]

Between the brackets supplied by these two statements,

an outbreak of 'neo-Empsonianism', best diagnosed by A. Alvarez,[43] raged like a low fever among undergraduate poets in Oxford and Cambridge (particularly the former), and in some of the work of Wain himself. Passion, logic, formal beauty and moral honesty (all of them genuine Empson qualities, some of them sincere aims for their own work of those who admired them in Empson's) seem now to have had less to do with the resulting poems than had a liking for Empson's tone of voice, certain of his stanza forms (especially the tight quatrain and the terza rima), some turns of phrase, and the flavour of individual haunting lines. Yet if poetic reflections of Empson (as, for instance, in Wain's 'Apology for Understatement' and George MacBeth's 'The Echoing Cave') were akin to those thrown back by a fairground distorting mirror, critical response to *Collected Poems* was steadier, stricture and admiration blending into a definite note of respect: large-minded in undergraduate Oxford, where *Departure*, though more in favour of the later poetry than the earlier, nevertheless reprinted the highly-clotted 1929 version of 'Letter IV'; more narrowly-based at Cambridge where, possibly, the influence of Leavis on a new batch of pupils caused the old favourites of 25 years before still to be singled out for praise.[44] Only G.S. Fraser, in *Vision and Rhetoric* (1959), saw Empson whole, calling him 'a consistently good poet'; but it has been unusual, since the publication of *Collected Poems*, to find any critic, however selective his approach, who does not judge Empson to be an important poet. Such a view of him has led, in the 'sixties, to a whole issue of *The Review* devoted to aspects of his life and work (1963), and in the 'seventies to a Festschrift (1974), embracing poems of tribute (including one, mellowly-forgiving, by Auden), biographical reminiscence, appreciation of his criticism, and the longest single essay on Empson's poetry, by Christopher Ricks, whose arguable thesis – that the poetry is deeply involved in the nexus of feelings to do with 'begetting life', and that the achievement by Empson after 1941 of real fatherhood caused its decline – gives rise to a host of separately valuable insights into a larger number of poems than any other critic has tackled.

What Ricks's essay throws into relief, however, is the

comparative lack of exegesis elsewhere. Many who have written provocatively, and shrewdly, on Empson's tone, style and treatment have felt little or no need to talk about his meaning. It may be possible to accept, however regretfully, the plain admission of this by Colin Falck: 'I have not been concerned here with what the poems actually say';[45] but the assertion by A. Alvarez that Empson's 'best early poems . . . are acts of the most subtle critical reverence to the whole concept, style', is rather too precious to be true, coming over, unintentionally no doubt, as a back-handed version of Louis MacNeice's 'inhuman'. Where a critic has tried, as A.E. Rodway did in 1956, to indicate some of his key themes, Empson has been grateful: 'I am glad that Mr. Rodway recognized that my verse sometimes tries to bring out these very sharp contrasts between one and another of our accepted moral beliefs; it is much pleasanter than being thought a Parnassian fribble.'[46] Nevertheless, apart from those discussed by Ricks in the course of his particular investigation, only some half-a-dozen poems have been treated in any detail, and then usually one to each commentator, so that they lie scattered in various magazines spread over the past 25 years. More than thirty poems have never been considered: some quoted perhaps, some dismissed as too difficult, but none analysed. For all Empson's generally agreed importance, there has as yet been no book in English[47] which attempts to examine all his poems; yet, if he is not to risk becoming a special case, a mandarin at whose language, in Aldous Huxley's phrase, 'we bow the head and do not understand', a poet whose general tone hovers above, but is not thought to arise from, the specifics of his poems, it is accurate and comprehensive explication of which his poetry stands particularly in need. G.S. Fraser, in a recent version of Eliot's view about 'true poetry' and communication, applied to Empson's poetry as read aloud a sensible distinction: 'Empson's *broad* semantics in poetry (the planting and repetition of words with a strong emotive charge) enable a listener to stop worrying about the *narrow* semantics, and to be carried on by the authority of the tone and the wonderfully effective . . . rhythms.'[48] But this should not cause the reader of the printed text, also carried and impressed by the 'broad semantics', to ignore the undulations above which he flies and which give his course its contour and direction: in Empson's own words, 'You think the poem is worth the trouble before you choose to go into it carefully, and you know more about it when you have done so.'[49]

VI

Such an assumption – that poetry which impresses also repays investigation – underlies the individual commentaries that follow. The discussion which gave rise to them has brought home to us the aptness to Empson's own work of his general statement that 'the process of getting to understand a poet is that of constructing his poems in one's own mind.'[50] The process is apt because of the kind of poetry Empson's most often is: a poetry of ideas and argument, always interesting, and usually animated by (or experienced as) strong feeling. It is rarely a poetry of natural visual description: the view of man, in the earlier poems, is often microscopic or telescopic, his life seen in terms of the insect world or the 'finite but unbounded' universe; in the later poems he is seen in relation to the moral and political pressures of 'real' life in historical time; but his physical surroundings are not usually taken into account. In 1963 Empson said that 'a visual image is hardly ever essential, I think',[51] and certainly observation of 'Nature' plays little part in his poetry. He describes, usually for non-visual purposes, the man-made – a building under construction, a wooden statuette of a Polynesian god, the Sphinx, the Beautiful Train; but the only natural objects that seize his attention for themselves are the magnolias of 'Doctrinal Point', and even then his admiration is used to emphasise man's difference, however regrettable, from them. Some landscapes, known well, are given varying degrees of notice: the flat alluvial stillness of East Yorkshire, the mysterious semi-woodedness of Cambridgeshire, the paddy fields and red eroded hills of central China. And it is the relinquished beauty of Nan-Yueh which spurs the most lyrical outburst in his poetry – an outburst all the more affecting for its brevity and uniqueness:

We have had the autumn here. But oh
That lovely balcony is lost
Just as the mountains take the snow.

Empson's habit of poetic arguing (which he once called, with typical self-deprecation, 'argufying') is related, by his own account, to his early response to Donne: 'I was imitating him more directly than the others were' and 'I really liked him because he argued'.[51] The element of argument generates much of the excitement in reading an Empson poem; it becomes a voyage of discovery and, as in Donne, it is furthered by verbal wit, ingenuity of comparison, and specialised reference to contemporary science and thought. But saying that Empson is like Donne, as has become a routine critical gesture, is no more or less illuminating than striking a match in a cellar: one gets one's bearings, but the light doesn't last long. Any similarity between them as poets affected by the science of their day (and Empson's science feels more central to his outlook, more engrossing in its own right) is counteracted by their difference as love poets. Empson rarely has the large confidence of Donne ('Camping Out' comes nearest to it), and is more usually indirect and restrained, gaining his power from compression rather than the grand gesture: simply, he has as a love poet a more unhappy and self-doubting temperament. Whatever Empson learned from Donne he soon assimilated. Neither is Milton (though mentioned in 'Description of a View' and quoted in 'Letter III') a distracting phosphorescence playing on the surface of Empson's poetry; it is a matter not of imitation but of affinity, as if in Empson the cosmology of Milton had been re-imagined with the aid of post-Einstein astronomy, and with a divine creator left out. Yet the Christian God, denied as a source of belief, haunts Empson's poetry, a phantom kept warm by recurrent allusion to the Bible and to Christian myths which clearly still retain emotional force.

Despite there being some truth in the view that *Poems* (1935) and *The Gathering Storm* differ in their frames of reference and in the nature and density of their ingredients (these differences being a function of Empson's changing experience and environments), it is more deeply true to say that Empson's poetry is an integral whole. Its underlying unity comes from two factors. One is Empson's rhythm, a characteristically grave yet immensely flexible iambic pentameter which gives his utterance an air both timeless and individual;

the frequent compression of these pentameters within strictly-rhymed three- and four-line stanzas results in a laconic memorableness which is utterly unlike the work of anyone else.

'Alas, how hope for freedom, no bars bind'.
'Too non-Euclidean predicament.'
'Glut me with floods where only the swine can row.'
'It is not human to feel safely placed.'
'Leave what you die for and be safe to die.'

The other unifying factor—also demonstrated in these lines, spaced out between 1928 and 1940—is Empson's pervasive pessimism, variously despairing (with the intense conceptual despair of youth), dryly dignified, angry, existentially open, and stoically courageous. 'I don't deny', Empson said in 1963, 'that the prospects of horror are always fairly large'.[52] Empson's concern in most of his poetry is the predicament of man, as species and as individual, in a universe and world which he must inhabit but which he neither controls nor can fully understand. Such a life 'involves maintaining oneself between contradictions which can't be solved by analysis';[53] yet, as Empson implied in 1937 when stating what was clearly the pressure behind his own poetry, man's intellectual pertinacity drives him to make the attempt: 'The first or only certain reason for writing verse is to clear your own mind and fix your own feelings'.[54] Empson's efforts to do so, whether or not they succeeded as therapy, have produced poetry both invigorating and moving, which reverberates in the memory and is likely to last.

NOTES TO THE INTRODUCTION

1. *Milton's God* (1961). Rev. Edn. (1965), p. 26.

2. Also influential was the new less well-known anthology *The Progress of Poetry*, edited by Ian Parsons. Published earlier in 1936 than Roberts's, it included 'Arachne', 'Legal Fiction', 'To an Old Lady' and 'The World's End'.

3. John Lehmann, *The Whispering Gallery* (Autobiography I), Longmans, Green (1955), p. 151.

4. 'Empson's Poetry', *Accent* (U.S.A.) IV, Summer, 1944. Reprinted in *Accent Anthology* (1946), p. 576. Eberhart's example is the second line ('The mighty handles and persensate dials') of the unreprinted poem 'UFA Nightmare' (*Experiment*, Nov. 1929.)

5. See *Burke's Landed Gentry* (18th Edn., 1972) III, pp. 292-93.

6. *Milton's God* (1965 Edn.), p. 111.

7. *Ibid.,* p. 10. Empson says that 'nearly all my little playmates thought the same', but has pointed out to us that 'little' was meant as a joke. He himself entered Winchester just before his fourteenth birthday.

8. Empson's activities may be traced in issues of *The Wykehamist* from 27 February 1923 to 27 May 1925.

9. Nevertheless, the Marvell Press record of Empson reading his poems (1959) displays a splendid photograph of him, in bearded middle age, running up to bowl with fierce determination.

10. In a letter of 1964 to J.H. Willis (quoted in his unpublished Ph.D. thesis, Columbia, 1967), Empson said: 'I had written some poems before going to Cambridge but feel sure that I destroyed them all.' The notion, voiced in some quarters, that some of Empson's *Cambridge* poems were written while he was at Winchester, thus appears to be erroneous. Nothing of Empson's appears in *The Wykehamist,* though four anonymous and rather sophisticated 'Epigrams', published in the issue for 27 May 1925, are tantalising. In one of them, 'Night', occurs the phrase 'many-fingered' (cf. 'Letter II'), and the jerky, many-comma'd syntax of 'Decoration (?)' adumbrates the author of 'High Dive' and 'Plenum and Vacuum'. However, Ian Parsons, who was contemporary with Empson at Winchester, is sure they are not by him.

11. Empson, Review in *The Criterion* XV, No. 60 (April 1930), p. 520.

12. *Cambridge Review*, 28 May 1926.

13. It should perhaps be added that there were more Firsts than any other Class, and that this was the general situation in Mathematics at that time.

14. This distinction was shared that year by M.C. Bradbrook, who as a woman (women were not then admitted to full membership of the university) was listed separately. Only eight male candidates received (ordinary) Firsts.

15. Report in *Cambridge Review*, 12 Nov. 1926.

16. Debate of 25 Oct. 1927, reported in *Cambridge Review*, 28 Oct. 1927, p. 58.

17. M.C. Bradbrook, in *I.A. Richards: Essays in His Honor* (1973), p. 69.

18. Kathleen Raine, *The Land Unknown* (1976), pp. 40-60.

19. Julian Trevelyan, *Indigo Days* (1957), p. 16.

20. Richard Eberhart, 'Empson's Poetry' (1944), reprinted in *Accent Anthology* (1946), p. 578.

21. *The Venture* brought out its first issue at the same time as that of *Experiment*. Two of its three editors, Michael Redgrave and Robin Fedden, were also at Magdalene. John Lehmann, of Trinity, who 'placed' it in the Cambridge spectrum, was closely concerned with it, as was Julian Bell of King's.

22. *Cambridge Review*, 1 March 1929.

23. *Cambridge Review*, 28 Oct. 1927, p. 49. It is interesting to compare this with Richards's subsequent view of *Poems* (1935) in *Cambridge Review*, 14 Feb. 1936: though 'much the most considerable of the younger poets', Empson had perhaps overdone the compression in some poems, particularly 'High Dive' and 'Sea Voyage'.

24. *Cambridge Review*, 2 May 1930, p. 375.

25. Julian Bell, 'The Progress of Poetry: A Letter to a Contemporary'. *Cambridge Review*, 7 March 1930.

26. Reprinted in *Collected Poems* (1955). Cf. a review by Empson in *The Criterion* XV (April 1936), p. 579: '. . . there have been puzzling borderline cases [of obscurity] in recent poetry; some failures have probably been due to mistaken theory; queer forces have been driving poets into obscurity or into paying a heavy price for clarity; . . .'

27. 'A Metaphysical Poet', *The London Mercury* XXXII, No. 190 (Aug. 1935), pp. 387-89.

28. H.A. Mason, 'William Empson's Verse', *Scrutiny* IV, No. 3 (Dec. 1935), pp. 302-04.

29. 'Mr. Empson as a Poet', *New Verse* No. 16 (Aug.-Sept. 1935), pp. 17-18. The review is signed 'L.M.'

30. It is significant that Empson's name is mentioned only once (p. 64, where his 'ambiguities' are oddly linked with those of Mallarmé) in Francis Scarfe's survey *Auden and After: The Liberation of Poetry 1930-1941* (Routledge, 1942).

31. Full recollections of Empson in Japan were contributed by

Professor Rintaro Fukuhara, his professor at Bunrika, to *William Empson: The Man and His Work* (1974), pp. 21–33.

32. 'Foundations of Despair', *Poetry (Chicago)*, Vol. 49 (Jan. 1937).

33. See *The China Reader, Vol. 2 (Republican China 1911-1949)*, ed. Franz Schurmann and Orville Schell, Random House, 1967, pp. 259-61.

34. 'A Chinese University', *Life and Letters* Vol. 25, No. 34 (June 1940), pp. 239-245.

35. Letter to Alex Comfort, July 1943. *The Collected Essays, Journalism and Letters of George Orwell* (1968), Penguin Edn. (1970) II, p. 348.

36. 'Puzzles in Verse: The Cult of Ambiguity', *T.L.S.* XXXIX (12 Oct. 1940), p. 522.

37. W.H. Mellers, 'Cats in Air-Pumps', *Scrutiny* IX, No. 3 (Dec. 1940), pp. 290-93/300.

38. A *Collected Poems* appeared in America in 1949; previous to this only six poems by Empson had been published there in magazines. Chatto & Windus had been unable to find an American publisher for *Poems* (1935), and the subsequent publication by Faber & Faber of *The Gathering Storm* sprang from Empson's hope that T.S. Eliot's influence in America 'would result in a combined American edition of both books.' (Letter from Ian Parsons to the authors, 6 May 1976.) Other factors must eventually have operated (Empson was greatly esteemed by the 'New Critics' and taught with John Crowe Ransom at Kenyon College, Ohio in his summer vacation from Peking in 1948), since it was Chatto & Windus, his usual publisher, who brought out the 1955 *Collected Poems*.

39. *The Review* (1963). Reprinted as 'William Empson' in Ian Hamilton, *A Poetry Chronicle* (1973), pp. 37-44.

40. *Ibid.*, p. 42. In fact, none of them did.

41. 'How to Read a Modern Poem', *The Strand* (March, 1947.) Reprinted in *Modern Poetry: Essays in Criticism*, ed. John Hollander. O.U.P., 1968, pp. 243-48.

42. Antony Thwaite, *Essays in Contemporary English Poetry* (Tokyo, 1957), p. 151.

43. In *The Shaping Spirit* (1958), Ch. III.

44. See Philip Hobsbaum's review, *Delta* No. 8 (Spring, 1956), pp. 31-37.

45. 'William Empson', *The Review* Nos. 6/7 (June, 1963).

46. Empson, 'Mr. Empson and the Fire Sermon', *Essays in Criticism* Vol. 6, No. 4 (1956).

47. Angelo Morelli's *La Poesia di William Empson* (154 pages) was published in Sicily in 1959. This is an attempt to translate, paraphrase and explain most of Empson's poems; the attempt deserves

respect, but though Morelli is equal to many of Empson's references, he is not always able to grasp their point, and some poems (such as 'High Dive', 'Part of Mandevil's Travels' and 'Autumn on Nan-Yueh') defeat him entirely.

48. G.S. Fraser, 'The Man Within the Name', *William Empson: The Man and His Work*, p. 63.

49. Preface to *Seven Types of Ambiguity* (2nd Edn., 1947).

50. *Seven Types of Ambiguity*, 3rd. Edn. (1952), p. 62.

51. 'Argufying in Poetry', *The Listener*, 22 Aug. 1963, p. 277.

52. 'William Empson in Conversation with Christopher Ricks'. *The Review* Nos. 6/7 (1963).

53. Note to 'Bacchus', *Collected Poems* (1955), pp. 104-105.

54. Empson, 'A London Letter', *Poetry (Chicago)*, Vol. 49 (Jan. 1937), pp. 218-22.

THE ANTS

First published, as 'Sonnet', in *Cambridge Review*, Vol. 49 (27 April 1928), p. 369.

This poem has none of the obvious surface difficulty of much early Empson — recondite vocabulary and allusions, complex syntax, a knotty rhythmic texture. Some lines ('How small a chink lets in how dire a foe', 'Winter will come and all her leaves will go') combine with instant memorableness — and thus an air of significance — the intellectual feel, however slight, given by antithesis and the 'singing' quality Empson has always prized.

Nevertheless, the apparent simplicity is highly deceptive. The basic *ant* situation, on which Empson felt it necessary to provide a note when the poem first appeared, is this: ants take from plant lice (aphids/greenfly) a sweet liquid which the latter produce as part of their own process of feeding on the juices of plants and converting them into protein. The domesticating relationship involved, a sort of parasitism at one remove, is described by W.M. Wheeler (*Social Life among the Insects*, 1923, p. 178): 'Many species of ants have learned how to induce the Phytophthora to void the honey-dew by stroking them with the antennae, to protect and care for them and even to keep them in specially constructed shelters or barns'. The literal framework of the poem is thus, clearly enough, a relationship between ants, aphids, and plants (tree and garden, in the terms of the poem). The reader's first difficulty lies in accepting this as the real subject of a poem, and indeed Empson's rapid dovetailing of the ants' tunnel or 'tube' with the imagery of the London underground seems to rule out the possibility here. 'Ants' soon take on a familiar metaphorical overtone, and we see busy office workers leading their harried subterranean lives, in artificially-circulated air and surrounded by advertisement hoardings: 'nostrum' as remedy suggests a life not altogether happy, but the life is also 'ours'.

This parallel between two ways of life, of ants and man, emerges fairly quickly. It is rather more difficult, however, to identify in human terms the two other elements in the three-fold relationship. The problem crops up in the very first line: who or what is the 'you' to whom the ants are tunnelling, to whom the poem is addressed, and to whom the aphids ('your aphids') belong? And where is the action of the poem taking place? These ants, the note tells us, 'build mud galleries into trees'; one presumes, then, that their 'station' (line 9) is just inside a tree trunk or branch, and is arrived at by tunnelling up and along. Similarly, though not exactly (since man's 'tapping' activities, of business or pleasure, are hardly carried on in tube stations), man tunnels to the city which provides his life. The crucial point is that though both ants and man tunnel 'out', they do not quite break through: the first eight lines convey movement towards something (the 'you' of line 1) and a parasitic activity which 'your branch must bear', which reads almost as 'put up with'; but the last six lines bring in a very different feeling, fear perhaps, but at least a prudent drawing back. From the 'view' available in line 8 there is a quick turning away in the gesture of denial in line 9: 'No, by too much this station the air nears'. But what is it that is being denied?

Empson's record-note to this poem calls it 'a love poem with the author afraid of the woman'. Christopher Ricks ('Empson's Poetry', p. 183) follows this up by making woman the 'you' who is addressed – it is thus she, on this reading, who is the 'branch' (and there are certainly two obvious senses in which she 'must bear' man); it is also possible to see her as both giving man his view of 'the garden' and as letting in 'how dire a foe' (since Eve was tempted by Satan and so brought on the Fall). Given all this, flight from her as something dangerous and challenging, as well as life-giving, might be likely. It would be unwise to ignore Empson's comment, but one notices that he does not say where the woman fits, and Ricks's equation of her with the 'you' of the poem leaves one still, in his own words, 'unhelpfully perplexed'. If ants are man and 'you' (the branch which bears him) is woman, who then are the aphids?

The references to 'the garden' and to 'a foe', so close together, suggest that the poem may most comprehensively be read as a sort of tailpiece to *Paradise Lost*, as a comment on the fallen human condition. The noonday 'through' which (that is, under which as well as during which) man tunnels, belongs to a perfection he can no longer reach or feel suited to; nevertheless he moves towards it, as the ant towards the surface of the tree, only to recoil at what he sees through his 'chink'. 'In one glance' suggests that his view, however comprehensive, is a hasty one, and is accompanied by a sense of mortality, the garden's, now, as well as his own. On this reading, the 'you' of the poem can be the Tree of Life (which provides his dew, but only indirectly), but also the Garden of Eden seen from it; ultimately, the 'you' of the poem is God, seen as having to suffer the 'all-but freedom' of disappointingly fallen man.

As a fallen creature man leads, most of the time, a suitably subterranean existence: 'the sweat of thy face' (*Genesis* iii, 19) is suggested by the images of tube travel, and it is to this limited but safer world that the tree's 'parasites' seem to return at the end of the poem. 'Carry . . . below' is presumably man's murmured injunction to himself, and it emphasises the contrast between the in-turned, gloomy meditations of the sestet and the more arrogant stance of the octave, as shown particularly in the line 'You may not wish their sucking or our care'. It is from his 'care' for these aphids (themselves parasitic on the juices of the tree) that man derives at secondhand the sweetness that he needs in the 'narrow darkness' of his life, and surely, on the poem's human level, it is women who are the aphids? The view of woman as benefactor (and thus powerful as well as pampered) is sufficiently established for Empson not to need to specify the mysterious sources of nourishment she makes available. It was Eve who passed on the deliciousness of the apple, as well as it penalty of exile. Perhaps it is in this sense that 'The Ants' is a love poem: man is grateful to woman for her solace in a shrunken world in which her original error placed him.

VALUE IS IN ACTIVITY

First published, as 'Inhabitants', in *Cambridge Review*, Vol. 49 (6 June 1928), p. 492

The present title embodies an allusion to Aristotle's *Nicomachean Ethics*, a quotation from which stood explicitly (insofar as its appearance in Greek allowed) as epigraph to the poem as originally published: 'τὸ ἀνθρώπινον ἀγαθὸν ψυχῆς ἐνέργεια γίνεται κατ' ἀρετήν'. That is, broadly speaking: a good man's function is to act well and rightly; such actions 'in conformity with virtue' are supposed to bring happiness. Empson's poem proves on examination to be a rather ironic gloss on this, and his present title represents at best a stoical acceptance of life's meaninglessness.

A month before the poem appeared, Empson had seen and reviewed Charlie Chaplin's film 'The Circus', and it is tempting to suppose that this furnished his initial image, especially in view of the atmosphere of its last scene: 'the end of this film, where he stands in the middle of the tarred circle, like a fairy ring, from which the circus, overnight so insistent, has evaporated, picks up the paper star of the hoop the heroine jumps through, and throws that away, surely strikes as clear a poetic note as Mr. Chaplin can ever have intended'. (*Cambridge Review*, 4 May 1928.) It is however a characteristically sardonic, rather than poignant, edge which Empson brings to his picture of the divine/human/insect circus.

The method of 'The Ants' (essentially narrative, but no more scrutable for that) is replaced here by a sequence of illustrative and richly resonant images. The open and ambiguous syntax of stanza one allows a large number of permutations, all meaningful and interrelated. The initial, splendidly Miltonic, 'celestial sphere' is, as object, the apple which the juggler (man) tosses; it is also, by apposition, the circus (earth) in which he performs his act; and the central phrase, 'An acid green canvas hollow', is all-purpose, since 'acid green' fits apple and earth, and 'canvas hollow' fits circus. In that the apple is a 'celestial' sphere it suggests the apple of knowledge, and its 'central smuggler' is the penalty of banishment from Eden lurking within if it is eaten. But as earth is itself a 'celestial sphere' (into which Satan smuggled himself to seduce Man), its juggler is God, whose artistry is exhibited in his creation. The total picture which emerges shows God tossing the earth in the heavens, earth's rotation tossing the juggler in his circus, and the juggler tossing his apple through the air: a scene of activity, with man at the midpoint functioning with athletic and artistic skill: the juggler's admirable ability to keep his apples flying in their planetary circle is aptly matched by Empson's own virtuosity with syntax.

Yet, for all his clever balancing (of his apples, on the surface of life), the juggler does not explore deeper, does not bite the apple of knowledge. Line 4 suggests (taking 'heeds' as both 'knows' and 'cares') that this ignorance may be bliss, though surely a juggler must eat and cannot keep juggling indefinitely; but the second stanza offers four other possibilities inside the apple. One may summarise these as (1) rottenness, (2) sterility, (3) something being eaten or about to be, and (4) fruitfulness (the original version reads 'close ripe pips'). Only the fourth, and that only vaguely, gives any incentive to discovery, though the image of 'caverns' suggests warmth for the 'mites' and, perhaps, in human terms, the sheltered if hollow comforts of cathedral interiors for insignificant man. On the whole, though, the likely rewards of knowledge are poor, and the unusual form 'raven', with its overtones of greed, war, and the 'rats that ravin down their proper bane' of *Measure for Measure*, provides a particularly strong deterrent.

On the evidence presented here, one assumes that the juggler (precarious man, perhaps man as artist) chooses not to eat his 'apple'. Empson completes his poem with a grim stanza describing the very different lives of lesser inhabitants of earth's 'celestial sphere': 'some beetles' who seem to do nothing but eat. These beetles, who burrow into felled trees and cultivate edible fungus gardens in them, are described by Wheeler (*Social Life among the Insects*, pp. 38-39), but one suspects that Empson may also have in mind termites, who not only cultivate fungi (Wheeler, p.270) but eat wood, and books, the final undigested residue of which, as excrement, 'can be used for nest-building'. (Haldane, *Possible Worlds*, p.66). Here, whoever's it is, the voracious demand for food (which, in human terms, may be knowledge in the form of books, since 'knowingly' smacks of self-conceit, and the 'halls' sound like libraries) outruns supply, until the insects' breathed out carbon dioxide can no longer be converted into oxygen by the depleted fungi and their suffocation (and/or starvation) results. (The exception to this rule – what, in the beetle world, survives winter and what, in the human world, in a sense survives death – is the pregnant females, but the exception is made dismissively, in brackets, and with a striking rancour: 'tupped' is the voice of Iago, and 'worming out', natural in insects, suggest low cowardice and treachery in the human race.)

What the poem seems to come down to is that there is nothing to choose, in a life nipped off by death, between eating and not eating, between the exploration of knowledge and the enjoyable juggling with surfaces. Nevertheless the ironic title is serious: man's two 'activities' (those, perhaps, of poet and scholar) are not equally purposeless but equally purposeful: their value lies precisely in their activity, since man must do something. Such an attitude, a courageous pessimism, is basic to Empson, and he stated it with particular relevance to this poem in a review of 1935: '. . . whether or not the values open to us are measurable, we cannot measure them, and it is of much value merely to stand up between the forces to which we are exposed'. (Review of John Laird, *An Enquiry into Moral Notions*, *Spectator*, 29 November 1935, p. 912.)

INVITATION TO JUNO

First published, with five stanzas, in *Cambridge Review*, Vol. 49 (4 May 1928), p. 387.

The stanzas originally placed after the present stanzas two and three, respectively, were inferior to the three retained, which make up one of Empson's most delightful and light-hearted poems; but they did make it quite clear what kind of poem it is – not a speculation on the possibilities of modern science as such (though Empson is interested in these), but a neo-metaphysical seduction poem. The goddess Juno, humbly and obliquely requested to try again the conclusions of a divine/human mating, is also a human girl who may perhaps be perplexed into bed by the wit and learning of her suitor. Subtleties of vocabulary, tone and rhythm, and the vocal mimicry of the two made-up quotations, are played with great skill against the apparent heaviness of literary and scientific reference, so that the teasing out of this yields only part of the poem's effect. The datum (itself a myth) of the poem is the attempt made by Ixion to mate with Juno (Hera) and produce a demigod: this was frustrated by Zeus' jealous sub-stitution of a cloud shape for the real goddess. The child of this unfortunate affair (for which Ixion was nevertheless bound to his fiery 'single wheel') later sired the centaurs; so instead of demigods Ixion's experiment produced demi-men. (Graves, *The Greek Myths* I, 1960 edn., pp. 208-10.) Lucretius, the rationalist, 'could not credit' centaurs (*De Rerum Natura* V, 878-98), for the sensible enough reason that the life cycles of man and horse would be out of phase. One surely agrees with him, intellectually; but Empson's use of 'could not' (suggesting limited imagination), of 'deemed' and 'superannuated' (donnish condescension), and his choice for most of the stanza of curt, 'no-nonsense' octosyllabics, all seem meant to pressure one's feelings against agreement.

Stanza Two moves from the ancient 'bi-cycle' to another would-be mixture, the real but primitive bicycle. According to Empson's note, Johnson spoke of this 'somewhere in Boswell'. Since John Fuller (who otherwise writes well about this poem) has asserted that 'no one as far as I know has found [the reference], so he is no doubt thinking of the flying machine in *Rasselas*', it is worth placing Johnson's view and (in this instance) Empson's reliability on record in full. On October 26th, 1769, "Mr. Ferguson, the self-taught philosopher, told him of a new-invented machine which went without horses: a man who sat on it turned a handle, which worked a spring that drove it forward. 'Then, Sir, (said Johnson) what is gained is, the man has his choice whether he will move himself alone, or himself and the machine too' ".

(*Boswell's Life of Johnson*, ed. G.B. Hill, rev. L.F. Powell, Clarendon Press, 1934, Vol. II, p. 99.) Empson's 'quotation' is clearly a précis of this, in magisterial Johnsonian pentameters which also (in the stress of 'Johnson could see') mock that ex-cathedra 'plain sensible manliness' of his. For indeed, although many early bicycles 'had to be propelled by pushing the feet against the ground' (*Encyclopaedia Britannica* III, 1966, p. 594), this one, however laborious and open to Johnson's sarcasm, seems to have deserved a little admiration. Nevertheless, no disagreement with Johnson here changes a bicycle into a demigod, however modern bicycles may refute his scepticism. Empson's illustrative references are witty conceits, not stages in sober argument. Certainly the line '*Gennets for germans* sprang not from Othello', denying as it does Iago's coarse taunt to Brabantio (Act I, Sc. I, 114), would hardly be cause, if taken seriously, for other than relief.

Yet science has now improved on less satisfactory earlier mixtures, and in stanza three offers the suitor examples he may turn to better account: his 'Courage' may be a rallying of the girl but is more likely a whispered exhortation to himself to persevere. Alexis Carrel's attempts to prolong life, (Haldane, pp. 151-2) and his transplant experiments with heart-muscle tissue, prompt some hope that two 'periodicities' (loosely, life cycles; strictly, elements differently placed in the periodic table) may combine. Equally hopeful are the crossing experiments of Darwin (*Origin of Species*, Ch. IV), which brought together 'annual and perennial plants, deciduous and evergreen trees, plants inhabiting different stations and fitted for extremely different climates'. One notes the Petrarchan subordination of would-be lover ('annual' and mortal) to wished-for mistress ('Perennial' and divine); but the last line, with its sexual suggestions of grafting and its strongly physical 'upon', is a reminder of the human situation, of what all this display of learning is *for*. It is, nevertheless, rather strange, in view of the poet's desired fusion of himself and his girl-goddess, that there is not a single perfect pair of rhymes in his poem.

THE WORLD'S END

First published, as 'Relativity', with an extra stanza and slightly different wording, in *Cambridge Review*, Vol. 49 (11 May 1928), p. 406.

Einstein formulated his Special Theory of Relativity in 1905 and his General Theory in 1915. During Empson's time at Cambridge Einstein's great follower and clarifier, Arthur Eddington, was Plumian Professor of Astronomy, and it is his description of space as 'finite but unbounded' that lies behind this and many other early Empson poems. The implications of Einstein were also stated, thus, by J.B.S. Haldane in *Possible Worlds* (1927), which Empson reviewed in *Granta* (27 January 1928): '. . . the extended theory of relativity seems to lead inevitably to the view that the universe is finite, and that progress in any direction would ultimately lead one back to the starting-point.' (p. 4.) In his prefatory note to *Collected Poems* (1955), Empson refers mellowly to such theories of space as 'the sane old views we were brought up upon', but 'The World's End' suggests a more dubious and pessimistic outlook: the human urge for freedom or escape, always hard to fulfil, is rendered quite futile if your world view offers nowhere on the other side of the fence to run to. Of course, such pessimism involves hyperbole (one could not, in 1928, get into space anyway, so it hardly matters physically what it is like), but the rather grand quatrains and the generalising references to Satan and Tantalus help the reader to take it on that level.

The original opening, 'Fly to the world's end, dear', called up lovers attempting to escape authority (parental or social), and on that reading 'variance' may have been meant, amusingly, as lovers' quarrels as well as non-conformity. Wisely, one feels, Empson changed this and produced a stanza capable of broader application: the mention of Milton's Satan in line 8, together with the inverted commas, strongly suggests a version of his address to the fallen angels in *Paradise Lost* I (Empson's note quotes lines 314-15); to this the 'topless cliff' adds a touch of Marlowe's Faustus. The lofty speech thus epitomises the human 'outward urge' (search for freedom, rebellion, even – as with Tantalus – trespass on divine property), and sets the tone which the rest of the poem mostly keeps to.

But in a modern world without limits or edges ('bars'), how can freedom (defined by its opposite) exist? Just as a round earth brings you back to your starting-point, so does a curved universe: 'padded' (not prison) 'cell' conveys a maddening predicament, for all its comfort of 'cushioned air' (curved like its container) and foetal snugness. In such a situation the 'metal' of your exploring plumb-line, and the mettle of your resolve to escape, prove useless, curving round and up again to 'bump you behind'. The mischievous overtone here of 'bumps your behind', and the possibility that 'lead' also means 'the man in front of you', offer a wry deflating humour amid the slightly operatic anguish. The punning of line 8 suggests the difference between present and past: Satan's words discomposed (but inspirited) his followers ('the whole of Hell'), but any rebel now is shaking, not the bars of a prison, but emptiness. Lines 11-12 put the matter geometrically, with 'rounded' earth standing presumably for space. The concept of a 'tangent plain', complicated by a pun on 'plane' and replacing the idea of a line by that of a two-dimensional surface, is not easy to grasp, but what is meant is perhaps this: since tangents can be drawn to touch a curve at any point, no single point on the curve can be designated the 'top'; thus any or none may be. Is this, perhaps, a space equivalent of trying to keep one's balance on a rotating ball? The 'point' reference is simpler: any point, in any direction, is the 'end' of this relative world, and any act of 'pointing' likewise.

Thus man is left, in the last stanza, with nowhere to go: 'the world's end' (spatial and temporal) 'is here'. The final image fuses Tantalus, punished for his challenge to the gods by being hung from a bough between inaccessible fruit and inaccessible water, with Adam, similarly unable either truly to enjoy his 'apple of knowledge' (Newton's, too, which led to Einstein) or to drink oblivion. Both gifts recede from him 'differentially' – in different directions, and keeping the same distance from him whatever movement he makes. But his 'shadow' (the literal one, and his fallen nature, and perhaps the shadow which, in Eliot's 'The Hollow Men', falls between desire and fulfilment) will not leave him, and the poem's grave ending shows man as an open prisoner in the curved universe his science has discovered.

PLENUM AND VACUUM

First published in *Poems* (1935).

This is a vexing poem; the two scientific 'illustrations' sound so cut-and-dried, the conclusion so convinced not only of its own rightness but of its logical connection with the 'evidence', yet the total effect is baffling. One may admire the texture: the fastidious elegance of the first stanza, the appropriate clottedness of the second, the self-assurance – as of the practised illusionist – of the last; but this is only partial compensation. Not that much cannot be explained. Indeed, perhaps the problem is that too much can: the poem abounds in ambiguities, but no single reading will either stand the weight of them all or impose itself with enough certainty to exclude some as irrelevant.

The 'plenum' of the title is a medium entirely filled with matter; the more familiar 'vacuum' is entirely empty of it. Evidently the poem is to be about opposite states, but the first problem is to identify the way these are shown by the two examples (since one assumes that is what they are), and which is which. Stanza one offers the familiar myth that scorpions, when surrounded by fire, commit suicide by stinging themselves. Whether Darwin (whom Empson refers to in his note) verified this we have not been able to trace; but Dr. Johnson, told the story by Boswell, was firmly of the opinion that they did not (*Life of Johnson* II, pp. 54-5) and J.H. Fabre, who did do the experiment, confirmed Johnson's view that the scorpion's apparent stinging of itself was an involuntary convulsion followed by a trance-like inertia; death, if it ensued, resulted from the already-convinced observer's failure to remove the surrounding fire. (*The Glow-Worm and other Beetles*, trans. 1919, pp. 401-08.) It seems clear, however, from Empson's note that he is not concerned with the truth or otherwise of the story, and the overtones of his language ('goose-step', 'patrols', 'weal') suggest that it is used as a convenient if inaccurate metaphor for (some) human behaviour. Empson's use of 'postpones' carries weight: the real emphasis is on the preceding narrowness of life, as man executes his ritualistic and often deadly movements ('goose-step' at this date may suggest Prussian rather than Nazi militarism) within the narrow circle ('wheel') of fire which Empson sees as his environment ('weal'). The scorpions' glass bell-jar (not used by Fabre but perhaps by Darwin), itself created by the effects of heat, represents the imprisoning bubble of man's physical world, blown in the fires of cosmic creation. Is this, then, the 'plenum': a world packed with men, seen (inevitably?) as scorpions, from which there is no escape except self-cancellation? But bell-jars also suggest vacuum experiments; obviously such a life is vacuous enough. And within this larger meaning there is perhaps another one: 'penned', taken with 'goose-step' (particularly when 'delicate'), makes one wonder whether the scorpions can be writers, exploring their literary territory under 'vaults' of various kinds: the sky, the awareness of death, the library, the hothouse world of undergraduate Cambridge.

The sense of strain, of incipient hysteria, communicated by stanza one provides a slight bridge of feeling into the otherwise very different microcosm of stanza two, which capitalises on Darwin's investigations into human facial expressions. The theory here is that the adult habit of involuntary frowning is a legacy of childhood when, in order to protect the eyeballs from bursting during a screaming fit, the orbicular and other muscles round the eyes contracted. (See *The Expression of the Emotions in Man and Animals*, 1896 edn., p. 192). Empson's point, as made in his note, is that such reflex activity in adults no longer relates to anything; unlike the bell-jar situation of stanza one, which contains something (the world of scorpions), the 'frowns' of stanza two are 'void-centred' and thus contain the 'vacuum' of the title.

Even if one were able to accept this schematisation, the resultant significance would be obscure enough, but in fact the ambiguities of lines 11 and 12 make Empson's note less than adequate. The reflex reactions are called 'stays' (which can mean either reliable 'defences' or painful 'corsets'), and their effect is such that 'no relief ensanguines' the eyes: that is (and the ambiguities come to the same thing), 'no relief makes the eyes hopeful', or 'the lack of relief leaves the eyes bloodshot'. Surely this suggests not an irrelevant protection but an inadequate one? And the further effect of these so-called 'void-centred' frowns is to 'burst wrinkled hold-alls', surely a violent reaction? Violent perhaps, but not clear: a hold-all might burst when full, so perhaps a paradox is intended here: this one bursts when empty, as in the school experiment of making a container collapse by pumping the air out of it. This could mean that a no longer needed gesture defeats itself; but the frowns, which produce wrinkled skin, are themselves in some sense the 'hold-alls': that is, the frowning reflex, even if prompted by nothing, has a bad effect on the skin which frowns, and leaves permanent creases in it. One seems little nearer a solution, but perhaps the words 'stays' and 'sphincter' give hints of what is behind the obscurities. 'Corsets' were the control devices of an earlier age, hiding the true human form and hurting the wearer: in *Milton's God* (p. 111) Empson reports his early horrified reaction to the painful practice of 'tight-lacing' by girls. 'Sphincter' suggests most of all the *sphincter ani* muscles, thus anal retention and concomitant retarded attitudes to sex: in such a context colloquial possibilities in the phrases 'wrinkled hold-alls' and 'guard their balls' suddenly make themselves felt. Can it be that the real impulse behind stanza two is a hostility to repression, which may be viewed as equally harmful whether it represses something or nothing?

The 'glass-cautered bubble' and the 'ringed orbiculars' may differ in their contents, but as well as acting as containers they are boundaries, and the last stanza, playing with the relationship between space and matter, seems to shift its attention to the idea of limits, edges and the effect the presence of these has on human life. Without Empson's note about relativity theory the first line would be very obscure, little more than a crossword-puzzle clue: the thing which matter punningly 'includes' is space, but space also 'encloses' matter. The instruction that 'the line is not meant to be read as anapaests' (or dactyls?) places the emphasis squarely on the word 'must', giving the reading 'Matter includes the space which also encloses ('contains') it'. Empson states that the inclusion is only 'logical', not spatial (i.e. 'matter has space as one of its constituents'), but reference to Eddington suggests that the inclusion is spatial as well, and perhaps gives another clue to the feeling of the poem: 'The revelation by modern physics [Rutherford in 1911] of the void within the atom is more disturbing than the revelation by astronomy of the immense void of interstellar space'. (*The Nature of the Physical World,* Everyman Edn., 1935, p. 13). Putting Empson and Eddington together gives a picture of space surrounding a thin rim of matter which itself surrounds further space; but this is complicated by line two. Empson's note suggests that the 'air-holes' are universes, bubbles embedded in a medium of solid glass (vacuums within a plenum); but 'air-holes' are surely more usually vents, breathing 'spaces'. The physics here is difficult to grasp (the clever sound similarity of the opposed '*inc*ludes' and '*enc*lose' obscures rather than assists); but the effect is of something being turned this way and that, inside-out and outside-in: plenum and vacuum seem interchangeable and equally meaningless terms in a modern view of the universe. (See Eddington, *Space Time and Gravitation,* p. 164).

Such sharp human application as there may be in all this emerges, if at all, in the last two lines. If space is a property ('consequent') of matter, then 'Heaven's but an attribute of her seven rainbows' ('seven' presumably because there are seven colours in a rainbow's spectrum, which seems rather affected): Heaven, the carrot of a repressed age, is an illusion, and only the visible arch in the sky exists, either a 'ringed orbicular' serving no purpose, or a glass bell surrounding men who patrol in circles. Hell, likewise, is non-existent; it is the fear of actual death, symbolised by the river Styx, which governs and represses his life. The force of the concept represented by Styx is made clearer by reference to F.M. Cornford, whose book *From Religion to Philosophy* Empson knew well: Styx is a barrier, 'a representation of Taboo', 'the "shuddering chill", the awful horror which is the negative, forbidding aspect of Power'. (p. 25). It is also, more crudely, the stick (sticks) with which man is beaten in a restricted and repressed life, lived according to reflexes, rituals and taboos still powerful but no longer meaningful in the world of modern physics where the concepts of space and matter (religion and logical positivism?) have become problematical. Unfortunately, the poem itself does not so much embody a fully-articulated meaning of this kind as act, through its separate parts, as an irritant, a spur to the reader to construct one; and this can hardly be judged success in poetic terms.

ROLLING THE LAWN

First published in *Cambridge Review,* Vol. 49 (4 May 1928), p. 388.

Published in the same issue of *Cambridge Review* as 'Invitation to Juno', this poem is similarly light-hearted. It assumes that human activity is without purpose, but accepts the fact with gay stoicism — grimness would ill suit the homely metaphor and the office-worker persona it employs. The ingenuity of its puns, together with its cheeky enlargement of scope at the end, convey an admirable feeling of human resilience in the face of 'flat despair'; and its technical insouciance (the head of a Miltonic sonnet joined to a tail of three Augustan couplets) reinforces this.

The first phrase, 'You can't beat English lawns'. is breezily colloquial ('you can't get better lawns than these. and. unlike the carpets they so resemble, you have to roll them'). but its further meaning ('they can't be defeated') leads nicely into the quotation from Belial's speech in *Paradise Lost* (II, 142-3). This daringly casual incorporation allows Empson simultaneously to deflate Miltonic grandeur (since 'flat' is what he hopes to make the lawn, at least temporarily) and to suggest the larger implications of his chosen metaphor: man (who should not therefore give up) has nothing to hope for. Calling the garden roller a 'Holy Roller' enables him to laugh at 'the English fetish' (the cleanliness of your lawn is next to

Godliness) and also bring in what was at the time probably a 'with-it' reference to the enthusiastic American revivalist sect. The phrase 'at the slope' (pushing the roller up the slope of the lawn) doubles as a sly dig at army drill, or at least order and neatness (akin to the office-worker's 'uniform' of bowler hat and rolled umbrella), which is renewed at the end when God (as inspecting general or public-school master) 'calls the roll'. The octave concludes with a comically religious image, as the poet kneels to pull up the daisies which deface his lawn's smoothness, before going to his daily 'office' of business.

Perhaps pulling up daises reminds him of 'pushing up the daisies', since the second section introduces throughts of mortality and how to avoid it. Line 9 rejects the usefulness of rolling 'the abdominal wall' — a recommended route, as his note indicates, to health in the 'twenties. The rejection, however, has only the most specious of reasons, turning as it does on two puns: the abdominal 'wall' is yoked by violence to the wall of Troy which 'Lead, since a plumb-line ordered, could destroy'. If indeed the walls of Troy were demolished by Greek cannonballs, it was hardly because a lead plumb-line helped in their building. From this he returns to his own remedy: healthy exercise constantly repeated, keeping down the burrowing moles (mining like Greek besiegers) and postponing ('ne'er' can clearly not be taken seriously) the day when he will lie, if not beneath the mole's 'tumuli', then under a graveyard version of them. 'Brawn', indicating a healthy body, may imply the 'mens sana' supposed to go with it; but perhaps it suggests instead 'brawn not brains', and thus, beneath the poem's good-humoured surface, the limited possibilities for man in a life without ultimate meaning.

The last couplet, with mock grandeur, treats the earth as though its rotation of itself (and of the lawns on it) were comparable to man's laborious routines. These routines themselves (presented by the soul to God as its credentials of a life well spent, or spent in the only way allowed) are compared to the gridirons, another form of metal, on which his martyrs suffered. Such an image brings in the idea of life as torture, but fairly lightly; equally present in it is any office-clerk's humorous resentment of his weekday chore, and perhaps also, if he is married, his wife's martyrdom to the kitchen stove (another kind of 'gridiron').

Like 'Value is in Activity', but in the very different spirit of 'grin and bear it', this poem praises effort for its own sake; technically this may be felt in the exuberant pointlessness of the sound repetitions within lines ('despair/therefore/ere'; 'holding the Holy Roller at the slope'; 'grub/grope'; 'roll/no mole'; 'tumuli/tomb'; 'World, roll yourself; and bear your roller, soul'). Empson's typically English mocking of English rituals is balanced, with equally English doggedness, by his acceptance and practice of them. The intellectual, however wryly, rolls up his shirtsleeves.

DISSATISFACTION WITH METAPHYSICS

First published, as 'Disillusion with Metaphysics', in *Experiment*, No. 1. (Nov. 1928), p. 48.

Unlike the earlier 'The World's End', which found the curved universe frustratingly restrictive, this poem seems to take some comfort from it: the concepts of the new physics, once accepted, provide a welcome alternative to the endless speculations of philosophy or the empty rituals of religion. Empson's note to 'Four Legs, Three Legs, Two Legs' quotes the description of a metaphysician as 'a blind man looking for a black cat in the dark which isn't there'; a year before the present poem he had reviewed the first five numbers of *The Monthly Criterion* (Vol. VI) in similar terms, that imprudently foretell its pragmatic 'disillusion': 'Mr. Eliot seems often to be saying that something, if he knew what it was, would be very important if it existed' (*Granta,* 11 November 1927, p. 104).

The basic contrast presented is between the Infinite, the immeasurable stock-in-trade of religion, mysticism and metaphysical thought, and the finite, the measurable world of physical science. Two images are used for the Infinite: in the first stanza the circle, radiating further and further outwards; in the second the line, stretching on for ever. In Islamic belief, bodies do not go to heaven; that of Mahomet, however, being too special for earthly burial, is believed to hover permanently somewhere above Mecca, and is thus the 'centre of the universe' for Mohammedans. Using the fact that the earth's elliptical orbit has two foci, one the sun, Empson satirises their belief by fancifully placing 'Allah's prophet's corpse' in the position of the other, so that the earth revolves around both. But by comparison with the warm and real sun, Mahomet is an 'empty focus', in that Empson does not believe in his divinity ('Allah's prophet's corpse' suggests he is at two removes from it), and in that he is cold because dead ('focus' in Latin means 'hearth', and Mahomet has left his real earthly life behind.) Nevertheless, none of this presents problems to religious belief; although Mahomet's wives (nine of them) are 'undone' (deserted, desolate, with their garments rent in Oriental fashion, and no longer made love to), concentric circles of devotion, getting further and further from his death in historical time, and ranged further and further from Mecca, widen out from him presumably to infinity. The word 'epicycle' is especially rich. To begin with, it has two astronomical meanings: one the geocentric path of a planet (so that Mahomet, in Ptolemaic fashion, is the earth around which his devotees revolve), the other a small circle which has its centre on the circumference of another (so that the devotees seem cogs in the large machine of religious observance; they also 'round him run' like servants ministering to his divine whims.) But, its technical meanings aside, the very sound of 'epicycle' calls up a host of echoes which enormously extend the range of Empson's incredulity: 'epicene' followers, profiting from the bereavement of his 'undone' wives; 'disciples', 'apostles', 'episcopal' (one hardly believes that only Mohammedans are being mocked); even 'epic cycles', the proliferation of holy writ, Koran or Bible, around the life and teachings of the dead Messiah. It is a splendidly close-knit stanza; even the incongruous rhyming of 'corpse' with 'universe' contributes its touch of irony.

The second stanza is also full of meaning, but less unified and so less satisfying. The object seems to be to debunk the very concept of Infinity by showing it as a pointless succession of the same things. The first line can be paraphrased simply as 'two mirrors with all the time in the world (infinity) to dine'; but the mirrors are also pictured as dining with a personified Infinity, and drinking much more than he does; they are also, in a sense, drinking *him*, so that he disappears. The idea seems to be that two mirrors, set face to face, create their own infinity of recessive reflections and thus, mere physical objects, outdo any metaphysical infinity imaginable. From this Empson passes to another illustration (surely non-metaphysical also) of the infinite line by means of Adam and Eve, who have given birth to an endless progeny all in their own image, like a simple mathematical series whose unexciting 1, 2, 3 progression is indicated by the 'dotted line' of 'and so on. . .' Incest comes in because we are all, ultimately, children of the same parents and so can only marry our siblings; such 'inbreeding' leads to insanity and 'dotted line' takes on the meaning of dotty heredity. The last line of the stanza collects the ideas of 'reflection' inherent in mirror-images and idiot repetition inherent in human reproduction in order to mock the metaphysical disease of 'all philosophers': the infinite coupling and re-coupling of (in the words of the note) 'a few fixed ideas'.

Empson's conclusion is to praise modern physics for bringing together, in effect, the best of both earlier attitudes, (circles and lines): the 'straight lines' of the present are 'safe' because they do not lead to futile infinity but are 'finite'. Their finity is what Empson emphasises; yet they are also 'unbounded', since curved, and their curvature, calculable by the laws of relativity, provides a known frame of reference preferable to the meaningless ever-increasing epicycles of metaphysics. Such a conclusion, however wittily enforced, is essentially a preference: Empson ranks himself with the 'new men' of the twentieth century, epicyclical to Einstein. The final lines (particularly the sudden appearance of Prospero) are more obscure, but perhaps indicate reservations. Prospero at the end of *The Tempest* drowned his book of magic (metaphysical enquiry?) 'deeper than e'er plummet sounded', an imaginary infinity; but deeper than this were the waters of the Deluge (a real event as well as a Biblical story) which 'flooded the plain' – the prehistoric world but also, perhaps, the 'plain series' of Adam and Eve's progeny up till then. That event, says Empson emphatically, was the true location of infinity; 'then corpses flew', and only then (not in Islamic fancy), borne high on the destroying waters of the flood. It is as if Empson wishes to put infinity 'in its proper place', localised in history or in a myth firmly set in the past, rather than in the speculations of the contemporary mind. Having once upset the natural order, God 'promised Noah not to flood again', not to intervene in his creation. The possible undertone here of God as a child who has long ago repented his 'naughtiness' may allow man to feel safely in control of his new, post-diluvian, post-Einsteinian universe from which infinity has been excluded; yet the last line sounds ominously flat, and promises may be broken. Perhaps the asseverated 'thens' protest a shade too much, and modern scientific man is himself presented with a tinge of irony.

POEM ABOUT A BALL IN THE NINETEENTH CENTURY

First published in *Magdalene College Magazine* VIII (June, 1927), p. 111. Reprinted in *Experiment* No. 7 (Spring, 1931), p. 59.

Empson's earliest printed poem, published anonymously in his college magazine, may disregard 'meaning' (as his note points out); but its handling of rhythm and sound-recurrence (the one extremely varied, the other taxingly limited) suggests the atmosphere and swirling movement of a Victorian formal dance with self-sufficient virtuosity. The poem is by his own admission an imitation of Gertrude Stein, whose Cambridge lecture of 1926, 'Composition as Explanation', was published later that year by The Hogarth Press; it seems likely, however, that the actual influence on Empson's rhythms came from one of its companion pieces, 'Preciosilla'. There are also touches of Hopkins's 'The Leaden Echo and the Golden Echo', and the poem's opening phrase, 'Feather,

feather', is what the sheep says to Alice in *Through the Looking Glass* (Ch. V) when she is trying to row a boat with knitting needles.

When the poem first appeared, there were no wide spaces between the last seven sentences, though they were, as now, printed on separate lines, not in a block like the long passage ending 'peacock a very peacock to be there'. The provision of spaces is a distinct improvement, not only giving the eye a rest but emphasising a real difference in feeling and pace. The large block of words (set out like a prose poem and visually an equivalent of the large crowded ballroom) conveys the rapid movements of the dance, here expansive and graceful, there slightly jarring as bodies ('well surrounded') bump into each other; and as the dance proceeds there are suggested fragments of overheard conversation ('I declare'), wisps of interior monologue (the punning 'will he become'), glances over the shoulder ('turning for dancing'), the excitement and danger of covert sexual awareness ('beware'), and, as Empson's oddly moralistic note indicates, the various kinds of vanity that keep the social circles revolving ('feathers for fair', 'peacock', 'to have become preferred').

The next four 'lines' (two rapid sets of four phrases, inter-locked by rhyme and rhythm, commented on by two tight-lipped sets of three single words) suggest a gradual slowing down: perhaps two people sitting out a dance, perhaps a snub or lovers' tiff. ('Reproof, recovered, solitaire', the latter word conveying apartness and/or retirement to the card-room, almost suggests in little a chapter of Jane Austen.) And the last three lines, with their lovely resolution on to a fading iambic pentameter, have an air of nostalgia, as if someone who attended the ball were turning over her memories: such a one, perhaps, as the Victorian mother whose 'cooling planet' Empson pays tribute to in 'To an Old Lady'.

There are certainly (words being what they are) elements of story in the poem: one may imagine the ball as a coming-out dance, with its attendant love-interest and its wedding prospects (phrases like 'to make one the pair', or 'for asking of all there' with its flavour of marriage-banns). Balls such as this also cost money and imply affluence and social cachet: one notes this further possibility in 'well surrounded', as well as in 'bearer share' and even 'preferred' (not just position or affection but stock). Yet such possibilities must be seen as arbitrary when the poem's non-logical use of syntax is taken into account: any 'story' (and each reader may see a different one) remains only a matter of tantalising 'hints and guesses', thrown up inevitably, but incidentally, by a verbal texture packed with rhythmical repetitions, alliterations and internal rhymes, whose essential concerns are impressionist and musical.

SEA VOYAGE

First published, without the last line, in *Cambridge Review,* Vol. 50 (16 Nov. 1928), p. 131.

There is some disparity between Empson's interesting note to this poem and what the poem itself, essentially ingenious and cerebral, manages to communicate with any force. The note suggests a wish to control, limit, and to some extent interpret the many possibilities of the poem's language, but in practice this is too elaborate to be so contained. Some of the glosses seem arbitrary, and the lack of focus in the poem tends to reduce it to a number of clever things said about the sea and man's connection with it.

The first sentence of Empson's note states that the 'cat's cradle' is an image for the sea's constant movement, but its 1955 version, employing a hyphen and a comma, is less enlightening than the original one in *Poems* (1935), which needs to be resurrected: 'The first and third verses are supposed to describe the sea — cat's claws and cat's cradles are foam tumbling and sliding back'. In the poem, however, the many suggestions of the first line complicate this visual image, and it seems from Empson's very first note, in *Cambridge Review,* that nothing so simple was intended: '(Verses 1 and 2: a new idea, at first elaborate and exciting in itself, should become with practice a simple unit, an indivisible tool. Verse 3: it should hold itself ready to be re-analysed)'.

Thus the poem, though based on an image of the sea, seems to have been originally meant to deal also with mental exploration, with the fascination of ideas (constantly shifting like a cat's cradle) and with how we use them. The original note implies that 'freezing' refers to the fixing of an idea into a usable 'simple unit' (i.e. such fixing is a good thing); but the phrase 'grave its filigrees' (with the 'indivisible tool' of a diamond) suggests not only engraving a pattern permanently but also killing (burying) it. Perhaps the second part of the original note ('it should hold itself ready to be re-analysed') provides a link between these two readings: one notes the apparently casual and parenthetical phrase 'Forbad be crystal' in stanza three, with its suggestion that a fixed form (in contrast with the 'crisp', but moving, 'silver foam' of the sea) is to be avoided. 'Crystal' also suggests clarity, so perhaps the very uncertainty of concepts (even the obscurity of much of this poem) is being recommended. Any idea that the present poem is about human thinking (with the sea as its metaphor) cannot be pressed very far, but some awareness of these earlier notes is necessary, since it reveals a divided, or altered, aim and thus explains some of the fuzziness of the final poem.

The cat's cradle image, of lines of cotton constantly changing their shapes between the fingers that manipulate them, conveys the sea's movement ('fleeting' because transitory, but also carrying fleets of ships and so introducing the idea of exploration dealt with in stanza two), but it is also seen as a conversation ('re-plyed' means 'doubled up' or 'folded', but also 'replied'; and 'extorted', literally 'twisted out', can be used of a reply). The conversation is also a kind of music, an ever-altering ('oft transposed') 'tune from plucked cotton' (reminiscent, because of the 'Deep South' connotations of cotton-picking, of Nigger Minstrels, or Negro Spirituals), which accompanies the 'dance' of the waves. These ambiguities (already too many to hold in the mind at once) culminate in the conceit of an 'abandoned kitten' (originally, and excruciatingly, it was a 'disownered' one), which is 'fostered' in the 'cat's cradle'. (The precise identity of the 'kitten' is unclear, as is that of the 'fingers' which have abandoned it; but as 'abandoned' also means 'wicked' perhaps the kitten is man, or at least his basic ingredients, thrown by God into the primeval sea to sink or swim.) The stanza ends with a further conceit: the sea's movement (seen as a 'flickering of wit', like the stanza itself) is imagined as freezing into a permanent design, equivalent to the knot that would result if the cat's cradle were pulled tight. Just before the lines meet in a knot they form a diamond shape: this is fancifully transformed into a diamond with which engraving can be done, but the connection between 'grave' and the earlier 'cradle' suggests a movement from life to death, from flux to final permanence, as well as the gradual emergence of animate forms (amoeba, fish, mammal, man) from the sea. Complicated (rather than complex) as all this is, it can be analysed; but many of the ambiguities seem merely frivolous, and the 'knot-diamond' collocation belongs with the story of the man who, having escaped from gaol, shouted till he was hoarse then jumped on the horse and rode away.

If the first stanza presents the sea, the second presents man. The cat's cradle which fosters and shapes ('dures') him gives place (via 'filigrees') to a cognate image from lace-making, which employs thin bobbins stuck into a curved (convex) 'pillow', across which the openwork lace is built up. The resemblance involved here, one feels, is to the earth as a globe, also convex, with the gulfs of sea covering much of it. Man is 'crucified' to this in that his life is a voyage of physical, mental, and (taking the hint of Empson's note) spiritual exploration: 'pillowed' on 'gulfs' (convex sea and concave depths) is appropriately paradoxical, and the 'exiguous bobbins' are presumably the fixed limits of birth and death and the thin thread of his fate. Man is both 'Son of Man' (like Ezekiel) and the 'Son of Spiders', in that he, like his human parents, hangs on a thread, spins webs of various kinds (like lace), and travels far and wide, though precariously. The crucifixion image is intended to suggest man 'in the tortures of his spirituality' (like Christ on the cross) generating energy (perhaps by sublimation?) which causes him to discover 'a better place': the image of holding out a red rag to make a bull charge is blurred into the idea of 'dobbins' (rather unseriously suggesting sea horses, horse power, and mechanical inventiveness) and that of a sail set to catch the propelling wind. Yet it is not Heaven which is the 'better place'; man remains 'earth-bound'. His explorations, mental or real, the 'trapeze' on which he swings like a circus performer, all take place on earth, which is moving not towards God (as Empson's note adds – the intention would not emerge otherwise) but towards the constellation of Hercules. (This astronomical belief of the time also figures in Leopold Bloom's meditations in the penultimate section of *Ulysses*, 1922).

The running over of stanza two into stanza three isolates and emphasises the phrase 'Earth-bound', as if Empson were at some pains to deny that man's 'voyage' could ever lead to spiritual rewards. The immediately following phrase 'Blue-sea-bound' seems to indicate a similar restriction on the foam whose movement was described in stanza one, but the connection is not clear, and the verse-movement suggests merely an abrupt return to the poem's opening subject. The idea of the lace-like sea as an aphrodisiac (eringo, its correct pronunciation ignored as cavalierly as 'amalgam' in 'Bacchus', is the candied root of sea-holly, used as this) is easy to accept, since we think of it as, among other things, beckoning and seductive. But the next image of the sea restraining its full strength under a silk-smooth surface, like a girl (another 'abandoned kitten') trying on her 'seven petticoats' (a kind of rainbow) and acting the vamp only in her bedroom, is harder to follow. The concept is a curious one, and that of the sea's being given the devil's task of making ropes out of sand (as George Herbert sees himself doing in 'The Collar'), and thus containing itself within the boundaries of its shores, seems little less arbitrary.

Somewhat tenuously, out of this odd context, the final lines emerge to make their individually valid points. As sand is used to make glass, seashores can by conceit be seen as a full goblet holding all the elements ('concentrate' like soup mix) from which the human line has derived, man himself being in large part water. It is thus appropriate that he should salute his origins in a liquid 'toast' (as the line read in 1935); but the present concluding line (1949) is far denser. The toast is drunk 'in port' – the haven of humanity which evolution has reached, from which its slow ascent through its 'degrees' (levels or ranks) can be summed up or seen as a whole (the banquet itself has gone through the degrees of soup, fish and meat); the 'port' is any harbour (like those of line 11) at which man the voyager arrives and celebrates his journey through the 'degrees' of latitude and longitude; and what is drunk is port, as if at a college banquet (of 'degrees' or academics) which has reached the stage of mellow retrospection. The late change from 'toast' to the more all-inclusive 'port' was perhaps prompted by a wish to use in his own work an ambiguity Empson had discussed in 1930 in *Seven Types of Ambiguity* (pp. 108–09), the one Pope had patented in *The Dunciad*: 'Where Bentley late tempestuous wont to sport/In troubled waters, but now sleeps in port'. Empson's new line is a worthy successor to Pope's couplet but a less satisfactory conclusion to his own poem, whose thoughts are neither clearly articulated nor emotionally persuasive. The product of a maturer and more disciplined Empson, it stands out, in its functional wit, against a general cleverness which on this occasion may be called, in a pejorative sense, 'undergraduate'.

HIGH DIVE

First published in *Poems* (1935).

On the face of it, this poem is one of Empson's most difficult: it bristles with off-putting technical terms ('irrotational', 'potential function', 'co-ordinates', 'phusis'); its syntax, particularly in lines 15–26, is convoluted and demanding; its cross-references and ambiguities are bewilderingly dense; and many of its phrases, those in brackets especially, have the blank-wall air of clues in *The Times* crossword. However, unlike 'Sea Voyage', it rewards the reader's application with a definite quasi-narrative into which most of the details fit. Its rhythmic vitality and variation reflects the changing directions and tensions of its theme, which is presented not as the general human condition but as a particular and momentous situation with an individual at its centre.

In conversation with Christopher Ricks, Empson described his early poems as being 'about the young man feeling frightened, frightened of women, frightened of jobs, frightened of everything, not knowing what he could possibly do'. That last phrase gives an ordinary meaning to the term 'potential function', and 'High Dive' is a poem concerned with the conflict between contemplation and action, the need to choose action, and the likely results of that choice. The poem's date is uncertain, but is probably 1928 or 1929: the 'enclosed bathing-pool' could be Cambridge (in whose literary life Empson certainly made a splash), the 'termite city' might be London, or at any rate the life of work and jobs into which the undergraduate must eventually move. Whatever the precise context, the bathing pool image is an admirable one, both sharply realistic and widely metaphorical, standing for one's peer-group, society at large, even (as in Empson's note) the universe. Its combination of broad range and personal immediacy and urgency makes 'High Dive', its difficulties notwithstanding, one of Empson's most important early poems.

Structurally it divides into three sections: stanzas one to three, stanzas four to seven, stanzas eight and nine: contemplation, the pressures to action, disenchanted comment on action. The poet stands on the diving board in an 'enclosed bathing pool' (line 18 implies it is partly open to the air), conscious of the noises and wave-motion ('greenish hollow undulation') made by those swimming. The disturbance they make is 'irrotational', since waves move in lines not circles; thus, viewed mathematically, one simple 'potential function' will 'give the rule' — express the movement of the water and in that sense control it. In lay terms, the scene is peaceful, able to be seen 'steadily and whole' by the non-participating observer. But even at this early stage the idea of pressure (a note that will become more insistent as the poem proceeds) is introduced in brackets: the swimmer's 'cry' and the sound of the word 'hollow' call up in the watcher's mind the 'Halloo' of the fox-hunt and the baying of hounds in pursuit. Nevertheless, contemplation dominates: the poet 'holds it' (waits, and preserves his potentiality), feeling like God whose 'spirit. . .moved upon the face of the waters' (*Genesis* i, 2);

65

'brood' also suggests a hen, hatching its future as it sits (cf. *Paradise Lost*, I, 21). As the observer is Godlike, the pool ('tank') is seen as an 'infinite', 'triple' like the Trinity and because it can be described by the three 'co-ordinates' of length, breadth and depth. The poet 'need not dive' into this watery infinite because as God, who *is* his creation, he already 'informs' it; as human, he does so at least potentially (*in posse*). The idea here may anticipate Empson's reference to Wittgenstein in 'This Last Pain', since Wittgenstein says that 'A thought contains the possibility of the situation of which it is the thought' (*Tractatus Logico-Philosophicus*, 1922 trans., proposition 3.02). At this stage, contemplation includes action (*in esse*) and thus makes it unnecessary; yet the proximity of the 'cry of hounds' cannot fail to bring to mind the 'Wild West' meaning of 'posse'.

Further images for the all-embracing 'potential function' are added in stanzas two and three. The poet becomes Phoebus the classical sun god, who (as 'chauffeur') heats the 'girdered sky' (the roof of the bathing pool as well as the over-arching heavens); the first two letters of his name also make the Greek Φ, the symbol for the potential function in calculus, here 'infinite-reined' (with a pun on 'reign') because of the large team of horses he drives. The poet is also Aton the Egyptian sun god, who is depicted as a solar disc emitting in all directions rays which terminate in human hands: the 'steeds' he drives here are the wavy reflections ('maggots') of the overhead girders. But Empson relates these watery horses to the water which (as tempest and whale) successfully pursued Jonah as he fled from God (*Jonah* i & ii); and the explanation of eclipses in Norse mythology, that the sun (the Norse Phoebus) was chased and eaten by wolves, is also referred to. Thus, by the end of stanza three, any comfortable feeling that one may remain with God-like power on the diving board, perfectly poised between inaction (keeping the moment) and action (murdering it), is increasingly under pressure.

The conflicting impulses of the next four stanzas lead the poet to his eventual 'dive'. One impulse comes from outside: the swimmers, now seen as hare-hunters in green coats (the water), have caught up with him and 'tear him down' (a phrase horribly emphasised by stanza eight). The welter of adjectives and the choppy rhythm of line 13 suggests, in any case, that the movements of the water are no longer controllable by the aloof (but only human) observer, and the phrase 'by gulf or rocks' may mean that it has overflowed its 'handy' container. But another impulse comes from inside: an attraction towards what society seems to offer. 'Rut' means the roaring of the sea (cf. Eliot's 'rote' in *East Coker*), but also sexual lust; 'crashing' and 'shocking' may imply pain and danger, but also, particularly when juxtaposed to 'gay' (the gay twenties) and 'musical', suggest parties (gate-crashing, loose morals). All this is summed up in the tension between 'Menacing' and 'Assuring'; one may be frightened of society (the upper-classes 'baying for broken glass' in Evelyn Waugh's *Decline and Fall* in 1928), but one is human and belonging 'assures' (insures, re-assures) the individual. From this sense of group-identity comes the image of the pool (a 'tin reverberant town "Thicker than water" agglutinate', in Empson's mimicking agglutinative phrase) as filled with blood, in F.M. Cornford's sense of the life-blood which unites primitive tribal society: 'By virtue of this descent [from one 'totem-ancestor'] they are of one blood; and we may conceive the blood as a continuous medium running through the whole group, as it were the material substrate of its solidarity'. (*From Religion to Philosophy*, 1912, p. 57).

The fifth stanza, dealing with this idea, is obscure in its details, but the drift seems clear: one may fear action, but one may also fear one is missing something, and if one does not act quickly to join a group it may disappear or close up (the full pool may empty or freeze over, the sticky blood, "thicker than water", finally clot). There is a further, and decisive, fear: that isolation and fixity may lead to neurosis. 'The Ark' colloquially represents antediluvian attitudes, and such 'Ark neuroses' are exemplified in doves, imagined staying indoors vacuously cooing to themselves, neither forced out, nor tempted out by the promise of the olive branch. (But 'forewarned' is double-edged, as if to anticipate the poem's conclusion.)

Such neurotic 'contemplation' may be avoided by taking action, which seems to promise something, if not everything.

Stanzas six and seven show the diver 'in act', moving as if in slow motion (the slowness both portentous and indicating unfamiliarity) into the diving position, conscious only of physical, not mental, strain: the rather artificial phrase 'the rein cone now handed' is a kind of diagram in which the cone shape formed by Phoebus' spread-out reins assumes the hands of Aton and narrows into the diver's extended arms.

Both syntax and idea are difficult at this point of the poem. The decision to dive seems to involve perceiving a distinction between one's 'shade' (two-dimensional fragmented reflection?) and one's 'image' (graven image like a god's? three-dimensional reflection?): but it is not clear whether the discerning of a 'shade' is a true perception (perhaps contrasted with Narcissus devotedly contemplating his image in the water – cf. lines 29/31 of 'Bacchus') or merely simple-minded – action is easier for the less imaginative. The main sentence in stanzas six and seven is almost hidden by the jungle syntax, but appears to be: 'Unless one unchart/chooses /leaves/dives' (though the transition from subjunctive to indicative is odd – perhaps a need to rhyme with 'phusis'?). 'Unchart the second' is obscure (in the manner of Dylan Thomas rather than Empson), but the word 'obstetric', taken by itself, suggests the dive as a form of rebirth (water including the motifs of amniotic fluid and of baptism). 'Isle equation' may be a twisted allusion to Donne's 'No man is an island', or, conceivably (since this gets a little nearer to the 'not frozen ford'), to the small off-shore island from which, in *Kidnapped,* David Balfour escapes at low tide. Escape from isolation is the main point, but one suspects the 'equation' is a verbal trick, the two lines of its 'equals' sign (=) linking island and mainland.

The final image of stanza seven shows the diver eluding his pursuers, the hounds of stanza one, by plunging under 'foamed new phusis' to become reborn. 'Phusis' (or 'physis', linked with modern 'physics') is a wide-ranging term dealt with by Cornford in *From Religion to Philosophy*: basically it means (in primitive societies) 'the nature of things', the 'material continuum' (p.x.) in which they all exist; early Greek philosophers defined it variously, as air, or as water (p. 7). It is also the life-blood of the tribe to which the diver now belongs; as Cornford also points out: 'Rites of initiation are regularly regarded as new births' (p. 95). But there are ominous undercurrents here. Concerned to escape his own fears and to avoid his pursuers, the diver by taking action becomes in effect one of them, and thus loses his identity; though it is possible to suppose that he 'receives reward' in his own 'memory' (congratulating himself on his decision and courage), it seems as likely that he is remembered, posthumously, by others. The element in which all things are joined may be death or infinity, the 'limitless thing' of Anaximander (Cornford, p. 7), and Empson may have in mind here Cornford's description of the 'eponymous hero', the primitive tribal hero who embodied its collective soul: 'The historical circumstances of his life and character. . .are the least important part of him, and may soon be forgotten. His actual achievements blend with the other glorious acts of tribal history in a composite memory that defies analysis'. (p. 107).

If such ironic self-cancellation is the consequence of action, it is small wonder that the poem's final stanzas are so dark and virtually return the poet to the stasis and quandary of its beginning. With fierce despair (projected by the startling apostrophes) Empson cites two examples of 'diving' that turned out badly: Lucifer (son of the morning and so of Phoebus) who fell from glory, and 'high' Jezebel (II *Kings* ix, 30–37) who was pushed, so hard that 'some of her blood was sprinkled on the wall' (thus 'splash high'). There is a savagely punning relationship (recalling Hamlet's 'not where he eats, but where he's eaten') between 'Fall to' and 'They feast'; between 'tired' as 'adorned' and 'tired' as 'torn by a beak' (its meaning in falconry) and as 'greedily eaten' (as the dogs – the final pounce of stanza one's 'hounds' – ate Jezebel). One senses a strong sympathy here for the two who fell to their foes, and Empson underlines it by medievally placing Jezebel's surviving skull on a pike, as a *memento mori,* an object lesson to himself on the rewards of diving.

The final stanza is quieter, more controlled in its accept-ance of what is clearly for Empson a hopeless situation, though one could wish the first two lines less enigmatic. It seems uncertain whether the poet's instruction to himself to journey to the 'termite city' represents a criticism of the tough measures urban man takes to protect his civilisation or common life-blood, a wish to adopt its hard shell of brick and bullet instead of his own 'scab' (thinner skin?), or a fear that the future will be harder to live with than the present has been. But the last lines are clearer, and even have a touch of humourless laughter: though the search for fulfilment in action must be made, the impetuosity of the callow human 'puppy' (like that of the puppy in the story) will find nothing under the water into which he plunges except 'the imaged solid of the bone' — not something good to eat, but his skull. And far from creating the 'irrotational' undulation of stanza one, his dive will produce a whirlpool, down which will vanish even that last reflection of himself.

TO AN OLD LADY

First published in *Cambridge Review*, Vol. 49. (20 April 1928), p.347. Reprinted in *Cambridge Poetry, 1929*.

In view of a bald statement by Alan Bold (*Cambridge Book of English Verse 1939* [*sic*] − *1975*) that 'The old lady is the moon', it is worth re-asserting what this poem's subject really is — Empson's mother Laura, who died in 1944. Empson himself makes this quite clear in his record note, and revealingly adds: 'When she came across it in print she luckily thought it meant her own mother, this showing that it tells a general truth'. The care implicit in this only half-humorous remark reinforces both the reverence of feeling and the distanced observation of the poem. Its distance, however, is not that of irony but of propriety and respect, and one may adduce here two statements Empson made while at Cambridge. In January 1926 he took part in a Union debate on the motion 'That the Victorians were greater than ourselves'; speaking for the Ayes (who lost), 'Mr. Empson in a very amusing and clever speech defended Victorian dignity. It was a genuine thing, so why shouldn't they be proud of it?' (*Cambridge*

Review, 29 January 1926.) Hence his injunction to 'revere'; but one should not intrude. Early in 1928 he reviewed Godfrey Winn's book *Dreams Fade,* which described Winn's break from his family to write novels in London; despite the break Winn had evidently sounded too pious about family closeness, for Empson commented: 'The family works very well if you don't force it, but to look for soul-mates there is a kind of incest'. (*Granta,* 3 Feb. 1928.)

Far from the old lady's being a metaphor for the moon (the 'social detail' of stanza four would hardly fit such a reading), it may even be incorrect to say that the moon is a metaphor for the old lady. The distance between son and mother (the 'generation gap' of recent parlance) is aptly expressed by the metaphor from astronomy, itself revelatory of the modern scientific interests of the young man who chooses it; but Empson nowhere mentions 'moon', only 'planet'. Since that planet 'shares my sun' it lies within the solar system; but the only planet with a goddess's name (alone appropriate for the old lady) is Venus; this seems unlikely, even indecorous, applied to her, and the planet Venus is in any case too close to the sun to have 'failing crops' or to be 'cooling'. One tends to think of the moon because of its serenity, its identification with goddesses (Diana, Selene, Ashtaroth), its worship by man, its visibility by night rather than by day; but it never had any crops to fail, and as the earth is the place whence the poet observes through his telescope, it is neither accurate nor proper to imagine his mother, as moon, circling as his satellite. One is left feeling that the old lady is part-planet (an extra one), and part-moon, that the poem uses whichever aspect best fits the human points it wishes at different times to make, and that at the deepest level (as distinct from the conceptual and structural one) the poem is unified not by its extended metaphor but by its old-fashioned dignity of tone, its reticent admiration, and its evenness of ceremonial pace. It is the only poem on his record that Empson reads with anything like gentleness.

The opening words from *King Lear* (V, iii, 10) are appropriately spoken by a child to a parent (Edgar to Gloucester), and taken from a play concerned with proper parent-child relationships; the authority of Shakespeare enforces Empson's implicit claim that the old lady has attained 'ripeness' (a ripe age, wisdom, and in this case five children), and therefore, though gradually ageing, is hardly 'wasted' (laid waste; with nothing to offer). To think she is would be presuming, in the sense both of impertinence and of jumping to conclusions. 'Do not presume' leads to 'keep at a respectful distance', and the Swiftian connotations of 'project' (the Lagado Academy of Projectors with their cloud-cuckoo 'scientific' schemes) suggest the futility of trying to get too close: such attempts (and a grave sadness enters here) will not arrest the ordered processes of nature ('Gods cool in turn'). The fact that earth, unlike the rest of the planets, is not named after a god is exploited to suggest that its inhabitants, lacking fixed beliefs and values, are particularly ill-suited to help the old lady (if help were required); if they did reach her they would be bulls in china shops (the phrase 'break some palace' sounds like Lewis Carroll but isn't), destructive but also ridiculous: the colloquial understatement 'seem odd' is quietly devastating, and fittingly unfitting, here. M.C. Bradbrook, describing the attitudes of her generation of Cambridge undergraduates (which included Empson), incidentally illuminates his choice of adjective: 'Our strongest term of disapprobation was "odd".' (*I.A. Richards: Essays in his Honor*, 1973, p. 71).

The reference to bees 'stinging their need', however, works less well; though it sharply suggests the indignant pride of an old lady when someone minds her business for her, and thus a final good reason not to interfere, it is as an image out of place in the planetary/human framework of the poem. Moreover, as an entomological illustration it seems both muddled and inaccurate, if Maeterlinck (*The Life of the Bee*, 1901 trans., pp. 82–86) is to be believed: if a new queen is introduced into a hive which lacks one, it is often accepted; if it is introduced when a queen is already inside, the former queen may sting it but the workers only imprison it between their massed bodies. It is hard to see the relevance of either of these situations to the poem, since the space-travellers, however ill-advised, are not 'invaders' of this kind. The line is a small but important error, of tact and tactics, in an otherwise scrupulous poem.

The central stanzas offer a respectfully-distant survey of the old lady's slowly-vanishing way of life, a 'ritual' gradually narrowing down from the exotic evocations of 'temples emptying in the sand', through the English Gothic romanticism of 'crumbled tracery', to its more prosaic current embodiment in the 'social detail' of running a house, playing Bridge, and the servant problem. The disproportion between such a life and the 'Wit' and 'tragic fervour' brought to bear on it suggests that the old lady's 'appanage' (in effect, the dignity, and dignities, she has inherited) has never been fully used; and there is controlled pathos in the ordinary meaning of 'uncalled-on': Empson's mother had been a widow since 1916 and had moved away from the family home. Yet the grave balance of these Augustan lines (especially 'And tragic fervour, to dismiss her maids', with its pregnant comma) suggests the two-fold operation of the mock-heroic mode: the old lady's qualities of soul and style ennoble the small world in which they operate. The seventh stanza strengthens this emphasis: she remains certain of her values and direction (like a gyro-compass set to true North whatever goes on around it), is unaware of limitations (and thus transcends them), and remains her own mistress, however 'failing' her crops: 'sole' suggests 'solar' and also 'soul', perhaps with a side-glance at that other heroic Victorian, W.E. Henley. The archaic-sounding 'precession' draws all the feelings together: the dignity of 'procession', the comfortingly-ordered world of 'precedence', the precession of the equinoxes as she as planet moves tilting round the sun, and the analogous movement of a top, spinning slower and slower as it slopes to its eventual fall.

The final stanza skilfully uses the astronomical metaphor to convey, in summary, the paradoxical distance between parent and child. Like planets, or like earth and moon, they share the same sun (the solar system of the family, with its joint experiences and group-memories). Yet like the moon the mother-planet is visible only at night, and thus in effect as inaccessible as the stars, so much further away and only visible then. The 'night' may stand for Empson's distance from home in Cambridge, whence he can contemplate the old lady with more clarity and understanding than proximity (the light and distraction of everyday contact) allows. Yet overtones of Milton's 'No light; but rather darkness visible' (*Paradise Lost* I, 63) add a sombre note to the ending: the tribute paid by the poem is rooted in an accepted separation whose inevitability its astronomical metaphor and solemn language press on the imagination; but there is a degree of sadness in the acceptance. In addition, 'darkness' and 'night' are unlikely not to suggest dark nights of the soul, and the resigned mood opens speculations on whether there were also human counterparts for the 'stars how much further from me'.

PART OF MANDEVIL'S TRAVELS

First published in *Experiment* No. 1. (Nov. 1928), pp. 38-9. Reprinted in *Cambridge Poetry, 1929*.

In 1957 Anthony Thwaite called this poem 'impenetrable'; Empson himself, in a letter to Philip Gardner ten years later, said it was 'meant to be lively and readily available'. The contrast between poet's expectation and reader's response is striking. The poem certainly looks difficult, with its density of unfamiliar and disparate reference and its apparently blank juxtapositions; but apart from a few enigmatic details (why specifically 'malachite' boulders in stanza 5?) and the obscure convolutions of stanza 2, the difficulties are not of meaning, nor to any great extent of tone, but the result of topicality. What was 'readily available' in 1928 has become less so with time, but the liveliness is largely restored if one digs backwards to identify the figures named, and troubles to read the book of which this poem is a freely-adapted 'part'. What is then revealed is a witty pattern of ironic parallels and contrasts, between ancient and modern, and between East and West.

The poem originated in three co-incident events of 1928, and cleverly if rather speciously assembles them so that they throw light on each other. The first was the publication of the Everyman edition of *Mandeville's Travels,* whose 87th chapter, describing the fabulous kingdom of the half-Christian Prester John, provides the material presented with ponderous archaic dignity in the odd-numbered quatrains. This material is 'commented' on by the deflatingly casual couplets of the even-numbered stanzas, which draw on the second and third 1928 events. The second was the visit to England, lavishly reported in *The Times* between March 14th and 31st, of King Amanullah of Afghanistan, a reforming and westernising monarch who, *inter alia,* visited a small-arms factory, a coal mine, a steelworks and the Liverpool docks, enjoyed an air display at Hendon which involved aerial bombing and, while travelling by submarine from Portsmouth to Southampton, personally fired two torpedoes. Amanullah's alleged remark (the 'motto' used by Empson as epigraph) was certainly not reported by *The Times,* which noted only a colourless 'best wishes from under water' sent by him from the submarine to his Queen following by ship; but it nicely satirises British armaments and 'progress', and by its form suggests the kinship between Amanullah ('half an Englishman') and Prester John, who 'hath not all the full beliefe as we have'.

The third event (the catalyst in the chemical reaction of Mandeville and Amanullah) was a report published in *The Times* of 28th September 1928 (Empson's note to the poem in *Experiment* erroneously gave the date as September 29th). This detailed some of the discoveries made by the German geologist Dr. Emil Trinkler, (Empson spells him 'Trinckler') who had been travelling in Chinese Turkestan (Sinkiang) in 1927/28 in search of traces of ancient civilisations. Trinkler had visited Afghanistan in 1923/24, and his account had appeared in an English translation (*Through the Heart of Afghanistan*) also in 1928; but though this refers to Amanullah's reforms with wary approval (cf. p. 115), and describes a glittering dry river bed oddly reminiscent of Mandeville's 'river of dry jewels' (p. 94), it is not to this book, but to the later report on Chinese Turkestan, that Empson specifically refers, adapting descriptions of 'a large belt of dead poplar trees covering 2,000 square miles' (stanza 4), 'enormous gravel deposits' (like Mandeville's 'gravely sea'), and 'five-fold layers of clay' (stanza 6).

These observations of Trinkler, a more scientific Mande-ville, are given a slightly ironic effect (two-way, perhaps) by Empson's juxtaposing them with the original Mandeville: 'the gravely sea', which runs turbulently three days a week, becomes glacial moraine deposits concealing 'some chipped flints'; the marvellous but deadly 'iron-fruited trees', rising and subsiding during the cycle of a day, are merely dead wood. Yet the two descriptions are basically alike: Prester John's kingdom (located in the early middle ages in Asia/ India) is something of a waste land, as is contemporary Central Asia, and since the poem (whose geography, according to Empson's note 'is as dim as Mandevil's') relates both places to Amanullah's Afghanistan, a certain wry tolerance seems extended to his journey westward, an inversion of Mandeville's, in search of wonders. 'Iron-fruited trees', which no man dare pick, are of little use, as are 'dead poplar trees'; if Amanullah truly lives in such a waste land it is hardly surprising that the West appeals to him: 'our deso-lation is of harsher steel'. This splendid line sardonically praises Amanullah's enterprise: England offers him a more efficient waste land, not natural like his but man-made: 'Tour well the slag-heaps, royalty, we own/The arid sowing, the tumultuous stone'. The mock-pride of 'own' is fused with the disenchantment of 'own up to'.

Nevertheless, the main emphasis of the poem is on Ama-nullah's misguidedness. Similarity between the world of wonders he discovers and that described by Mandeville is conveyed by Empson's sly inclusion in stanza 3 of a reference to 'dock-side cranes' which tower as a Western equivalent of Mandeville's mirage-like spear-trees. They too are 'all cliquant' — an invented word suggesting metallic clicking noises (like robots?) and the French 'clinquant', used to describe tinsel and tawdry glitter. The glamour of Western technology is deceptive, and perhaps no more securely based than the trees, 'brief by waste sand upborne', which disappear by nightfall. The absurdity of Amanullah's desire for arma-ments is hyperbolically underlined by the last two stanzas. The 'fish of another fashion' enjoyed by Prester John really were 'of full good savour', but Empson turns them into deadly 'mail-dark fish' — torpedoes, 'spawned in grit-silted grotto' of factories. Deadly, but also useless, as he laconically indicates: unlike Shakespeare's fanciful Bohemia, but like the real Afghanistan, 'Paradise. . .has no coast'.

The references to Paradise, and to 'Adam' at the end, bring a clinching element of generalisation to the poem's pattern of topical juxtapositions and contrasts: to its odd particularities (the fantasies of Mandeville, the geological discoveries of Trinkler, the 'progressive' ambitions of Amanullah) is added the oddity which embraces them all: the curious predicament of fallen, searching humanity, the 'man-devil' of Empson's significantly-spelled title. The kingdom of Prester John is located by Mandeville next to 'Paradise Terrestre', from which the 'dry river' flows to 'Pantarose' (the macaronic name suggesting a land where everything is rosy); 'Paradise Terrestre' (earthly paradise) is Mandeville's name for the Garden of Eden, which he also calls the highest place on earth. This virtual identification of kingdom and Garden gives Empson, in turn, poetic licence to place both on 'the Roof of the World', and thus, loosely, in Afghanistan. If Amanullah is Prester John, he is also 'King Alleluiah' (perhaps an irreverent Cockney garbling of his name, difficult because foreign), bent on the improvement of his country: the 'bowlers' of stanza 8 allude, freely, to the prescription of frock-coats and top-hats which was one of his odder reforms. But, more comprehensively, Amanullah stands also for Adam, 'bent' as a result of his wish for knowledge, who leaves behind the innocence of his Garden (however arid in this instance) and journeys to the fallen world of Western man. Like Adam's, Amanullah's improvements brought him little good; in 1929 he was deposed by reactionaries, and when Empson's satirical poem was reprinted that year in *Cambridge Poetry* he added to it the sympathetic note: 'This was written when the King seemed a successful reformer, and calls for apology now'.

CAMPING OUT

First published in *Experiment* No. 2 (Feb. 1929), p. 15.

If, as Empson said in 1963, he spent much of his time at Cambridge thinking 'it would be very nice to write beautiful things like the poet Donne' and sitting 'by the fire trying to think of an interesting puzzle', the reception there of 'Camping Out' must have been very gratifying for him. It seems to have been a poem which particularly exercised the wits of his university contemporaries: Richard Eberhart called it 'a brain-tickler which exercised many hours of drawing-room discussion in Cambridge, and withheld its ultimate ambiguous secrets for years' (*Accent Anthology*, p. 571). The reaction was not only to the puzzle-element and to the profusion of neo-metaphysical conceits; as George Rylands, then a young don four years Empson's senior, has testified, it was also to the shock-effect of its first line: 'And now she cleans her teeth into the lake': to the sheer effrontery of a poem which dared to plunge *in medias res* in such an unexpected way. What a topic to start a poem with!

Such an opening was not unprecedented: a similar shock must surely in its time have been given by Donne's 'Mark but this flea'. Empson's method in this poem is more than usually like Donne's, in moving from the ordinary, or the startlingly unpoetic, through a series of ingenious comparisons to a sweeping conclusion which astonishes by its apparent distance from the point of origin. One remarks the spaciousness of gesture and rhythm in stanza two, compared with the broken texture of stanza one (interrupted by colons and brackets); one notes the hyperboles of stanza two, in which poet and reader are in a world (updated by Eddington) where 'She's all states, and all princes, I;/Nothing else is', compared to the quieter attribution of qualities to the girl in stanza one. Yet the claims of divinity made by both stanzas are equally large, and the imagery of the second (stars, Heaven, Madonna) is established by the first. The tightness of interconnection is emphasised by the unusual form: given that the poem is of love, its fourteen lines might have been organised as a sonnet, but instead they are divided into two exactly equivalent blocks, each economically rhyming aab aaab.

Part of the effect of the opening line lies in the questions its abruptly-stated situation leaves unanswered. The two people are camping out, but are they together by the lake or is the poet watching unsuspected from his tent? And the line's various possibilities of emphasis also tease. If she 'cleans her teeth' into the lake 'now', was she washing in it before (which would explain stanza two's 'soap tension' better than toothpaste)? If what she is doing 'now' is 'cleaning her teeth into the lake', what (elsewhere than the lake) might she have been doing previously? No answers are supplied, but what does emerge from line one is that whatever the girl does it is for the observing poet a wonderful spectacle, as if she were giving him a present.

The physical situation is fairly plain. The girl, balancing on a couple of rocks, cleans her teeth into the water; as she does so, flecks of toothpaste from her sleepy brushing fall into it. What this activity deposits on the water resembles a pattern of stars, as if a reflection in miniature of the Milky Way. There are, however, no real stars reflected in the water, since the pale mist of morning (with a pun on 'pale' as fence or boundary) 'debars' this (prevents, and physically excludes it). The logic of conceits therefore makes it possible to think of the girl as like God, generously giving the lake what the misty sky does not, or as restoring the water's ability to mirror heaven, like a looking-glass, which Nature cannot at this hour do. The interpolated 'that Will could break' is obscure — perhaps a rather pointless allusion to the supposed effects of concentrated will-power, able here to break something which the girl's powers can nevertheless mend. A 'glass' is of course a container as well as a mirror (or window), and as such can be shattered by a sustained high-pitched note; having 'restored' it in the sense of mended it, the girl can then 're-store' (refill) it with watery stars.

The final lines of stanza one seem to credit the girl with a supreme ability: that of lending Heaven something it does not have. 'Her pattern', which she graciously 'lets Heaven take', is both her own reflected image and the pattern of stars she sheds on the water. 'Milks' and 'straddled sky' would together normally suggest a sky over-arching her, a heavenly cow to which she is milkmaid; but here the 'sky of stars', created by her 'milking' or squeezing of the toothpaste, or made of the milky liquid itself, is beneath her in the water and straddled by her. Thus the 'dimming' of Heaven seems not only a natural early morning dimness but a replacement of its light by her own; and the phrase 'half awake' may not only indicate her sleepiness but imply that her power is only half switched-on. Clearly the girl is divine, and 'milks' suggests her as a mother-figure. (The Greek root of the word 'galaxies' links the idea of milk to that of stars).

Having gradually built up the girl's prosaic activities as evidence for her deification, the poem suddenly speeds up and takes off as from a launching-pad. The 'soap tension' relating the various milky solutions on the water widens and enlarges ('magnifies') the pattern of mimic toothpaste stars which have replaced the sky and makes them move apart like an expanding universe. 'Magnifies' (as 'praises') calls up the Magnificat, and the girl is revealed as 'Madonna' (her reflected head haloed with stars), who 'through-assumes the skies' she has created, soaring upward to be received into Heaven like the Virgin Mary. By association, of mother with son, and of reflected sky below with true sky above, the widening stars are also seen as the tomb from which Christ rose and the opened 'vaults' of Heaven which 'achieved' him (brought his earthly life to a successful conclusion).

Such a divine hyperbole might have suited Donne, but it suddenly seems not to Empson's taste. As if his ingenuities have led him astray, he switches in the last four fluent lines to the heaven of modern astronomy which is more congenial to him, his abrupt negative (cf. 'The Ants') putting the divine one in its place: 'No, it is we soaring explore galaxies'. The emphasis is as much on 'we', as if he realises that the apotheosis contrived for the girl excludes him and is, after all, that of a virgin goddess (as it is of a celibate God). What he wants is a joint trip to the stars, as the 'bullet-boat' of the lovers' ecstasy (its compound combining wave- and particle-theories of light, and recalling the lake from which the poem started) accelerates well beyond the speed of light and leaves behind the systems of the ordinary universe. The last line, reminiscent in its soaring trajectory of sound (if not in its optimism) of Johnson's magnificent 'They mount, they shine, evaporate and fall' (*The Vanity of Human Wishes*) is one of Empson's most memorable, its grandly-expansive 'See', like a gesture of the hand directing a fellow-passenger's attention from a speeding vehicle, serving as conclusive advertisement for the journey proposed. The slangily-metaphysical overtones of 'die' suggest that what is 'outsoared' may not only be the stars, but the sexless consummations of Madonna and Lord; if only in the universe of his imagination, the poet attains union with the girl whose ablutions he has observed with such devoted care.

LETTER I

First published, as 'Letter' and without stanza 4, in *Experiment* No. 1. (Nov. 1928), p. 4.

Of Empson's five verse 'letters', written in studiously-differentiated stanza-forms, two were published in 1928, two in 1929, and the last in 1934. All are love poems of a sort, and three (the first two and the last) employ the letter convention not only to address the beloved but to discuss the question of communication itself. There seems little doubt that they were not originally conceived as a sequence, since 'Letter I' and 'Letter II' were both first printed simply as 'Letter'; and in fact the presently-titled 'Letter I' was the second to appear, six months after what is now called 'Letter II'. In the absence of the external evidence which would date their composition or identify their 'recipient(s)', the poems must be treated as diverse responses rather than as episodes in a continuing story.

'Letter I' is an interesting but unsatisfactory poem. It moves rather uneasily between epistolary casualness (the beginnings of the first two stanzas) and the intimations of bottled-up passion which conclude stanzas three and four, creating a sense of randomness rather than of tension; it illustrates its theme (essentially, the proper distance between two people in a relationship) by analogies, not entirely convincing, from astronomy and from Cornfordian primitive 'physics', but its most resonant lines (the last two of stanzas three and four) derive their force not from the arguments they complete but from the self-contained emotional commonplaces they express. The poem also displays irritating local obscurities (though 'who' in line five seems merely perverse), some clumsiness (as when the aside on Mars in stanza two forces the poet-lecturer to repeat after it the phrase 'for messages' which precedes it), and two particularly drastic ellipses ('Hanged on the thread of radio advances' and 'your circumambient foreboding'), whose very necessary glossing by Empson's note only increases one's sense of their crossword-clue arbitrariness.

J.B.S. Haldane had begun his first essay in *Possible Worlds* (1927) with the words: ''Le silence éternel de ces espaces infinis m'effraie', said Pascal, as he looked at the stars and between them, and his somewhat irrational terror has echoed down the centuries'. (p. 1) Empson's quotation of Pascal (*Pensées,* iii, 206) at the start of stanza one may well echo Haldane's, since he seems to share Haldane's surprise at such a reaction, contrasting with his own approval of 'dark spaces between stars' the fear which the girl (despite her self-conscious amusement) feels towards them. Empson's phrasing in lines 3-4 seems not to allow the girl's feeling to be one of awe, like Pascal's: Eddington, in *The Expanding Universe* (1933), called space 'a network of distances' (p. 101), but Empson's jokily literal-minded 'net-work without fish', his 'extended idleness' (suggesting prolonged laziness as well as spatial emptiness), and his 'pointless places' (lacking any definite locations, and futile) proffer the girl's feeling as a pragmatic impatience with the apparently useless. The purpose of such infinite spaces, empty even of galaxies let alone anything nearer, is perhaps conveyed by line 5, though the unhelpfully odd usage 'possiblized' (rendered as 'possibilized' in two printed versions of the poem) presses guesswork into service. Such spaces, one hazards, have been created in order to invite the gaze of speculation ('made possible in order to bear faces', 'made capable of bearing faces', perhaps even 'accustomed to bare faces'). Their very emptiness is thus a virtue, and even the girl might take advantage of it, looking upwards and reflecting the moonlight out into the void from her face. Whatever the girl's attitude to 'infinite spaces', it is clear that the poet admires her.

His own attitude (recalling that in 'To an Old Lady') is presented in stanza two, where the astronomical references start to reveal their metaphorical purpose. Gaps between stars (people) are necessary and proper, serving as a spatial hedge which ensures privacy (though not, it would seem, isolation). They also 'carry glances/Through gulfs'. As a statement about space this seems fatuous, but a deeper human meaning, turning on the contrast between 'glances' (rapid, on the surface) and 'gulfs' (depths, differences), seems likely: distances deepen the commonplaces of close contact into mystery. This is not quite the romanticism of 'distance lends enchantment': the bracketed illustration (the original reading 'renown' is restored in the 1977 printing of *Collected Poems*) suggests that the 'wise tact' of communication over distances gives people credit for qualities (such as Mars' reputation for wisdom, based perhaps on its 'canals' and fictionally assumed by H.G. Wells) which they may not possess. Such imputed qualities could disappear if one got too close; thus they 'hang by a thread'. In terms of the illustration the 'thread' is both the actual radio contact with Mars which we might achieve, and (because threads are thin) the thin chance that we will ever achieve it (the 'never' in Empson's note hardly fits his gloss). Distances are thus preferable to proximity: the approximate 'messages' they permit are equated with the findings of 'common-sense', here considered as something kindly and reliable, which puts the best construction on things. But there is some strangeness here, both in the equation of warm 'common-sense' with a metaphoric infinite space (which leaves the girl cold), and in the preference revealed, surely unusual for a young man confronted with a young woman.

Up to now the poem has sounded rather complacent – the poet's 'approval' contrasted favourably with the girl's 'fear', itself tinged with sophisticated amusement. The corollary of her fear of space has not been stated, but the tone suggests that she prefers human proximity and that the poet is fending her off in a kind of intellectual game. Stanza three reveals stronger feelings and a different situation, and the word 'banishment' (suggesting that the poet is apart from her and making the best of it, hence perhaps this letter) sends one back to 'privacy' and reveals its undertones of 'privation' and 'deprivation'. The distance between poet and girl (already implied in their differing attitudes) may be imposed rather than sought; and even if sought, it is only tolerable if the 'common-sense' of messages travelling across it belongs to a world, a 'space', they truly have 'in common'. Empson's metaphor for shared beliefs is the same as that used in 'High Dive': Cornford's concept of primitive 'phusis', a continuum of life-blood (akin to the sacrament of communion) in which all members of the tribe are joined in a relation to a common 'totem-ancestor' – in modern terms, the meaning- and value-systems (scientific, philosophical or religious) which unite them. The semantic link (based on 'phusis' as life-blood) between physics, metaphysics and 'physician' ('the "leech" who lets blood') is brought out by Empson in *Some Versions of Pastoral* (1950 edn., p. 78), and it is easy to see how comforting, in separation, would be the knowledge that one was living in the same world as the girl. But how the beliefs of such a world would function for her, differently, as a 'showman' (which Empson's note glosses as 'tragic hero') is baffling, unless perhaps she is simply meant to be seen as an extrovert and thus different from the poet in his 'banishment'. Whether they share anything at all seems, in any case, doubtful: their predicament (or Empson's own) is 'too non-Euclidean' (which, though it refers back to the 'space' metaphor, is perhaps here no more than a fashionable way of saying that it is complex and peculiarly modern: in *Space Time and Gravitation* (1920, p. 8) Eddington explains 'non-Euclidean' as 'in popular phrase, warped').

The last two lines of the stanza return to the initial images from astronomy, but now in a more emotionally-charged manner. Empson's wish for 'darkness' is both positive and negative. One kind (like the 'bars' in 'The World's End') would define light (that of her face in stanza one) by contrast – which seems a further boosting of his argument in stanza two. The other kind is more complex: it would help him to forget her; but since 'such' darkness does not exist, she need not be afraid — whatever darkness there is would only enhance her. Such statements, romantic rather than scientific, seek perhaps to unite the differing viewpoints of poet and girl, but the interrogatives leave everything up in the air.

The unsatisfactoriness of the poem up to this point lies in its failure to embody within its response the situation it responds to; this absence of a central focus makes the response itself blurred and difficult to evaluate. The addition of stanza four, after 1932, was perhaps an attempt to clarify matters, but it does not entirely succeed, despite its impressive emotional gestures. The two 'lovers' are seen, now, not in terms of the universe but of the solar system. But what is happening to their sun? He is 'jovial' (like Jove, since he rules the system, and with the grinning face of children's drawings), but will not long remain so. 'These times are critical' may in part be a private joke (by 1932 Leavis, Richards, and Empson himself were in full critical swing), but one assumes that its essential reference is to the contemporary ferment of astronomical theory, which included speculation on the origin and likely future of the sun. It also suggests an object's 'critical mass': Eddington had calculated (Haldane, p. 6) that a star heavier than five times the sun's weight would burst (so presumably the sun itself would 'avoid exploding'); but he also pointed out (*The Nature of the Physical World,* Everyman, p. 91) that 'matter is gradually destroyed and its energy set free in radiation', and it is this basic idea that Empson adopts. Lines 4-5 (taking 'while' as 'whereas', which seems necessary) suggest that, instead of staying 'packed with mass' and thus containing its radiance (presumably a humanly-viable degree of heat and light), the sun will gradually expand as its mass burns up into a radiance which will 'Flame far too hot not to seem utter cold'. In the process (since, as Eddington pointed out in 1933, 'the conversion of material mass would start a contraction' in the size of the universe) the separating space around it (the darkness the girl disliked earlier, here called, with a wrenching of the usual meaning of the possessive adjective, 'your circumambient foreboding') would rapidly diminish; but the effect would be destructive.

What this final illustration (a more compact and powerful one than that of the first two stanzas) must be attempting to convey, as metaphor, is that emotion is kept at its best temperature at a distance: too close a contact between people defeats its object and leads to one of them (since extreme heat and extreme cold feel the same) hiding 'a tumult never to be told'. The difficulty, no less than with the first two stanzas, is whether such extreme analogies apply convincingly to a human situation, especially one so shadowily presented as this is. If the girl fears 'dark spaces', the poet equally fights shy of proximity, and the *cordon sanitaire* he advocates conceals his 'tumult' no less effectively than its reduction might. One may well feel that, however Empson's cautionary tale about the sun recommends the virtues of distance, a sun which barely 'avoids exploding' is a fine natural symbol for frustration.

LETTER II

First published, as 'Letter', in *Cambridge Review*, Vol. 49 (6 June 1928), p. 485. Reprinted, as 'Letter', in *Cambridge Poetry, 1929*.

Whether 'Letter II', the first of the letters to be published, was in fact the second to be written one cannot say, but it does suggest some reasons for the 'concept of necessary distance' which is so puzzling in 'Letter I'. The sense of evanescence it conveys is depressing; but though its examination of human closeness may imply in the poet a temperament prone to boredom, the lack of strain in the poem's imagery, and the melancholy of its tone, help to build up a moving individual situation which has some degree of universality. Most relationships end; this one simply ends sooner.

The image that unifies the first four stanzas is that of the girl's face (or rather its various changing expressions) seen as a 'cave gallery' covered with primitive rock-paintings, through which the lover walks, picking out each one with a torch.

The idea may have been suggested by the rock-paintings of Altamira in northern Spain, discovered in 1868 and authenticated in the first decade of this century; at Altamira there was a large cave containing paintings of bison together with various side galleries, also painted. The comparison, striking and unusual, is also rather odd, as however the girl's expressions change her face remains stationary, whereas each painting is on a different part of the cave-wall and the observer moves past them in turn. But it works quite well, perhaps because the reader responds to the gallery's extension in space as the equivalent of a relationship's duration in time. This act of instinctive translation enables him to obey the poem's instruction to 'only walk on': time is irreversible, though in space one can go backwards; and though paintings co-exist whereas expressions follow each other, the latter is made plausible in terms of the metaphor because a moving torch can illuminate only one picture at a time. The poem's slow, inexorable progress through the 'gallery', allowing no second thoughts and little lingering ('the sands are shifting as you walk'), contrives to create an air of inevitability in the human situation it mediates.

The blurred syntax of line two suggests a film in which one shot 'dissolves' into another and various meanings overlap. The inclusion of 'which' before 'ravishes' (Empson's suggestion in his note) indicates what later phrases confirm – that the observer is ravished by only one fresco at a time, since the most comprehensive reading of the lines ('My torch meets fresco after fresco which ravish and rebeget me') is precluded by Empson's use of verbs in the singular. 'Ravishes' (colloquially suggesting the girl's 'ravishing' face) here recalls Donne, since it stands next to the word 'rebegets', whose rarity cannot avoid reminding the reader of 'A Nocturnall upon St. Lucie's Day'. Donne is 'rebegot/Of absence, darkness, death', Empson of beauty; but the beauty is momentary. These primitive wall-paintings ('fresco' blends them with Renaissance wall- and ceiling-paintings, hence the 'heaven' of line 4) are not only illuminated but 'crumbled' by the torchlight: they are themselves ravished as well as ravishing. The suggestion (inspired perhaps by the faintness of primitive pigment) is that close scrutiny is destructive.

The second stanza expands the literal element of the meta-phor (the paintings, however beautiful, are too faded for one to appreciate fully the 'triumph' of the 'stocks', the primitive people who produced them) to suggest that facial expressions (externals of behaviour?) body forth only faintly the person behind them, and there is little for the 'sketchbook' (memory perhaps) to record. The jellyfish image combines the ideas of sliminess (the wet cave walls) and colour (the hues of the creature, the paintings, the girl's face) with the idea that a thing loses its life and beauty once it comes to the surface. What is left is (virtually) 'bare canvas', unsuitable for elaborate framing (worship? permanence?). The original form of the line ('Bare canvas the gold frame disdains') emphasised this reading; but Empson's expansion of it provides the opposite possibility, that primitive pictures, and the girl's fleeting expressions and phases of behaviour, disdain to be framed: their fragility and informality is their beauty. The ambiguity suggests, at any rate, the poignancy of transience.

The movement of poem and searcher resumes in stanza three, but the associations of 'golden frame' lead to the cave's now being seen as a portrait-gallery, perhaps in a great house: the 'primeval stocks' turn into human ancestors, whose various faces (all dead now) are recapitulated in the varying expressions of the girl. ('Wealth' and 'style' work to link her range of faces with money, the grand gesture; 'sense of character' links the admirable with the acted.) All the searcher can do, however, is 'walk on' through this series of new portraits, not yet 'bleached' or dazzled to death by his torch; the 'process' (of life, of a relationship) cannot be altered. The phrase 'in general terms' suggests that this irre-versible process is in fact speeding up, the examination growing more cursory if equally destructive (familiarity breeds contempt?). 'Only walk on' is more urgent still; the relationship is declining, its basis becoming insecure, fewer things (and those less important?) are left to see. All human life, the last line implies, is a 'darkness', but the darkness of the future offers less beauty than that of the past. The pessi-mism of this view, imaginatively persuasive, is nevertheless intellectually arguable, and the literalness of line two is perhaps an effort to convince the reason that this one case of pessimism, at least, is justified by circumstances: 'Whom lust, nor cash, nor habit join, are cold'. The pejorative implications of 'cash' (mutual interest, self-interest) are reduced by its echoing of the earlier 'wealth'; 'lust' may well be sheer sexual enjoyment (cf. Donne's slightly envious, but not hostile, use of the word in 'A Nocturnall'); 'habit' can be sustaining as well as dreary. Empson's line suggests the possibility of all these links between people; here they have either never been discovered or, as seems more likely ('the greater part have gone'), have been exhausted.

The last stanza replaces the richly-exploited but now worked-out image of the cave-gallery by one of 'desperate stars' — the death-throes of the relationship's end. The world of this stanza is plural, as if to include as an active participant the girl who before was the object observed; it is also a world (of lovers generally) which the poet comments on as well as belongs to, and one notes that it is not 'finite but unbounded', but rather finite and bounded. The various adjectives suggest hopeless attempts (star-crossed lovers, double-crossing, the pursuing 'hounds' of 'High Dive') to escape the inevitable, attempts which are greedy ('nose-sailing', on the scent of something to 'devour'), promiscuous ('fingered by many', perhaps, as well as 'having many fingers') and destructive. 'Worms dying in flower', recalling the 'invisible worm' in Blake's sick rose, is also connected to 'ravishes' in stanza one: sex consumes both ravished and ravisher. All this frantic impressionism, expanding the personal case into a general statement and conveying the end of life as well as of relationships, turns on a tricky piece of syntax: 'those worms dying in flower/(Which) ashed paper holds'. Stars and worms may be images for human activity, and between them may comprehend cosmic and sub-earthly; but what kinds of stars are also worms, and what kinds of worms are actually 'held' by 'ashed paper'? The answer, satisfyingly embracing all the verbal connotations in a single spectacle, is surely fireworks, bursting out, up and around as rockets and catherine-wheels from their paper/cardboard cases, exploding in the shapes of flowers, lighting up for a while the night sky around them as the torch lights up the 'frescoes', and leaving behind only darkness and ashes.

THE POEMS OF WILLIAM EMPSON

VILLANELLE

First published in *Cambridge Review*, Vol. 50 (26 Oct. 1928), p. 52. Reprinted in *Cambridge Poetry, 1929*.

Empson is more associated with the villanelle (and for that matter the terza rima) than is any other twentieth-century poet; significantly, it is in these forms that any parodies of him have been composed – Dylan Thomas's 'Request to Leda' (*Horizon* VI, July 1942, p. 6), Richard Kell's 'Empsonium' (*London Magazine* VI, Oct. 1959, pp. 55–6), L.E. Sissmann's 'Just a Whack at Empson' (*The Review*, June 1963, p. 75). What prompted Empson to adopt this early French verse-form is not clear, though its technical rigour – its alternating refrains and its two rhyme-sounds stretched over nineteen lines – was no doubt a challenge. As is made clear by comparison with nineteenth century practitioners of the villanelle, Austin Dobson, Wilde and Dowson, Empson's specimen is very much his own. With the exception of Dowson in 'Villanelle of Marguerites', his predecessors employ lighter, three- or four-stress lines, and their villanelles, graceful, nostalgic or bitter-sweet, lack the plangent fullness given by Empson's pentameters and heavy monosyllables.

Powerfully conveying the unhappiness of an ended relationship, the poem is more immediately accessible, in feeling, than any other in Empson's first volume. But its method is by no means obvious – not until the final stanza is the reader fully aware of the situation from which the feelings spring – and the refrains are not just formal echoes but reveal new aspects of meaning as the poem proceeds. The first line, which functions as an emotional ground bass for the poem, may gain some of its force from the way its shape and movement recall Othello's 'It is the cause, it is the cause, my soul'; but the emphatic and characteristically Empsonian use of the 'it is. . .' syntactical formula seems essentially intended to deny any mellow assumptions that what survives a relationship is the pleasure and happiness it brought. The second line reinforces this view by comparing beauty to (presumably) an acid which destroys human resilience. The word 'chemic', however, pertains as much to alchemy as to chemistry, and its ambiguity is exploited later by, on the one hand, reference to the modern-sounding 'toxin' and, on the other, the old-fashioned, almost fairy-tale quality of 'allures' and 'poison draught'. The girl is an enchantress; her beauty, ('poise', 'grace') brings a sickness (the similarity of 'poise' and 'poison' emerges in the juxtaposition of lines 14 and 15) for which her own 'kindness' is, or was, the 'salve', and against which no 'later purge' (perhaps work, perhaps a future girl) seems likely to be effective.

Balanced against the poem's generalising refrain is the particular incident which has acted as its spur: 'Poise of my hands reminded me of yours'. Your hands? Your poise? The poise (pose, position) of your hands? It does not greatly matter, and the vagueness adds an appropriate air of intimacy to what is, after all, a love poem addressed to an audience of one. What is important is the disproportion between transient, fortuitous pressure and the permanent pain which it sets off. In stanza three the pain is compared to an 'infection' which one thinks under control, either because one is used to it ('custom') or because one has been distracted from it ('change'); it is, however, somewhat like malaria, only awaiting the chance stimulus which is bound, some time, to make it flare up again. That 'pain's secondary phase was due' suggests both that it arrives according to its own inscrutable schedule, and that its occurrence is a proper tribute to the girl who has caused it.

Further point is given to the unavoidableness of painful reminders by stanza four, which demolishes the pretensions of conscious memory. The present tense 'assures', necessitated by the rhyme-scheme, is misleading; the pastness of such assurance is made clear by the ironic 'How safe I felt'. Conscious memory, which thinks it has the girl's grace ('your grace' is surely also honorific) 'by heart', like a piece of rote learning, is entirely vulnerable to the sudden attacks of involuntary memory, which reveal her beauty as a dangerous force alive in the bloodstream rather than as a treasure kept 'safely' in the mind. The apt placing of stanza four's refrain baldly stresses the power of pain over retrospect.

The last stanza, recalling her kindness, which could once

'the old salve renew', also makes clear that it is no longer available as an antidote to pain. Her paradoxical inaccessibility is rendered with terse poignancy in lines 16-17. 'Beyond adieu' means, physically, 'on the other side of goodbye', hence 'immured': for whatever reason, the love affair has been ended. But the phrase equally suggests the impossibility for the poet, in emotional terms, of saying goodbye to her. 'We miss our cue' (where 'we' refers to people in general as well as to the two in the poem) may imply the failure of human beings to synchronise in a relationship, to say the right thing at the right time, or perhaps to part eloquently, as often in drama. Perhaps, also, there is a wistfully-ironic backward look to the misplaced confidence of 'safely by heart' in stanza four: the situations of real life find the lover speechless and inadequate. Whatever the details, enough has been said to show that the relationship has not worked out, and the two refrains are all that the poem needs to complete its perceptive and moving treatment of the psychology of disappointed love.

ARACHNE

First published in *Cambridge Review,* Vol. 49 (6 June 1928), p. 490. Reprinted in *Cambridge Poetry, 1929.*

Ever since its first two stanzas were quoted approvingly by F.R. Leavis in a review of *Cambridge Poetry, 1929,* 'Arachne' has belonged to a small group of early Empson poems (also including 'To an Old Lady', 'Legal Fiction' and 'This Last Pain') which critics have been disposed to comment on and to praise. With part of its fourth line misprinted ('the velvet roof to streams'), it was also selected by Yeats to represent Empson in *The Oxford Book of Modern Verse* (1936). Empson himself, however, omitted the poem from the record he made in 1959, for a reason he stated to Christopher Ricks in 1963: 'I'd come to think that it was in rather bad taste. It's boy being afraid of girl, as usual, but it's boy being too rude to girl.'

Empson's explanation makes it clear that, for all its apparent philosophising about man in the first three stanzas, 'Arachne' is essentially a love poem, and the title indicates in what its 'rudeness' consists. Various aspects of the Arachne story are open to interpretation, but the outline is clear: Arachne was a princess so proud of her weaving that she challenged the goddess Athene, whose consequent destruction of her rival's perfect tapestry caused Arachne to hang herself; whereupon Athene turned Arachne into a spider. The girl of the poem is thus presented as proud, presumably of her beauty (though this is 'vain', in the other sense of 'futile', without someone to admire it), and as a female spider, who in the last line is imagined as likely to devour her aspiring lover before, during or after the sexual act.

The route by which the poem reaches its personal conclusion is ingenious and oblique, and though its metrical shape is satisfyingly rounded (the central line of the last stanza completing the terza rima pattern by rhyming with the outer lines of the first), the shape of its 'thought' is top-heavy. The poem is like a funnel, gradually narrowing from the metaphysical rhetoric of man's midway state down to the rather tenuously-connected case of the suppliant lover. With this altering of focus goes a shift of tone, as the lofty sonorousness of generalisation is displaced by the insinuations of special pleading, and in the contrast of weight and scope between the first three stanzas and the last two (all these illustrations of human precariousness to persuade one girl into bed) one may even suspect intentional bathos, or mock-heroic. At any rate, the metaphysics of the poem (its likeness to Donne flaunted in his word 'hydroptic') resides less in its philosophy of man than in its exploitation of this for amatory ends.

The essence of man's state, as depicted in the first three stanzas, is its precariousness, but though the clashing opposites between which he exists are strikingly rendered by verbal and sound-patterning, much of what is actually said is, if taken as serious statement, unsatisfactory. The first line starts with a cliché, the second is abstract shorthand, the fifth

93

involves an inexact parallel: the spider must avoid 'bird and fish' for rather different reasons from those prompting man to avoid 'god and beast'. And though the scholastic philosophers are supposed to have speculated on the number of angels (nine?) that could dance on the head of a pin, it seems unsuitable to drag this story in here and to show man, as an angel, balancing on such an 'extreme' in line six when the previous lines have established his midway state between extremes. It is necessary to take the first two stanzas not as careful argument but as a rapid sketch of the human predicament, linked to what comes later by the 'king spider' image for man's act of delicate balancing.

Stanza three introduces the 'bubble' image on which the rest of the poem's development turns. The bubble is at once the thin globe of the earth's surface (made of water as well as land, and so connected to both lines three and four) and the Cornfordian social continuum ('tribe-membrane') whose existence involves human interdependence. Like the individual, it is seen as precarious: as the earth's surface is marred by storm and earthquake, so the social 'surface film' (frail as a cobweb, and perhaps 'the bubble reputation') is easily shattered ('breath' may suggest also the breath of scandal). It may be protested that this view is arbitrary, and that earth and society are tougher than the poet chooses to admit here: the objection is valid, but it is assertions of fragility that better suit his present purpose.

This the poet begins to reveal in stanza four. If social bonds sustain individual existence, one may go on to claim that the most exciting and beautiful relationships ('bubbles gleam brightest') exist between the smallest number of people, that is, when the bubble is thinnest. One molecule (used here in the sense of a single independent atom, and thus the individual) is not enough to create the necessary surface tension; the minimum required is two, and in the abruptly personal 'We two suffice' the poet reveals his hand in what Hugh Kenner ('The Son of Spiders', 1950) has well called 'an astonishing *peripeteia*'. The phrase's force comes partly from its sudden brevity, partly from the fact that 'suffice' not only conveys the lovers' potential to combine in terms of the 'scientific' bubble metaphor but also the older and more vibrant assumption of lovers that they are an exclusive and self-sufficient unit. Any sense of triumph, however, is momentary, since the poet is clearly unsure whether his feelings are reciprocated: the bubble of this relationship is perhaps only a beautiful dream, a film soon to disband. Against this possibility the last two-and-a-half lines make their strongly sexual suggestions, in an uneasy mixture of appeal and boast. As soap and water are both needed to make a bubble, so girl and poet need each other, and though 'meagre water' may imply his sense of inadequacy, her insatiably thirsty ('hydroptic') soap may be grateful for whatever it can get. Neither, certainly, is of any use in isolation (no less precarious a state than the relationship itself may be), and the last line (with a one-sided eye, one may feel, on the main chance) advises the girl not to terminate matters before the lover has had a chance to demonstrate his capabilities.

THE SCALES

First published, as 'Poem', in *Experiment* No. 6 (Oct. 1930), p. 12.

This is a cryptic and elusive poem, ambiguous in its details, variable in its angles of vision, confusing in its fluctuations between literal and metaphorical. Though the coherence of its imagery gradually reveals itself, its circuitous argumentative logic, moving through 'but', 'and', 'why' and 'rather', is apprehended much more slowly. Both title and first line are particularly blank-faced, so that the reader gains little to carry him forward; but while the title becomes clearer in relation to Alice in line 2, the first line has a number of different, indeed contradictory, meanings while only emerge in terms of the whole poem. Unfortunately, the rest of the poem is hard to grasp without some initial understanding of the first line.

   The title is to be taken in much the same sense as that of the first essay in Haldane's *Possible Worlds,* 'On Scales', which deals with systems of measurement, the 'scales' by which we both perceive and render an object's size, that of the earth, for instance, reduced to the scale of a globe or map. Empson's poem is concerned not with relationships between things but between people, specifically between himself and a girl whom he connects, in line 2, to Alice in Wonderland, who is constantly changing size and whose sense of scale becomes consequently confused, as in her encounter with the 'enormous puppy' in Chapter IV. In 1959 (record-notes) Empson described the poem as 'an excuse to a woman for not showing enough love'. The explanation is more gallant than exact: it would be truer to say that the poet offers love of a kind the girl hesitates to accept. But certainly the poem is about an imbalance of affection between them: on the girl's side something childish ('charming for nurse'), on the poet's something more adult, either intellectually or sexually more demanding. The first line may thus apply to both of them: each seeks the 'proper scale', the appropriate system of measurement, that would 'pat you [i.e. 'one'] on the head' in a gesture of reassurance. (The scale that would literally do this is the kind found in a clinic, doctor's surgery, or matron's room in a school, which is equipped with a sliding rule to measure height).

Had Alice been the 'proper scale' (or, as she puts it, the 'right size') in her encounter with the puppy, she would have been able to pat it on the head. Instead, the reverse seems likely, so Alice hides behind a thistle and distracts its attention from herself by holding out a stick for it to play with. Given Empson's Freudian explanation of *Alice in Wonderland* (*Some Versions of Pastoral*, 1950 edn., pp. 270-71), and the obvious maleness of the playful puppy (a 'pup' is also a young man), Alice's fear is clearly sexual; the point is emphasised by the equation of the stick with the bough with which Ulysses, shipwrecked on Nausicaa's island (*Odyssey,* Bk. VI), delicately hid his nakedness from the young girl. The momentary, and confusing, exchange of roles may be meant to suggest that the poet also wishes to avoid an erotic confrontation, but the rest of the poem hardly reinforces this feeling. For the girl, the 'proper' scale is that of decency or propriety, the safe paternal or avuncular pat on the head of a child; it may also be the girl's pat on the head for the 'good dog'. Both, actively given or passively accepted, are condescending pats, unacceptable to the young man. The girl's avoidance of a more adult relationship (the scale of equal sizes) is only 'wise with dread', a negative wisdom with which may be compared implications of the later 'Solomon's gems'. The pat on the girl's head from the man's 'proper scale' (that of reality) would be one of congratulation to her on having grown up.

The rest of the poem, complicated though it is by shifts of perspective, gives a physical setting to the unsatisfactory relationship of which Alice and the puppy have furnished a literary paradigm. Judging from the reference to 'castle sand' (line 9), the action seems to be taking place on a beach – a place, suitably, where sticks are thrown to amuse, and distract, puppies. The girl's stick is her 'gulf-sprung mountains', surely a blown-up metaphor here for sand-castles rising above sea-water-filled moats. Such juvenile occupations on the part of her charge might amuse a child's nurse, but 'I am not nurse just now': the form of the admonition implies a long-suffering young man, who puts up with such behaviour for much of the time. ('Rose-solemn dado band', a flowery wallpaper pattern running round the lower walls of a room, may suggest the nursery.) But in view of the perspective developed in stanza four (the human body seen as a mountain landscape), the girl's 'gulf-sprung mountains' are also her breasts, lifting up from the hollow of her waist: one imagines the poet lying near her, seeing her body in enlarged close-up. 'Snow-puppy curves' brings together whiteness and puppy-fat (with her, now, as the puppy); in this context one wonders whether the 'rose-solemn dado band' is, literally, the coloured material of a bathing-costume, as well as, metaphorically, the solemn rose-coloured spectacle of a sunset, or a sunrise, over snowy mountains. Such breasts would be 'charming for nurse', if the girl were one; but the lover does not wish to be nursed. Nor is he another kind of 'nurse', which in an entomological sense (reasonable to imagine, given the references of other Empson poems to ants and beetles) means 'a sexless worker ant'. On this reading of the stanza (sharpened by the mention of 'tunnels' in the next two), the girl is distracting the poet by means of her secondary sexual characteristics from her primary ones, or from her adult potential generally.

Sandcastles, or breasts, can be patted, mountains strode across. Both activities would be superficial – no more than a pat on the head. Stanza three recommends that, like a mountain summit, the girl is better (and more quickly) reached by train, however roundabout the 'climbing tunnels'. Tunnels may indeed, as Empson's note says, 'stand for difficulties of communication', but equally they are sexual, as is the 'train' which uses them. Line 9 returns the reader to the less extreme actuality of the beach, the lovers lying on either side of the sand-castle (here functioning rather like the sword placed between Tristram and Iseult), their fingers tunnelling under, if they will, to make contract.

The problem for the poet is to persuade the girl that such communication is advantageous to her. The word 'rather' suggests a retraction of stanza three's 'train' as premature (as indeed line 9 has already implied). His strategy now is to speak of tunnels less as routes of access than as containers of hidden riches or marvels in the girl which may profitably be opened up. The imagery of line 11 is taken from Chapters XVI and XVII of Rider Haggard's *King Solomon's Mines* – the diamonds in King Solomon's Treasure Chamber (a basket of which is brought by the three men to the surface), the rows of ice-like stalactites in the cathedral cave, the petrified bodies of dead Kukuana kings in the adjacent one. The latter image is eerie in the book, and hardly seems attractive here; but 'white vistas' (connected perhaps with the earlier 'snow-puppy curves'?) suggests something beautiful, and 'Solomon's gems', as well as being diamonds (a girl's best friend), may represent wisdom. It was through the humble artifice of a 'jackal sand-hole' that the diamonds, and the men bearing them, reached the surface in Haggard's novel; here the poet would be the jackal, revealing to the world and to the girl herself ('your air') the wonders concealed beneath her surface, buried but for him. 'Jackal' suggests self-deprecation (like the 'meagre water' in 'Arachne'); 'flung wide' connects his wished-for activity with that of a puppy, digging up its prize of a bone.

It is perhaps the (roughly) Central African location of *King Solomon's Mines* that leads the poet to his final image of the Upper Nile, a place as potent, fascinating and unknown to early explorers as the girl is to him. 'Does enormous things' is suitably grand and vague, embracing a mysterious source, forceful and dangerous cataracts, the lost splendours of ancient civilisations, and a desert made fertile by the flow of water. All these, the deeper resources of the girl, as yet untapped, are proffered by the poet as his last argument. The bracketed indirect statement '(she suspects)' reads puzzlingly after the direct 'your air', but may convey the poet's whispered caution to himself — 'she suspects my drift, or my motives; I haven't much time to convince her, I must make the most of it'. The frankness displayed toward the reader by this interpolation, and by 'slyly' earlier, have the effect of disarming criticism of the lover's tactics, which are seen to spring from a winning mixture of desire for the girl and a concern that she fulfil herself. The last stanza's image of the alluvial Nile north of Cairo, bringing only 'delta and indecision' in its uncertain movement to the sea, links up with the beach on which Alice/Nausicaa plays immaturely with her sand-castles and tries her lover's patience. In the face of such a picture (or picture-postcard), his advocacy that she become a woman ('Nile' concealing perhaps the compliment 'Cleopatra') seems only reasonable, though the poem's delicate obscurity may well, one feels, have weakened its powers of persuasion.

LEGAL FICTION

First published in *Cambridge Review*, Vol. 50 (30 Nov. 1928), p. 171. Reprinted in *Cambridge Poetry, 1929*.

Generally praised, though not frequently analysed, this is one of Empson's most compact and disciplined early poems, and perhaps his most cogent early expression of man's existential state. Some of its ideas give the poem a family likeness to 'This Last Pain'; but its feeling is better suggested by a line from 'Plenum and Vacuum': 'Matter includes what must matter enclose.' In 'Legal Fiction', what matter includes (physically, and finally) is mind; but despite this, mind is driven to control and make sense of external reality, to behave as if it were all-encompassing. The dualism which is the poem's subject — man as mind, man as matter — is reflected in its *modus operandi*. The intellectual content is conveyed to the reader's mind by the initial legal metaphor and by the geometrical figure developed from it; while his emotional response is evoked by homelier means — the basic opposites 'long' and 'short' in the first line, their richer equivalents, flashing lighthouse and wavering candle, in the last, the effectively tendentious (and rather sinister) harping on 'rights' and owning, the various connotations of 'Heaven', 'Hell' and 'Lucifer'. Empson's view of mind's pretensions, and of man's predicament, is mixed, involving elements of satire, admiration, and fear.

A 'legal fiction' is a concept which, though not strictly true, is accepted as true for purposes of convenience. The particular concept implicit here, and elaborated geometrically in stanzas two and three, is that man possesses not only his property on the surface of the earth (referred to as a 'farm' in line 11, perhaps because Empson's forebears were country squires), but also the air above it and the earth beneath it. The notions of 'airspace', and of mining or oil rights, give this fiction some legal 'truth', so that the first line can be taken as a literal statement about 'Law' in the technical sense: legal assumptions extend man's physical control. The figurative language used, however, is too rich to be limited like this: 'stakes' suggests property, and links up in this sense with 'fenced out' and with 'claim', but it also suggests the idea of risk or gamble (human life as a bet or race), and thus man's precariousness. 'Long spokes' are not only the geometrical, quasi-literal extensions of 'stakes' downwards to revolving 'earth's centre' and upwards into the universe, but also suggest 'long speeches', both the Law's long-winded dignity and the elaborations of other types of fiction by which man attempts to exert control over the world. It is, thus, necessary to take the word 'law' not just in its narrow legal sense but as including all those forms of ordering and organisation by which man enlarges his horizons. But though such 'law' makes something long (in a sense) out of something short, the very word 'makes' is ambivalent, conveying both creation and coercion, a positive and necessary activity yet also, as the poem concludes by showing, a pathetic and temporary falsification.

Having announced his text pithily on line one, Empson presents in the rest of the stanza the example of it which interests him – not physical property but the metaphorical 'real estate of mind'. The phrase conveniently blurs together the technical term 'real estate', the general term 'state of mind', and the old-fashioned dignity of 'estate', but may also be intended to prompt the reader to question whether man's mind is his 'real' estate (the end of the poem suggests it is not). Empson, giving this mental 'real estate' a physical presence, sees it as neatly divided from its neighbours, and incapable of being either overlooked or undermined. The literal source of the image is suburbia, encroached on by blocks of flats and railway lines, over- or under-ground: the 'nomad citizen' is surely that spreading phenomenon of the twenties, the commuter, whose world is also touched on by 'The Ants' and 'Rolling the Lawn'. What the mind prizes seems, from this image, to be privacy (not being overlooked suggests also a snobbish, or squeamish, gentility) and the feeling of uniqueness. To 'leave behind', however, is not only to depart from somewhere but to go faster than something; thus the end of the stanza asserts a power peculiar to the mind, the ability to comprehend, to keep up with, everything.

Stanza Two exploits the legal fiction about physical property to explain why the 'estate' of the mind is neither overlooked nor has trains running under it. What emerges is a typically Empsonian hyperbole, given characteristically 'scientific' form. The production, upwards and downwards, of the fences surrounding a property creates an enormously long cone, narrowing to a point at the centre of the earth, widening ever outwards ('without bound' since the universe is 'finite but unbounded') into the universe; viewed two-dimensionally this cone is the 'sector' of line 12. Empson's presentation is repetitious: first the traditional concept (line 6) that the mind contains part of Heaven and Hell in itself, then (lines 7–8) a rather muddled scientific version of this, in which 'stars' are arbitrarily separated from 'cosmos', and the phrase 'the same' is loosely used to mean "ditto". The geometrical analogy conveys the 'rights' (or merely claims) of the mind over the physical universe (cf. Cornford, *From Religion to Philosophy*, p. 60).

Stanza Three repeats the general ideas of Stanza Two, but with more emphasis on the narrowing end of the mental cone: whereas the separateness, and adventurousness, of each mind's view of the world is conveyed by the 'growing sector' which comprehends 'galaxies' (literal or metaphorical ones), the mind's 'rights' also 'reach down'. Line 3 defines this point, in terms of the geometrical figure, as the 'root' from which his property grows, the motionless ('still') axis on which it continually revolves. This might sound reassuring did not Empson envisage the central point as 'Hell', an 'exclusive conclave' where 'all owners meet'. There may be Biblical undertones here (ownership excludes from Heaven), or Miltonic ones (the 'secret conclave' at Pandemonium, *Paradise Lost* I, 795); but more striking is the sardonic contradiction-in-terms of 'exclusive conclave': some conclaves *are* exclusive (like the College of Cardinals), but this one is a private room which contains *all* owners, since the lines dividing their 'properties' unite at this point. Ultimately, man's claims to individual mental control of life come down to no more than this.

Control suggests fixity, but the last stanza asserts that man is 'nomad yet' (and thus, after all, no different from the 'nomad citizen' of line 2), despite the large claims of his 'law'-making compulsion. The word 'yet', however, has a strangely defiant ring here, as though Empson were not unduly dismayed by this realisation, as though man's precariousness were even a source of gallantry. The cut-and-dried geometrical figure representing man's claim to mental jurisdiction (the legal fiction he needs in order to live) is cleverly transformed into two shapes which, though geometrically similar (each an aspect of the earlier cone), convey the reality of his life very differently and with far stronger emotional effect. What man truly owns is not the world he lives in but a revolving 'lighthouse beam' which illuminates it at intervals. Virginia Woolf's *To the Lighthouse,* with its moving central section 'Time Passes' in which the lighthouse beam fitfully reveals the deserted Ramsay house, had appeared in 1927, and may have influenced Empson. Whether it did or not, his image here is a magnificent one, suggesting both the power and velocity of the human mind and the extent of the surrounding darkness. 'Lucifer' brings in the pride, and failure, of Satan, and the idea of 'Lucifer' matches. Man's state is both splendid and doomed, and as he is 'nomad', so the rotation of the earth is not on a fixed axis (central point) but around a central line drawn through the poles, which shifts and tilts with the passage of time and its own course around the sun. The subterranean 'end' of man's 'lighthouse beam' (a brightness of many units of candle-power) narrows, as the 'end' of death approaches, into a 'dark central cone', which may be either the shadow cast by a single candle, or the darkness discernible within the candle-flame itself.

So the poem comes full-circle: man's mind extends the power of a short life over matter, man's physical limitations extinguish his mind. The image of the flickering candle suggests the reduction of man's pride to a child's fear as it goes upstairs to bed, and the end of the poem may be an echo of Alice, as she worries about shrinking (*Alice in Wonderland,* Ch. 1): '"For it might end, you know. . .in my going out altogether, like a candle. I wonder what I should be like then?"'

SLEEPING OUT IN A COLLEGE CLOISTER

First published, as 'Sleeping Out in the Cloister', in *Magdalene College Magazine,* Vol. 9 (March, 1929), p. 46. [Published in *Poems* (1935) as 'Sleeping Out in College Cloister'.]

This poem first appeared, over Empson's initials only, in the 'house organ' of his college magazine; its first title, in that context, implies an origin in specifically Magdalene College experience which would be recognised by other members of the college. In the absence of anything properly describable as a 'cloister', one assumes Empson is referring to Magdalene's second court, whose lawn is bounded on one side by the college dining-hall ('Hall') and on the opposite one by the Pepys Library, with its arcaded ground-floor frontage; its other two sides being separated by walls from the Fellows' Garden and the River Cam. Tall trees rise outside the court, but not so many as to suggest by day the disquieting nocturnal perspectives recorded in the poem. Not that disquiet predominates, however: the 'uncomfortable view of night' also 'charms', and the relaxed and conversational blank verse gives on the whole a pleasant, if uncharacteristic, inconsequential air to the various observations and reflections.

Empson 'places' his own experience of sleeping out by relating it to that of Robert Louis Stevenson: the first five lines, casual yet lyrical, and beautifully paced, are a précis of part of Stevenson's chapter 'A Night Among the Pines' from *Travels with a Donkey in the Cevennes* (1879). The key passage runs: 'At what inaudible summons, at what gentle touch of Nature, are all these sleepers thus recalled at the same hour to life? Do the stars rain down an influence, or do we share some thrill of mother earth below our resting bodies?. . .Towards two in the morning they declare the thing takes place; and neither know nor enquire further. And at least it is a pleasant incident. We are disturbed in our slumber, only, like the luxurious Montaigne, "that we may the better and more sensibly relish it". We have a moment to look upon the stars'. . .(Tusitala Edn., 1924, p. 207). His own version of this mood of quiet ecstasy is delicately built up by Empson only to be deliberately jarred by the content and rhythm of lines 6–7: these lines do not 'debunk' Stevenson (there is nothing automatically ludicrous in his feelings), but they do indicate that Empson's 'small hours' experience was very different, as he steps accidentally in the dark ('stamped' and 'chose' are surely comic exaggeration?) on a fellow sleeper while moving his mattress to a more congenial spot. Such 'an animate basis for one's mattress' may be intended as a wry, men's college fulfilment of Stevenson's wish for a loved female companion to lie beside him (p. 208); sharpening the comedy of *that*, the phrase may also allude to Stevenson's description of his donkey, Modestine, as 'only an appurtenance of my mattress, or self-acting bedstead on four castors' (p. 147). The farcical incident, made single and specific by the past tense, is followed by Empson's perception, whose greater seriousness and wider relevance is emphasised by his contrasting use of the present tense; its difference from Stevenson's is appropriately suggested by its occurrence later than his hour of two o'clock. What Empson perceives is not night's beneficent atmosphere but the optical effect night creates, changing the sense of scale so that the court seems shrunken, the trees enlarged. The nice ambiguities of 'shelters' (cosiness or fear) and 'How much more foliage appears' ('shows itself', or merely 'seems bigger') create an eerie expectancy.

The second section, discussing size and perspective, seems less a digression than an attempt to offer examples of disorientation in order to decide whether they are analogies for the present case. His picture of earth first as globe then as *terra firma* recalls Satan's view in *Paradise Lost* III: 'A globe far off/It seemed, now seems a boundless continent' (lines 422–23). Either size, the one too remote to be worrying, the other so close as to allow recognition of familiar features and create a relationship, can be mentally classified (the phrase 'the Globe' suggests the comfort of labels) and thus not force the imagination to confront it. It is the phase of growth from one size to the other (finely and scaringly imagined by Empson's lines) which threatens to overwhelm the mind: the frightening quality here is only marginally reduced by the bracket about swallowing, which suggests a child about to have a pill forced down its throat. What does reduce it (creating relief rather than bathos) is Empson's transition from his 'nightmare' image, by the sleight-of-hand of 'in the same way', to a homelier example of a halfway state: the 'creepiness' (the slangy understatement is just right) produced by the odd failure of Cambridge(shire) scenery to achieve the look of woodedness, despite having trees (of which it nevertheless has too many to look bare). Such scenery, of course, literally illustrates the phrase 'you can't see the wood for the trees'. 'In safe hands' is obscure, but

105

may suggest that nature, who once knew best (when, and if, the county was 'virgin forest'), has been despoiled by man. Such a reading at any rate provides a shaky bridge into the last section, which seems to turn on the idea of man-made bareness (clearings and civilisation) being 're-engulfed' by nature.

Unfortunately, the first four lines of the last section are confusing, and indeed confused. Where does the main emphasis fall in the first line: on 'opposite', or on 'charms'? On balance, the second alternative seems likelier, since 'creepiness' (and it is the 'scenery', rather than the globe, which seems referred to here) is hardly charming. In what sense, then, are the two 'disorders' opposites, and in what way, for that matter, are they 'disorders'? One can only suggest that 'Cambridge scenery' (nature) fails to achieve the appearance of order represented by 'woodedness'; whereas the court fails to achieve the opposite order of 'airy and wide open space' planned by the college architects. These 'chosen proportions' have 'grown cramped' through night's shrinking effect (1.9); but, in addition, the planned open space 'seems stifled under traditions' – cluttered up, that is, by man himself. ('Seems' was the original reading in *Magdalene College Magazine* and *Poems* (1935).)

The bracketed '(Traditor)', glossed by Empson's note as 'betrayer', complicates an already blurred meaning by its uncertainty of application. One is unsure whether it is a mere punning reflex triggered by the stimulus of 'tradition'; whether it is designed to suggest an ironic link between the accretions of college history and the fading of pristine intentions; or whether it is the poet's mock-serious self-reproach for letting the college down by thinking such things and finding this 'opposite disorder' charming. Certainly the last four lines, with their irreverent post-Victorian reference to Tennyson (a Trinity man) and their joking identification of the court next to 'Hall' with the "*high*" (High Table?) hall garden of *Maud XII*, suggest an altitude mildly iconoclastic, one which is not sorry to see the nocturnal forces of nature reclaim, if only by optical illusion, the 'palace and campus' of college buildings and grassy court. (The very word 'campus', not recorded until the *O.E.D.* supplement of 1933 and then with purely American examples of its use, must in 1929 have sounded impiously Transatlantic, for all its Latin meaning of 'field'.) One does not feel that the 'uncomfortable view of night', related as it may be to the physical discomforts of lines 6-7, gives much discomfort to its perceiver; though neither does he proffer it too seriously to the reader. That would have required more clarity, and a less delightful image of drowning than the 'flounces and bell-calm of trees' with which he chooses to conclude.

EARTH HAS SHRUNK IN THE WASH

First published in *Experiment* No. 2 (Feb. 1929), p. 45.

Despite its (wryly) facetious title, and such a distracting local effect as the excruciating rhyme 'cancer'/'plants, or' in stanza three, the general tone of this cautionary tale about modern scientific 'progress' is concerned and pessimistic. It is, one should say, the 'science' theme that dominates; if there is another ('Civilised refinement cutting one off from other people', as Empson's note claims), it is present only in stanza one, after which the postulated 'earth now asteroid' is used as the basis for a fable, rather than as (presumably) an image for individuals no longer in contact with one another. It seems likely, nevertheless, that the poem does basically re-present a response to both things – the rate of scientific dis-covery and the pace of life in the 'twenties – as in some sense linked: there is obvious metaphorical application in a world literally without atmosphere (stanza two), gravity, or back-bone (line 10).

The title, lamenting earth's shrinkage in terms of once all too common domestic calamity, is amusingly flippant, and one sympathises with Empson's inability to resist it; but it creates problems for the reader. The laundry may shrink clothes, but what kind of 'wash' will make the earth smaller? To say that it, like the clothes, is well-worn and dirty and needs 'washing' has some emotional point; but such metaphorical washing would produce only metaphorical shrinkage, whereas the poem's story is based on an earth literally shrunken ('earth now asteroid'), which implies a wash of a literal sort. The collocation of title with first line reinforces this expectation: things (one does not know what 'they' are until the end of the stanza) which 'pass too fast' can create a 'wash' — such speed, say, as wears away the banks of rivers. Thus the shrinking of earth to the size of an asteroid could be taken as the result of some astronomical accident. Recounting, in *The Nature of the Physical World,* Sir James Jeans's theory of the origin of the solar system (a star passing the sun, and causing it to throw out filaments of matter which have condensed to form the planets), Eddington uses a sentence sufficiently like Empson's to have provided him with a point of departure: 'it [the star] must not have passed too rapidly' (1935 edn., p. 176). If Empson did extrapolate from this a theory of what might happen if some celestial body passed the *earth* too quickly, there is no apparent support for it in the astronomical speculations of the time; thus earth's shrinkage in the poem (on which much is made to hang) seems to have no cause other than Empson's wish to assume it for purposes of polemic.

What the first stanza essentially presents is a decrease in human communication brought about by an increase in the speed of life. The abrupt first phrase makes the point about speed very appropriately, conveying an impression of regret as it flashes past, but no precise meaning until this is established by lines 3–4. Meanwhile, in a sort of colloquial shorthand, two images of communication are put forward: the common romantic notion of slowly passing ships ('sighing' suggests 'ships that pass in the night'), which can at least 'speak' each other across the gap; and the cinematic fantasy of the agile hero (Douglas Fairbanks) who leaps from moving car to moving train. Such land and sea contact, rare or unsatisfactory as it may be, is displaced by Empson's aerial image of contemporary isolation: earth envisaged as an asteroid, an atmosphere-less ('dry') minor planet in orbit with her fellow asteroids ('flying mates', the 'they' of line 1) who pass her too quickly for sight or messages. 'If they miss her' is a very pregnant phrase here. In the context of 'sighing' and 'mates', 'miss' has its emotional meaning, calling up a lonely world of separate individuals, yearning but unable to communicate; but a strong stress placed on 'If' implies people unwilling to do this.

Most obviously, however, 'miss' means 'fail to hit', and it is this meaning which assists transition to stanza two, where the literal aspects of 'earth now asteroid' begin to be explored, first in terms of what would happen if one of earth's 'flying mates' did collide with her. (It may be that here Empson is thinking not of asteroids but of meteorites: there were more meteorite falls on earth in the 'twenties than in any previous decade.) Lacking an atmosphere – the 'air' that once protected the surface ('breasts') of mother Earth, God's over-arching but fragile rainbow, the vanished beauty of a once-promising world – asteroid-Earth is entirely vulnerable ('breasts' also suggests 'breastplate' and 'breastwork', which once fended off harm from outside); but the catastrophic result (oddly reminiscent of 'Landing you break some palace' in 'To an Old Lady') is reduced by the domesticity of 'skylights', as if a burglar rather than a bomb had fallen through the roof. There seems also, though, a strong sexual element in the description ('striking breasts', 'straddling', 'burrow', 'spill all'), as if with modern humans as with Empson's asteroids the only possibilities were separation or violent collision – in either case, hardly communication.

Risks of collision apart, life on such a world would be horrible enough. Direct sunlight ('airless' suggests suffocation, while meaning an absence of protective atmosphere) would produce not a sun-tan, which the transferred epithet 'bare' makes one think of, but skin cancer; lack of gravity consequent on earth's diminishing size would create curvature of the spine; and the food available would be useless. The diabetes reference in line 12 is explained by Empson's note, though the awkwardness of the line itself is still a blemish; in *Experiment* it was no less awkward, though its play on 'missing the beat' appeared more clearly in the form 'Miss (dia)beat(ic) down odd carbon chain'. Line 11 may have been prompted by a passage in Haldane's essay 'Enzymes': 'Many molecules which are attacked by [enzymes] are asymmetrical, . . . We can often make the mirror-images of these molecules, and we then find that the corresponding enzymes will only attack them slowly if at all. On going through the looking-glass, Alice would have found her digestive enzymes of no more use on the looking-glass sugars than her Yale key on the looking-glass locks.' (*Possible Worlds*, pp. 46–47).

The point of Empson's use of imperatives in stanza three, as if to proffer man a repulsive world he has in some way deserved, becomes clearer in the next section, an interpolated comment which seems to imply that man is well on the way to producing such a world: the 'here' of line 16, which one takes to refer to the present, is surely meant to contrast with the 'there' of line 9, the world of future possibility already presented so as to make the poet's warning in the last stanza more powerful. Life on other planets (a speculation line 14 entertains) may 'moderately' torture its creator, but it is certain that man, made in his image, does so on this one and, Empson ironically exhorts, 'has much more to do', by means of such disastrous experiments as the introduction of rabbits into Australia in the eighteenth century. 'Entail' is punningly related to rabbits, but more seriously suggests that the consequences of man's ill-advised actions may, like an entailed estate, be a burden to his successors. And there is surely sarcasm in the idea of a trail of fresh catastrophes which are always 'unforeseen'.

Empson's indictment (its triple rhymes and 'superior' tone conveying a pained boredom with man's follies, as well as some anger) culminates in his return to the original stanza form by means of the devastating short phrase 'And cannot tell'. Recalling the poem's opening sentence, and echoing the shape and sound of 'can so much entail' as well as completing its syntax, the phrase powerfully expresses man's blindness, his ignorance of where his discoveries will lead. The poem ends with a sombre warning to 'He who all answers brings', the modern scientist, his witch-doctor status suggested in the Red Indian-sounding periphrasis – though the answers he brings may be no more than a conjuror's 'rabbits'. Such a one's 'great taskmaster', one may conjecture, is not the God of Milton's sonnet on his twenty-third birthday (though that God may watch him nevertheless), but the world's desire for scientific progress, or his own for scientific fame. His researches, however, may well have mixed results, even cancel out, as Empson indicates in two quasi-examples (not necessarily linked) and one finely functional pun. Though he may 'dowse' for water (the scientists as laudable discoverer, but also, perhaps, inspired guesser), he may also 'douse' the candle (Empson grants him nothing brighter) of his illumination. (Cf. 'Legal Fiction'.) Likewise, while performing such a necessary act as pumping water out of a tunnel (the scientist as engineer), he may in some way drain off the water of the fertile valley under or out of which it runs.

It is a grave and impressive conclusion, made so by Empson's allusion to Milton and his skilful rhetorical balance. But one may doubt whether the dryness with which the poem ends (produced as it is by an action whose technical likelihood is by no means obvious) can lead, other than in terms of hyperbolic fantasy, to the extremer dryness with which it begins. Empson's concern about the two-edged sword of scientific progress is understandable, and the situation he presents in the first three stanzas as an example of its dangers would indeed be serious if it could happen. Worries about science, however, even in a poem, need some basis in science, and this worry is implausible. It is a pity that Empson weakens his case by overkill.

FLIGHTING FOR DUCK

First published, with numerous differences of wording and punctuation, and with eight more lines between the penultimate and final sections, in *Magdalene College Magazine*, Vol. 9 (Dec. 1928), pp. 19–20.

In late 1928 and early 1929 there appeared in *Granta* a series of humorous pieces, by various single or multiple hands, concerning a young man called Montague Slumberbottom and his father Alexander, who strongly recalls that indefatigable writer of Letters to the Editor, 'Disgusted'. Empson contributed one of the episodes, entitled 'Has Slumberbottom Sinned?' (30 Nov. 1928), and collaborated on two others

(12 Oct. 1928; 25 Jan. 1929). Montague is referred to once as 'the notorious Slumberbottom, the human spider of the fens', and his father's address is given as 'Dank Place, Nr. Drain, Drippingley', which seems close enough to Empson's low-lying birthplace on the Yorkshire Ouse near Goole. It is this part of the world that Empson deals with, seriously, in 'Flighting for Duck', published over his initials in his college magazine while the Slumberbottom story was still continuing in *Granta*. Empson's only poem of natural description, it gives the reader used to his complex intellectual manner an initial impression of flatness; but further acquaintance reveals it as skilful in structure, sensitive in feeling, and rich in suggestion. While one can hardly agree with J.H. Willis (unpublished Ph.D. thesis, Columbia, 1967) that it is 'the most Yeatsian of Empson's poems' ('The Wild Ducks at Goole', perhaps?), there is much more to it than is suggested by Empson's typically throwaway account when the poem was anthologised twenty years later in America: 'The magazine of my college at Cambridge asked me for a poem, and as this seemed a gentlemanly sort of public I thought they would like a poem about shooting, so I turned one out.' (*Modern Poetry,* ed. Kimon Friar and John Malcolm Brinnin, New York, 1951).

The eighteenth-century flavour of the poem, most obvious in the splendid pastiche of heroic couplets in section three, is particularly appropriate in view of the two activities described – 'flighting' (shooting wildfowl) and 'warping' (fertilising land with alluvial deposits) – since both present man as controlling his environment rather than just as observing it. One notices, in this connection, how the two bracketed phrases (lines 3–4, 5–6) describe the same flat and undramatic scene: the first in precise visual terms which yet give it a quality of timelessness and magic; the second practically, in terms of what is being done to it. Indeed, the landscape in 'Flighting for Duck' is to a large extent in the process of modification and 'improvement' by man ('constructed marshes'); similarly, though ducks which are 'out of shot' give pleasure to the eye, those within range furnish the pleasures of the table. Though Empson's attitude to man's supremacy is not unequivocal, it is recurrent ideas of order which provide the poem with its thematic unity: the infertile thistle-specked marsh which is 'not yet mastered' by man's 'alluvial scheme'; the human eye which 'orders' the 'unreachable chaos' of the flying ducks; the 'proper homage' paid by the dead ducks to 'Reason's arm'. (The realisation that this last is a periphrasis for 'gun' gives a nice ironic sting).

Atmospheric unity is created by the poem's slow progress from twilight, against which the darker objects of pinetrees and barn show with mysterious clarity, to misty moonlight ('one whole pearl embrowned') in which the poet's black hatband is similarly visible, standing out with enigmatic significance and relating surrounding objects to itself. And the movement up to and away from the climactic third section, with its sharp report and clipped couplets, is managed with unobtrusive ease: first the scene-setting, in blank verse which is given an effect of rhyme by its equal, though not always alternating, masculine and feminine endings (ten of each); then the arrival of the ducks, announced in staccato phrases and nervous, accidental-sounding rhymes; and their diverging movements in the sky, paralleled by the widely-varying gaps between the different rhyme-sounds. In the last four lines of section two the sentence structure and the two close rhymes 'amuse' and 'Ouse' combine to create a quatrain from which the poem's modulation into (mock) heroic couplets is credible and smooth. After their parody of Augustan balance and inversion, which conveys good-humoured dissent from the complacent convictions of sportsmen, and may be intended to recall Pope's description of hunting in 'Windsor Forest' (ll. 119–34), the last six lines form a complete contrast, in their slow-paced movement and rhyme-scheme and their mood of detachment and reflection.

To describe the poem's general effect thus, in terms of motifs, sound and mood, is to suggest its unusual place in Empson's work. Interestingly, he was prepared to concede in 1951 that: 'It might be said [to be] a better poem than the ones I take more seriously, but this wouldn't be a refutation of my position.' It is indeed a good poem, but not without devices found elsewhere in his work, and so not entirely an uncharacteristic one. A visitor does not, for instance, find it easy to see the 'high road' dividing the present fertile fields that have resulted from the warping as 'Egyptian banks', which Empson in 1951 glossed as 'Egyptian diggings. . .which may be up to forty feet deep and a mile or two long.' But the fanciful exaggeration has the effect of comparing the ferti-lising Ouse (its very name a useful pun on 'ooze') to the life-giving Nile, and thus adds an extra dimension to the phrase 'cult of Ouse' (worship, as well as the mud 'culture' trans-ferred from it to the fields) in section two. The word 'pomp' (line 5), in the context of 'Egyptian banks' and 'high road', functions in its Greek meaning of 'procession', and makes sense of the comparison of side banks ('transept' is fittingly dignified here) to a 'castle guard' who march up to meet the main one (the phrase 'even file' in the original line 11 brought this out more clearly.) The whole pattern of references places 'the further warping' (one feels no irony in the technical term) in a long perspective of civilising acts and rituals.

More contemporary fancies occur in section two. The 'hint of anti-aircraft' refers presumably to the farm dog's barking, as if at approaching danger, stilled ('disarmed') when the 'drumming' is revealed as the welcome ducks whose arrival 'repays' the hunters for their long wait. A reminder of Empson's astronomical imagery elsewhere is given by the magnificently-grotesque comparison – a realisation akin to 'I knew the Phoenix was a vegetable' in 'Note on Local Flora' – of the scattering ducks to the stars of an expanding uni-verse. (Since radio astronomy started no earlier than in 1931, 'their voices harsh' can only be a joke, applied to the stars – perhaps at the expense of the 'music of the spheres'.) The word 'surfaces' has a technical ring, as if Empson the mathe-matical scholar were savouring the ducks' complex geo-metrical evolutions – flat planes crossing each other, then expanding into three dimensions. The last four lines of section two are as ingenious as anything in Empson, with their richly-confused syntax, their overlapping phrases, and their conceit of the flying ducks as resembling exhaled cigarette-smoke ('turning clouds' may suggest that elegant and vanished brand 'Passing Clouds'), and being a kind of incense both offered to the Ouse and breathed out by its manuring mud. ('Manure in smoke' may function grammatically in the same way as 'sermons in stone'; but since 'manure' is related etymologically to 'manoeuvre', it may be intended as a verb, to describe the ducks' avoiding action.)

The last section, however, is not amenable to this kind of analysis. It is the surviving sestet of a sonnet, and the omission of the octave, though sharpening the technical and atmospheric contrast between the last six lines and the preceding six in the present version, has made the poet's attitude less explicit, as these omitted lines (the last three of the octave) suggest: 'When the punt splashing and far words between/ Meant hunt for corpses, like themselves unseen,/I walked the bank, the pines dimmed from view.' The poet, though on his home ground, seems an odd man out, remote from the duck-hunters whose activities he has earlier described. But what exactly the experience is that the present conclusion conveys is not clear. Neither the physical situation nor the illumination that arises from it is explained; one is simply left with the feeling of a solitary, non-intellectual revelation which is sufficient to itself.

Whether the 'black band', which leaps to the reader's eye as to the poet's, provides a clue to the quality of the last section seems uncertain. That it briefly shows 'everything by' may be no more than a visual impression, but one is so unused to this alone in Empson that one tends to look further, and see the band as indicating mourning. As the warping referred to in the poem was carried out on the Yokefleet estate in the 1920s, and as the only member of Empson's family to die anywhere near that time was his father, who died as long before as 1916, mourning seems an unlikely explanation for the quiet mood of the conclusion. Nevertheless, some motive of filial tribute may be at the root of the poem as a whole, since Arthur Reginald Empson had at the age of 41 himself treated this subject in a creditable version of eighteenth-century pastoral. At Yokefleet Hall in 1975 hung a watercolour of a marsh scene – a duck hunter in a boat hidden behind reeds, five ducks flying overhead, a low sunset reflected on water. Under the picture was pasted a poem, dated May 13th, 1894 and signed 'A.R.E.' It brought together the motifs of cultivation and shooting, employed varying verse forms, and was entitled 'Warping':

> He stood and watched the weary waste
>   Disdainful geese flew screeching o'er
> Not e'en an ass would stoop to graze
>   The weeds and thistles that it bore.
>
> The rushing river pours; leaving behind
>   The wealth of many tides. Wild duck and snipe
> Plover and curlew feed. Salmon and eels
> Abound. Deep through the mud the sportsman wades.
>
> Ah! Now he sees a different scene
>   Fair waving corn and scented bean
> Rich mustard and potato fields
>   The fruitful soil ungrudging yields.

LETTER III

First published in *Experiment* No. 3 (May, 1929), p. 7.

This poem, which shares with 'Letter II' the use of 'heaven' as an image for the loved girl's face and qualities, also vies with it in being the best of the five letters. With dense language, intricacy of cross-reference, and literary allusion (all these elements highly functional) it combines neatness and economy of structure and a strong main line of emotional argument throughout. Its more positive attitude to the love relationship is in refreshing contrast to the gloom of 'Letter II': while the poem belongs partly to the tradition of metaphysical compliment (like Donne's, Empson's mistress is 'more than moone'), there is a distinctly personal note in its grateful celebration of love as a bringer of sanity and courage.

Since it is addressed in stanza one but described in the third person in stanza two, one is not sure at first whether to take the 'moon' as literal or metaphorical. The noon of stanza three, also in mixed fashion, is called 'sane day' and

116

'daylight of your calm'. Lying between moon addressed and moonlight described, Empson's use of the word 'simile' (rather than 'metaphor') provides the clue to the most satisfying and all-inclusive reading of the poem. The girl who is the 'you' (line 15) of the poem is first seen as 'like' the moon, which has powers akin to her own, then, as the limitations of this comparison are registered (lines 10–12), she is seen as like dawn ('you a full sky unfurl') and like 'shadowless daylight'. Meanwhile, the literal time-scheme of the poem parallels these mental realisations. moving from moonlit night to sunlit day and, in terms of the poet's feelings, from fear of the daytime world to greater confidence in it.

The unusual word 're-edify' draws attention to itself. and serves also to announce a habit of multiple meaning which is particularly strong in this poem. 'Edify' usually means 'benefit', 'improve' or 'instruct', and it is clear enough that the moon/girl uplifts and strengthens the poet who appeals to her against the 'discomposing' effects of the sun's beams: her value is broadly therapeutic. The usage is sufficiently unidiomatic, however, to make the reader suspect the less familiar Latinate meaning, soon confirmed by the phrase 'the designer's sketches', of 'rebuild' or 'reconstruct'; for this, within the architectural metaphor set up, 'discomposes' provides an exact opposite (it also resembles 'decompose'). The poet sees himself as a building, enabled by the steadying influence of moonlight ('beams' are solid wooden supports, as well as the girl's smiles) to endure the harsher light, or heavier pressure, of painful daily reality. The nature of the girl's steadying effect is indicated by line 2: as moonlight shows a building not in its details but in outline, as in an architect's preliminary drawings, so the girl returns the poet to some pristine state, the 'order' (design or command) before it is put into effect. That the 'designer' may be God, and the state that of Edenic innocence, is suggested by line 6, which quotes Milton's description (*Paradise Lost* IV, 606–609) of the light that shone in Paradise as Adam and Eve, not yet fallen, enjoyed their first nuptial embrace. Like the moon, whose reflected light derives its power from the sun ('that altar'), the girl is an intermediary, through whom the painful brightness of reality is transmitted in a bearable form.

The last two lines of the stanza were originally in brackets, as befitted their startling shift in imagery and their intimately sexual flavour (emphasised by the word 'darling' instead of 'therefore'). They share with what precedes them the idea of the girl as the poet's protectress, from whom he derives what savour and powers of survival ('may do yet') he has. There is a tenuous associative logic linking 'moon', via 'beam', to 'cedar' cigarette box, but the leap from poet as building to poet as cigarette is much too abrupt and cavalier.

It is not, however, this 'simile' which Empson suddenly turns away from in stanza two, but that of the moon. He abandons it not so much because it is a false representation of the girl's powers (it *has* given him 'pleasure') as because it is an inadequate one. If moonlight can simplify things it can also distort them, its soft light creating shadows and a self-indulgent romanticism ('deep velvet'). He sees it in lines 3–4 as illuminating, only a shade less theatrically than lightning ('only lightning beats it'), the stone lacework of Gothic ruins, alike dear to the hearts of eccentrics and recluses (a possible interpretation of the slang meaning of 'parties'), and the stock-in-trade of evening 'mystery tours' in charabancs. ('Gothic' manages to encompass such things as Tintern Abbey, the creepy décor of the Gothic novel, and the 'nightmare' reference of stanza three.) As if rejecting the nocturnal comforts of stanza one as an evasion, Empson declares that the perspectives the loved girl opens up are not 'lunacy' (moon-madness, as well as moonlight), nor like jerkily-moving shots from some remembered film ('flick'). Instead her 'restoration' is a steady 'glow' which brings 'full relief' – a complete cure for his problems, and a clearly-lit building of which everything, outline and details, can be seen. The layered richness of lines 13–14 defeats linear paraphrase, but splendidly communicates the poet's appreciation of the girl's life-giving powers, which are summed up in the word 'restoration', with its fusion of the motifs of health, architecture, and royalty. For as well as restoring the poet, the girl is herself restored, being identified now not with the moon but with the dawn, the wholeness of whose 'full sky' lights up the poet's fragmented self ('my each face') and brings sight to his blindness. The 'blind' may also cover his window, and the 'pearl' (rather odd if taken to describe the eye) recalls the opening of *Paradise Lost* V: 'Now morn. . ./Advancing, sowed the earth with orient pearl.'

Some confusion in the poem's situation and chronology ensues with stanza three. Though aware of the dawn, Empson describes himself waking at noon, the hour favoured by the sensible lovers of Pope's anti-romantic line (*The Rape of the Lock* I, 16; Empson has sneaked his own word 'when' into it), who lose no sleep over love. Pope's lovers are apart, so presumably Empson and his mistress are too (the innuendo of stanza one notwithstanding). But unlike them, perhaps Empson genuinely was 'sleepless': the cigarette image, and his picture of shadowy moonlight (perhaps decorating the facade of a college court?), suggest insomnia as the source of his meditations. (One of Empson's uncollected undergraduate poems, published in April, 1929, was entitled 'Insomnia'.) It may perhaps be inferred that only in the early light of dawn, reassuring on this occasion, was he able to get to sleep, and so woke late, into 'diffused shadowless daylight' of sanity and calm, having put behind him (or avoided, as the variant forms 'past'/'passed' allow one to think) both 'nightmare' and the 'cold bitter pallor of daybreak' which may have been his more usual lot. A reference in Julian Trevelyan's *Indigo Days* (1957) is suggestive here: describing an overnight drive from London to Bolton, made with Tom Harrison and Empson in about 1937 for the purpose of 'Mass Observation' work, he notes that 'about five in the morning, Bill became restless, and we had to stop in a café, so that he should not see the dawn that upset him strangely.' (p. 83).

Precise circumstantial details apart, what the girl is being praised for in stanza three is apparent — her sensibleness and sanity, pouring its gentle heavenly light into the poet's 'square garish sky-sign' — a modified version of the earlier architectural metaphor. For all the 'round of pearl' of stanza two, his awkwardness is not totally transformed, but at least it can receive what the girl has to give. (In an 'additional note' to the 1956 impression of *Collected Poems* Empson

119

explained the now-obsolete 'sky-sign' as 'a prism displayed for advertisement, open on top, with a mirror on the back face and some writing on the front one, which was thus illuminated without expense.') Her light is more than sunlight, it is something earlier ('before sun or focus', the 'focus' either earth or moon), related by Empson to Pope's line which may be said to describe, in its commonsensical way, the re-creation enacted by daily awakening. The final couplet, three compliments which give the girl a triple crown, express her gift of light in terms of (blind) Milton's invocation at the beginning of *Paradise Lost* III: 'Hail, holy Light! offspring of Heaven first born'. Created and creating, she is the primal source of life and inspiration. She is also solidity, either the 'terra firma' which Earth *is* or, perhaps, the 'terra firma' around which earth revolves, the sun. And finally, in terms of Greek legend, she is the 'Gate of Horn' through which all true dreams come.

THIS LAST PAIN

First published, without stanza 5, in *New Signatures* (1932), p. 68.

Reviewing *Poems* (1935) in *The Criterion* (XV, No. 58, Oct. 1935, pp. 144–45), George Every singled out 'This Last Pain' as 'probably Empson's important contribution to English poetry'; subsequent critics have nearly all endorsed his judgement, at least to the extent of thinking the poem among Empson's best. It is easy to see why: the poem has the air of saying something important, appears to present it in logical sequence and with relative clarity, depending little on ambiguities of wording and syntax, and employs a crisp, elegant quatrain (an expanded version of that used by Marvell for his 'Horatian Ode on Cromwell's Return from Ireland') whose alternation of pentameter statement and octosyllabic comment has the effect of continuous epigram. There is, however, a considerable difference in clarity between the first five stanzas, with their witty but confusing analogies and their jerky, stop-start movement, and the last four, which form a smooth, if repetitious, train of thought, all too detachable from what precedes it. It is these later stanzas, and particularly the last two, which critics have been disposed to comment on and quote, finding in phrases like 'an edifice of form' and 'a style from a despair' ready-made aphoristic summaries of Empson's 'philosophy'. Yet the general feeling of the poem is cleverly serious, rather than profoundly so; it advances a set of provisional assertions ('let me foretell') rather than a watertight proof, and the words 'pain' and 'despair', which begin and end it, carry intellectual meaning but no great emotional weight. Empson's reading of the poem on his record (1959) conveys not grave pessimism but sardonic relish.

The idea was drawn from I.A. Richards, as George Every recognised: for him 'This Last Pain' was 'the most vivid poetic presentation possible of the dilemma of those who accept the view of the poet's position presented in I.A. Richards's *Principles*.' Both *Principles of Literary Criticism* (1924) and *Science and Poetry* (1926) distinguish between the scientific use of language, which is concerned with verifiable fact, and the poetic use, which conveys attitudes, emotions and beliefs, 'fictions' necessary to man but not capable of verification. For these two uses of language *Science and Poetry* advanced the terms 'statement' and 'pseudo-statement', the latter having the unfortunate effect of suggesting a degree of falsity, or at any rate inferiority, in the beliefs and emotions presented by poetry. This was not Richards's intention; on a number of occasions he makes clear that the two views of the world can co-exist: 'The use of fictions, the imaginative use of them rather, is not a way of hoodwinking ourselves. It is not a process of pretending to ourselves that things are not as they are. It is perfectly compatible with the fullest and grimmest recognition of the exact state of affairs on all occasions' (*Principles*, 1930 edn., p. 266); and again: 'That an objectless belief is a ridiculous or incomplete thing is a prejudice deriving only from confusion'. (p. 280.) For Richards, both kinds of statement are valuable, but it is vital that one should not be taken for the other: more precisely, that the 'beliefs' of poetry not be taken for the 'realities' of science. Nevertheless, it is hard to escape, in all this, on the one hand the feeling that the problem is semantic rather than essential, and on the other the suspicion that beliefs, including religious ones, are assumed for no clear reason to have been displaced by a prevailing scientific view of the world. Empson's own prose version of the intellectual dilemma of the time, expressed in the *Oxford Outlook* in March, 1931 (Vol. 11, pp. 54-7), is open to the same doubts as Richards's; the problem is 'that true beliefs may make it possible to act rightly; that we cannot think without verbal fictions; that they must not be taken for true beliefs, and yet must be taken seriously; that it is essential to analyse beauty; essential to accept it unanalysed; essential to believe that the universe is deterministic; essential to act as if it were not.'

This, of course, is a pretty accurate description of Empson's poem, walking its narrow line between total intellectual disbelief in God and 'all those large dreams' and total emotional belief in them (or enslavement to them), and thus in the process preserving both the poet's intellectual self-respect and his emotional health. Structurally, the poem can roughly be divided into the first four stanzas, which deny any 'real' basis to beliefs in God, eternity and the soul, and the last four, which present the human need to create such beliefs; with stanza five, added later (it was not in the *New Signatures* version, nor in the poem as published in Japan in 1934), acting as a pivot or bridge-passage.

The poem takes off from the Patristic idea ('found' suggests it is a last refinement of theological sadism) that the sinner's worst punishment in hell was to be able to imagine the heavenly delights he was deprived of, and applies this to man's state on Earth: heaven is non-existent, and its pleasures are known only here. The 'prying housemaid' image, undermining man's dignity and rather oddly elevating the soul (the housemaid's mistress), is useful in emphasising the line of demarcation, the locked door, between man and what he contemplates, stooping or kneeling; but the reference to a lost 'key', available neither to him to open the door nor to the soul to block the keyhole from the inside (which literally is not supposed to exist), invites profitless speculation; nor is

it easy to imagine why man should feel relieved ('He's safe')
at this state of affairs. The ramifications of the image distract one from the main point, which is simply that imagination of such 'divine states' (Empson's note) is all man has.

If he is not careful, however, (assuming that, like Empson
and Richards, he feels it is important to be careful), man
may fall into the false belief that what he imagines really
exists, since, according to Wittgenstein, "What is conceivable
can happen too". Wittgenstein, who first studied with
Bertrand Russell in Cambridge in 1912, returned there in
1929, the year Empson went down, and became Professor
of Philosophy ten years later. His *Tractatus Logico-Philosophicus* (1921), which greatly influenced the Logical Posi-
tivists, was translated into English in 1922, and Empson's
line is his version of proposition 3.02. (The 1961 translation
runs: 'A thought contains the possibility of the situation of
which it is a thought. What is thinkable is possible too'.)
The enlisting of Wittgenstein in the argument is convenient,
but a conscious trick, since he did not intend his proposition
to cover metaphysical situations, these being in his view impossible, or at any rate not conceivable by language. Hence
Empson's warning 'But wisely': we must take care what we
apply the proposition to, or we may end up self-deceived.
Some conceivable things can happen; others cannot. A third
category, indicated in line 10, is that of things which happen
but are not conceivable. Here a complimentary aside, presumably to a girl, enables Empson to get in a jocular dig at
philosophic omniscience, though the idea is picked up more
seriously by the 'miracle' of the last stanza.

Stanza four is the hardest in the poem, with its jumbled
references to Christ's crown of thorns, crackling thorns under
pots (*Ecclesiastes* vii, 6), fools' pots that soon boil and
watched pots that never boil. One is tempted to rely on
Empson's note: 'The folly which has the courage to maintain
careless self-deceit is compared to the mock-regal crown of
thorns'; but as this does not make clear whether the courage
of self-deceit is praised or its folly criticised, one is little
further forward. In *New Signatures* stanza four began 'Those
thorns being crowns', which was awkward but indicated a
connection with stanza three (in addition to the connection

with stanza one established by the word 'crowns' itself).
One may conjecture, perhaps, that the result of forgetting the
difference between the merely conceivable and the real (that
is, of believing that imaginary 'divine states' exist) is that one
receives a 'crown' of bliss, but that this crown is, what
Christ's crown of thorns was intended to be, a mockery;
nevertheless, the fool who deceives himself is easily satisfied
– the thorns boil his pot quickly, and his pleased laughter
sounds like their crackling. But however long the wise man
(the modern intellectual?) looks at such a pot, he can never
agree that it truly sings ('song' as set against the emptiness of
foolish cachinnation); nor, perhaps, can he by staring trans-
form his own pot (the 'conceivable', if not the 'potential')
into the actual. The identical rhyme sounds at the end of
stanzas three and four, even more the parallelism of 'wisely/
long' and 'wise and long', direct attention to some link between them, and to the need for care; but although it is true
that fools rush in where angels fear to tread, it may equally
be true that where ignorance is bliss, 'tis folly to be wise.

Stanza five wrings further use from thorns, though hardly
with precision, since the thorn-fuel which heats the 'frying
pan' of life is compared to man who is inside it. Both, however, turn to ash, and something can be made of them, thorns
literally, man metaphorically, as a 'cleanser'. If, dissatisfied
with what he has, a life without 'true beliefs', man leaps
'from pan to fire' – not suicide or hell, here, but dissipation,
or a life without any beliefs at all – this need not be final.
An opposite course is open to him, equally dashing if not
apparently so: that is, to come back to the frying pan and
turn his experiences to advantage. (Quite how he will clean
the pan is not clear, though his sufferings may have purged
or purified *him*.) What may lie behind this proposal is both
the *fin de siècle* view that rebellion and sin are better than
mediocre passivity, and a more dogged existential code in
which man proves his courage by accepting the limits of his
fate (the sides of the frying pan): the attitudes may co-exist,
since the return to the pan is only possible for those who
have jumped out.

The less witty but more disciplined imagery of the last
four stanzas, describing man's style of life in a world lacking

the confidence of 'real' beliefs, requires less guesswork from the reader. Men need dreams ('large' suggests 'generous-minded' as well as 'vague and idealistic') in order to 'live well' and to survive; but they are projected forward on to chaos by man himself, and what is 'real' is not the wide picture but the small slide: either a fiction or system made by the artist for himself, or the mass-produced article, buyable as it were at Woolworth's, which will satisfy most people's aspirations — systems of religious belief (God made in the image of man), humanistic ethics and the like. Enjoying the chiaroscuro illusion of the screen image man may forget that it is himself who casts it; he seems, here, not to be thought a fool for this willing suspension of disbelief, unless there is a touch of irony in 'feasting'. 'Feasting' and 'dappled shade' together conjure up Manet's 'Le Déjeuner sur l'Herbe'; certainly Empson's rhyming of 'shade/made' is a deliberate recollection of Marvell in 'The Garden' 'Annihilating all that's made/To a green thought in a green shade.'

There is sufficient comfort in such a spectacle for one to sympathise with the poem's concluding imperatives. Something (a feigned belief) is better than nothing, and an 'edifice of form' (formalism, the devices of art, 'good form', the externals of behaviour) may preserve adequately the ghosts of once-real beliefs. The syntax of line 30 is teasing: 'act that' might mean 'act as if', but a more plausible reading would be 'Act that state (situation, state of mind, human dignity) which only exists in one's conception of it, and is not 'real'.' The reference back to the form of Wittgenstein's proposition in stanza three is extended by the last stanza, where man is asked to imagine, as the poet does, 'what could not possibly be there'. To conceive the impossible (Wittgenstein would also call it the inconceivable), to hope against hope, is a necessary human assertion, a 'style' of behaviour, even though a miraculous balance is required to sustain it, and a 'miracle' to make the objects of its belief come true. Such imagination, like all the 'gifts' of (imaginary) gods, is double-edged; valuable in giving life meaning, but dangerous in that one may be deceived by its propaganda. (Yet the joke in stanza three about the 'you' who happened but whose happening was not 'conceivable' may prompt, in those less wedded than Empson to the idea that the desired must be impossible, thoughts of a God who happened 'by miracle' without having been conceived).

The humorous flavour of the last stanza's bracketed line offsets the touch of solemnity with which the poem ends. Empson himself is the lower-case 'god' who exhorts the reader, and his the 'ambiguous gifts': *Seven Types of Ambiguity* had appeared in 1930. The phrase 'a despair' has not the force of 'despair' or 'one's despair', and the poem's discussion of belief is illustrated throughout by images (housemaid, pots, pans, slides, haunted house) that are youthfully ingenious rather than emotionally sombre. Nor is its argument by analogy either so clear or so cogent as a cursory reading might suggest. In that it is adroit, lively, thought-provoking, and has some splendid local effects (stanza five's surface is brilliantly polished), 'This Last Pain' is a good poem; but there are many loose ends, and it is hardly profound as a philosophical statement. Strong reservations about this aspect of it were certainly voiced by Empson himself to Christopher Ricks in 1963: 'Somebody told me it was like Oscar Wilde saying that you ought to wear a mask and then you'll grow into your mask. This seemed to me positively embarrassing. . . I do feel it's writing, as it were, to a theory without my being quite sure what the theory comes to, or what it means or something. I felt rather doubtful whether it meant anything very sensible'. (*The Review*, Nos. 6 & 7, June 1963).

DESCRIPTION OF A VIEW

First published in *Experiment* No. 6 (Oct. 1930), p. 13.

This poem appeared in the same issue of *Experiment* as 'The Scales', and the uncertainty about comparative size expressed in lines 3–4 suggests some tenuous link between them, as may also its mention of 'the beam of Justice' (another meaning of 'scales') in line 15. Apart from prompting such hazy speculations, the poem is as inscrutable as the building it describes. The references of section two are not difficult to explain, and one is tempted to think the poem conveys a dislike of skyscrapers and a warning against *hubris*. But there is a sinister quality in the stillness of the scene – white unfinished building, intensely blue sky – which is not comprehended in such a utilitarian reading, and it may be this atmosphere of muted menace, rather than an opinion, that the poem is designed to express. Yet there remains a suspicion that the poem is no more than its flat title suggests – a visual description; it being always understood that in an Empson poem such description is likely to entail literary allusion and scientific analogy. Empson's note gives away nothing of his intention; he does not even identify the building.

Leaving it nameless, Empson presents it as a 'specimen of building', both an example of a skyscraper (a 'vulnerable sky' gives extra point to 'scraped') and like a scientific specimen laid on a labelled glass slide, in this case a wide shop-front with the name of the shop above. (Though Empson's claim, in his note, that the making of concrete involves boiling in acid is erroneous, it is true that specimens of fossil-bearing rock are cleaned in this way, and comparison of new building to extinct fossil is nicely ironic.) 'Concrete' is what the building is made of; it is also concrete rather than abstract, real not a mirage. Nevertheless, since there is nothing for the eye to measure it against, its large reality is hard to take in; alternatively, its combination of white concrete and dazzling windows may look like 'nothing' – an enormous blank. The anthropomorphic phrase 'was not sure what size it was' makes the building seem rather pathetic, despite its looming bulk, and lines 6–9 add further human attributes: the faculty of choice (whether to scrape the sky or not) and the capacity for self-restraint. 'Plain', 'firm' and 'cleanly' (adjective not adverb) suggest both the building's solidity and whiteness and a kind of sincerity and decency in its behaviour, in keeping with the level firmness of the 'stretched string' by whose aid the workmen build straight and observe the architect's intentions. ('Cleanliness is next to Godliness'?) But ambivalence in the presentation of the building is shown by the sequence of lines 8 and 9. Though suspicions that the building may have an overweening urge to touch the sky are denied by the protestation of 'It would not think of doing such a thing', with its tone of injured innocence, they appear again in 'On trust, it did not try'. Observed, the building is on its best behaviour; but what will happen when the observer turns his back?

These various thoughts have accompanied the gradual movement of the observer's eye upwards, from the 'labelled strip' of the ground floor up the 'ladder' of the windowed storeys to the crane whose arm stretches stalk-like (echoing the 'stretched string' of section one) along the unfinished building's top. Strictly, as Empson's note admits, the pencil-thin arm stretches *along*, but 'stretched in' makes sense also, since the metaphorical bridge, beam and Zeppelin are implicit *in* the literal arm of the crane which suggests them. Before the metaphors enter, however, the visual possibilities of the crane arm are exploited, though pointlessly and with unduly schematic compression. The horizontal rusty brown metal 'stalk', poised over the white building, is like (vertical) stalks of dry brown grass, salted by sea-spray, growing on the downs above chalk cliffs (Beachy Head, the White Cliffs of Dover); it is also, though this is only barely sketched in, like brown hair ('down') on white flesh.

The equivocal nature of the building – a sort of Franken-stein's monster with potential for good or evil – is conveyed in section two's main metaphor: the crane above it (in effect, the building itself) is the beam holding the scales of Justice, perpetually balanced over London. Beam and building are compared to the bridge described in *Paradise Lost* X, lines 294–318, the sole route (invented by Milton, as this building by modern man) by which Sin and Death pass from Hell to earth: aptly, the bridge is called 'a ridge of pen-dent rock' and is attached to Hell by 'asphaltic slime'. They are also compared to the hanging menace of a Zeppelin air-ship. If he is here using the term 'Zeppelin' strictly, he is referring to the many Zeppelin bombing raids, some on the City of London, carried out from 1915 onwards; if loosely, perhaps to the R.100 (built at Howden, a few miles from Empson's home), which was briefly visible over the Thames on 28 January 1930. (Nevil Shute, *Slide Rule*, 1954, Ch. 4). The section's final image is of the building as a high white mass of sea, rearing threateningly over London despite God's promise 'not to flood again' expressed by his curved rainbow. Here the flat-topped building, brown and white, is a 'level rainbow', and one is strongly aware of the aimed-gun overtones of 'level'.

The word 'deluge' in section two is, perhaps significantly, unrhymed, and the feeling of suspense this creates is prolonged by the unrhymed feminine endings of lines 19–21, which give an aural equivalent of the shimmering silvery-blue sky the lines describe. The movement of the final line, with its masculine ending, resolves some of the tension, and it may be that the 'larger concrete' of the sky is meant to offer a context in which the building will appear smaller and safer: the observer's eye has moved upwards again, the perspective has altered, and the 'low and vulnerable' sky of the opening has been forgotten. The real, concrete building is now contained within the 'dome' of the sky (was Empson's eye straying along the Thames to St. Paul's Cathedral?). This sky 'dome' is a 'larger concrete' both in that it is a larger, more comprehensive and perhaps more generous reality; and in that it glitters with innumerable almost visible stars, the 'sands' of which its 'concrete' is made, as the building's concrete consists (partly) of ordinary sand. It is a beautiful ending, though not an entirely peaceful one: the hypothetical 'palace walls in Grimm papered with needles', to which the bright sky is compared, are magical but sinister, and not less sinister for the total absence of any real counterpart from the 600-odd pages of *Grimm's German Folk Tales* (trans. Magoun and Krappe, Southern Illinois U.P., 1960).

HOMAGE TO THE BRITISH MUSEUM

First published in *Poetica* (Japan), Jan., 1932.

Kathleen Raine has described how, during Empson's vacations

from Cambridge, they would meet in London, when, among other things, they 'walked together among the oriental gods in the British Museum' and paused in front of a 'hideous idol'. It is this idol which provided the starting point for Empson's poem. Wryly concerned with the baffling plethora of beliefs and systems available to man, it is offered partly in ironic homage to a particular all-inclusive 'Supreme God', but essentially, as its title indicates, to the British Museum itself, of whose all-embracingness the god is an example.

The first section is literal description, though unless one seeks out the thing described it is likely to mislead: 'Supreme God' conjures up something large, and 'faced with a blank shield' sounds as though it means 'with a blank shield in front of it'. In fact the god is quite small, a light brown wood figure only a few feet high, and the 'blank shield' *is* its face, not empty but lacking a face's normal attributes. (The figure is not now to be found in the British Museum in Bloomsbury but in its Ethnography Department in Burlington Gardens). It is a carving of the Polynesian sea god Tangaroa, depicted in the act of creating the other gods and men – hence a 'Supreme God'. A decidedly bizarre figure, its chest and stomach are disproportionately elongated and, like the face, decorated with little gargoyle-like shapes which line 6 describes, variously, as 'lice', 'dolls' and 'local deities'. These take the place of navel, mouth, eyes, nose and ears (the idol's sexual 'organs of sense' are naturalistic), and also adorn nipples, knees and other points. The back of the idol, similarly covered, is detachable; the original function of the hollow belly within was to house a 'Pantheon' of smaller god-figures who thus partook of Tangaroa's divine power. In a crudely literal way, then, the 'Supreme God' represents a system of belief which comprises all others.

So, on a larger scale, does the 'ethnological section' which contains this image as one of many; so, even more, does the Museum itself. (Since the Roman 'Pantheon' was circular, one is reminded that the Museum needs its belly to include the Reading Room, with its quota of critics, those 'lice on the locks of literature'.) The second section shows man 'attending there', trying to comprehend within himself the many 'cultures' and 'codes' presented to him. 'Attending' suggests regular visits, waiting (for understanding), and religious observance ('attending' church). The description of his effort is as much physical as mental: he 'absorbs' cultures (bacterial as well as intellectual and artistic), and 'dissolves' codes. 'Codes' embraces systems of thought and behaviour from Courtly Love to Bushido while nicely implying their arbitrary and cryptic nature; but the verb with which it is paired brings in a possible play on 'codeine'.

The rich diet of cultures and codes, however, far from being absorbed and dissolved usefully into individual 'judgement', causes clogging: 'a natural hesitation' is a sly euphemism for constipation, referring one back to the god's 'hole behind' and bringing a ruefully comic recognition of the difference between divine and human anatomy/physiology. This specific lack of a 'way out' is wittily fused with man's inability either to provide solutions to general human problems or to direct particular enquirers, lost in the maze of the British Museum, with any certainty to the exit. Dazed by too many possible beliefs, man is at a standstill with 'no road', and might as well admit it.

But this conclusion causes Empson not even the vestigial despair of 'This Last Pain', published in the same year. The repetition of 'admit' suggests not only confession (of incapacity or indecision), but the opening of a door – a 'way in' which recalls, and perhaps takes the place of, the earlier 'way out'. 'Everything', even if indigestible, is at least 'something', and should be regarded as better than nothing. Even if, in our 'natural hesitation', we doubt whether it is, we should behave as if it were, and make the moderate best of ourselves. There is in the colloquial 'give ourselves the benefit of the doubt' a further meaning. Doubt is a midway position, between total credulity and total negation, and has its benefits, among which can be the saving of life. One aspect of this is illustrated by the behaviour of persecuted early Christians who, afraid completely to affirm their faith and deny the Roman gods, offered the latter a ritual 'pinch of dust' in what appeared a gesture of belief. It is such a prudential course (laudable given his dislike of extremes) which Empson recommends, his 'pinch of dust' resembling salt thrown self-deprecatingly over the shoulder to avert bad luck. Unable to choose between beliefs, the poet extends instead an amused tolerance to any or all of them, combining a polite bow with a sceptical shrug. Throughout easy in its movement, cool and sophisticated in its tone, the poem ends by in effect leaving such matters to those that comprehend them: the British Museum and its toad-shaped presiding deity, oddly touching in its combination of 'Supreme God' pretensions and modest size.

NOTE ON LOCAL FLORA

First published in *Experiment* No. 5 (Feb., 1930), p. 26.

This densely-packed poem, witty in idea yet grave in expression, begins and ends with a tree, which also provides its central aperçu, offered to the surprised reader with delightful impudence in line 8. The tree is the same throughout: it is 'local flora' in the sense of being 'native in Turkestan' or Western China, but also because a specimen of it is encountered by the poet in his tamer, and perhaps incongruous, local environment of the Botanic Gardens at Kew. The habits of the tree, whose cones 'ripen only in a forest fire', are transcribed imaginatively from a label 'affixed to it by the management', according to Empson's 1959 record-notes. The transcription, which starts in the manner of a fairy-tale, is done with an impressive show of eloquence: one notices particularly the slow, heavy monosyllables, the alliterations and assonances, of lines 3 and 7; the old-fashioned rhetoric of parallel clauses; and the delaying syntax of lines 6-7, in which the 'hard cold cones' await the 'forest fire' which is an 'image of time's end'. Here the Apocalyptic idea that the world will end in fire (cf. *Revelation* xx, 9) is expressed in a phrase which recalls Kent and Edgar's response to the entry of Lear 'with Cordelia dead in his arms': 'Is this the promised end?'/'Or image of that horror?' (*King Lear* V, iii, 263-4).

That the grave manner of the long opening sentence is not intended to be taken altogether seriously is suggested by the sharp contrast it makes with the dry plainness of the poem's title. There is a suspicion of mock-heroic, and one begins to be reminded of 'Part of Mandevil's Travels', with its correction of the fabulous by the scientific. The purpose of the seven lines is to build the reader up to a revelation which has already, before he devised his skilful piece of poetic engineering to express it, dawned on the poet. Since the tree's cones are not 'wards to time' – that is, they are not looked after, like those of most other conifers, by time's natural processes – they require the rare heat of a forest fire to force them open and expel their seeds. For Empson, quick to spot a comparison, this makes the tree a botanical equivalent, or explanation, of the Phoenix, reborn from its ashes. The splendid off-hand arrogance of 'I knew the Phoenix was a vegetable' (which conveys the meaning 'I always suspected it, and now this tree proves me right!') in part deflates the legend of the miraculous bird, especially as the generic 'vegetable' is so much funnier than the specific 'tree'; but the total effect is not so simple. Empson's triumph at being 'proved' right about the myth also transmits keen pleasure in the reality, that a tree like this can exist, and thus in its own way prove the fabulous true. The grandeur of his description of the tree is deceptive on one level, genuine on another.

However subtle or double-edged the poem's tone, its subject is clear enough up to this point: the tree itself, its quaint behaviour, and the comparison to the Phoenix which this prompts. And the last line of the poem can be read as completing this meaning: the captive tree in Kew, like its free counterparts in Turkestan, waits for the forest fire (an uncapitalised 'red dawn') which will enable it to reproduce itself. There is something odd – ominous, pathetic, or funny – about such a paradoxical 'thirst' for regeneration via destruction in a neatly-ordered place like Kew. Taken simply as a poem about a tree/Phoenix, 'Note on Local Flora' is handsome, and satisfying enough. Empson himself, in a longish commentary on it, included by Elizabeth Drew and John L. Sweeney in their *Directions in Modern Poetry* (1940, pp. 81-2), endorsed this basic view, calling the poem (rather too modestly) 'a mild little epigram', and later asserting that 'the facts about the tree are surely striking in themselves, and make you feel "So life's like that, is it?"'. Between the two statements, however, Empson's comments on the poem range widely among the implications it clearly had for him, some of them only vaguely or tangentially apparent to the reader: the Freudian overtones of cones unwilling to 'leave their mother' except for 'good cause' (the irresistible fire is one, but in an ironic sense); the notion of 'hard cold cones' as prudent, self-sufficient people who yet 'positively enjoy a big smash-up' at the end of life. Such personal applications, summed up by Empson's claim 'I felt that other people were *like* the tree in Kew', are not so much functions of the whole poem as chance thoughts that parts of it might provoke in different readers.

There are, however, other elements mentioned by Empson which do have to be taken into account, since they are more or less visible in the poem and provide subsidiary enrichment, in varying degrees, to the main stem of its meaning. One is the equation, established by lines 6 and 8, of the tree/ Phoenix with the classical myth of Semele, Zeus and Bacchus: the child-cones are seen as Bacchus, the tree as Semele, the forest fire as Zeus, the 'father god'. The last two lines ('So Semele. . ./As this. . .') work reciprocally: thirsting tree and yearning Semele are presented in terms of each other, and a bizarre element of eroticism thereby infiltrates Kew Gardens. But the mythical parallel is far from exact. Semele's stubborn and ill-advised wish for her previously mortal-seeming lover to appear in his true form (which turned out to be in thunder and lightning) brought her more than she bargained for – she was consumed, and her six-month-old foetus Bacchus (already 'fathered' by Zeus) had to be rescued from the flames by Hermes. Semele wished for her own immolation no more than the tree (really) does; and unlike the tree's seeds, Bacchus, far from being 'fathered' by his 'forest fire', was almost destroyed by it.

The other element in the poem – the identification of the tree's patient waiting and eventual ripening by fire with the country or countries in which it is found – is intimated by the attempt Empson makes in line 2 to push the tree 'native in Turkestan' as far east as he can. West Turkestan was the former name for Soviet Central Asia, East Turkestan for the

Chinese province of Sinkiang; the 'Tree of Heaven' is a deciduous Chinese tree with 'magical powers' (according to Empson's 1940 commentary), and a line drawn east from Turkestan would pass through Peking ('Tree of Heaven' suggests the Chinese idea of the Imperial 'Mandate of Heaven'). The juxtaposition of Empson's Turkestan tree to the Chinese one seems intended to emphasise its magical qualities while presenting it, too, as essentially Chinese. His commentary brings out his intention more explicitly than one can claim the poem does: 'Turkestan is cold, China is slow in growth and unwilling to change its way of life. . . One way and another the countries are supposed to fit the habits of the tree'. (This may help to explain Empson's large claim that he 'knew the Phoenix was a vegetable', since not only – as his commentary makes clear he knew – does the scientific name for another tree, the date palm, happen to be *Phoenix dactylifera,* but also, as Marvell said in 'To His Coy Mistress': 'My vegetable love would grow/Vaster than empires, and more slow.') Such slow-growing empires, like the patient hard-coned tree, need a fire to bring them to fruition – that of war or revolution. Russia had its 'Red Dawn' in 1917, and the Chinese Communist Party was founded in 1922; thus one may envisage the expatriate Russo-Chinese tree as a sort of Communist fifth-columnist, waiting hopefully in Kew Gardens for its 'salvation' to catch up with it. The conclusion's sudden overlapping of political catch-phrase on botanical Phoenix (involving perhaps a dig at left-wing leanings on the part of Empson's contemporaries?) is ingenious and amusing, rather than sinister, and clinches the conviction that the poem is what its title suggests, a clever tribute to an unusual tree.

In view of the tree's centrality to the poem, it is unfortunate that it can neither be located nor identified. Kathleen Raine, in a letter to the *London Magazine* (Vol. III, March 1957, p. 67), gave rather confusing directions as to its whereabouts in Kew Gardens, but a thorough search in 1975 failed to find it. The standard work on conifers, *A Handbook of Coniferae and Ginkgoaceae* by W. Dallimore and A.B. Jackson (1923; second edition 1931), confirms, in its section on the 'true pines', that 'in some species the cones remain on the trees unopened for many years, the scales ultimately separating when scorched by forest fires' (1966 edition, p. 386). But it lists no such species 'native to Turkestan'. Since Dallimore held a senior post at Kew for many years, one is loath to question the all-inclusiveness of his very large *Handbook*, and is thus left to infer poetic licence, an inaccurate label on the tree Empson saw – or perhaps a tree whose thirst for a forest fire has been quenched.

LETTER IV

First published, dated May, 1929, as No. 1 of *Songs for Sixpence* (1929). Reprinted, with many small alterations, in *Collected Poems* (1949). [Original version reprinted in *Departure* (Oxford), Vol. 3, No. 9, Spring, 1956.]

Songs for Sixpence was a series of six poems which Heffers of Cambridge published individually in cardboard covers. Edited by Jacob Bronowski and James Reeves, both associated with *Experiment,* it seems to represent an unequal collaboration, or truce, between that magazine and its rival, *The Venture*: four of the poems were by 'Experimenters' – T.H. White, John Davenport, Bronowski, Empson; two by 'Venturers' – Michael Redgrave and Julian Bell. The poems of these latter ('Water Music for a Botanist' and 'Chaffinches' respectively) deliver some of the lyricism intimated by the series-title; but, even with a cicada at the beginning and something like the music of the spheres at the end, Empson's tortuous and baroque 'Letter IV' was hardly an auspicious first contribution to a set of 'Songs'. Empson was not satisfied with the poem, and in *Poems* (1935) his note on 'Letter V' opened with the curt statement: 'I left out the fourth, thinking it bad.' Eventually, in 1949, he reprinted it, changed in details but not in form or conception, with the rather apologetic note: 'I have tinkered with it a bit . . . , perhaps making it tidier rather than better.' Not always tidier, the new version remains obscure and problematic, the point of even the explicable references often not apparent. Dressed in the heavy brocade of its elaborate verse-form – a Spenserian stanza lacking the seventh line – the poem moves stiffly, its archaic manner ill-suited to its modern scientific analogies and hampering their clear expression and argumentative effect.

Its omission from *Poems* (1935) was retrospectively explained by Empson himself on the grounds that 'it seemed sententious' (with which view it is easy to agree), and that 'the basic feelings seemed to have nothing to do with the moral, arrived at by allegorising Eddington.' Here one can only envy Empson, who is troubled by the disjunction between two components of the poem; for the reader, the problem is to be sure what the two components are. The 'moral' lacks sharp definition, and the 'feelings' are almost lost in the proliferation of metaphoric detail, though they may involve a sense of cold isolation which gives way to a gratitude for warmth imparted by the girl addressed. What tenuously holds the poem together is a gradual upward movement perceptible throughout: the 'long climb' of the cicada through the earth, the ascent of vapour from sea to sky, the conclusion of 'stars' and 'rounded universe'. Yet this continuity of direction is confused by changes of material along the way, as the poem passes from entomology through meteorology to modern astronomy. There are hints of a possible secondary pattern in the various motifs of voiding ('urine' and 'waste' in stanza 1, vomiting, the 'Roman feather' in stanza 2, 'bowels' and 'digest' in stanza 3, perhaps even 'putting its eggs' in stanza 4), but it is hard to be certain that deliberate cross-referencing is involved, or what it might be meant to signify.

Stanza 1 is derived from Chapter II of J.H. Fabre's *Social Life in the Insect World,* translated in 1912, which tells how the cicada, having spent four years in the larval state underground, tunnels up and out to undergo metamorphosis in the branches of a shrub. The cicada's ingenious process of boring, which creates a smooth lift-shaft connecting its burrow with the surface, is thus described by Fabre: 'As it digs and advances the larva waters the powdery debris and converts it into a paste, which is immediately applied to the walls by the pressure of the abdomen'. (p. 24). To this paste Fabre applies the word 'mortar', and the conversion is effected by what Fabre calls 'urine' – moisture periodically sucked by the larva from an exposed root nearby, which swells out its body and is discharged as needed. Hence Empson's odd-sounding but meaningful phrase 'parturient with urine', his reference to the assisting root as 'this lover', and his transitive use of 'coheres': the cicada organises the dark 'chaos' in which he exists ('the dust that smothers' and 'the incumbent shade') into 'an ordered Nature' – in effect, the tunnel – by means of 'his own waste'. (The proximity of 'waste' and 'ordered' makes a pun on 'ordured'.) The tunnel, however, is not constructed as a way of life but as a means of escape ('only to evade'), and Empson seems to admire the cicada's enterprise and courage: his use of 'brave' praises the root, but is also transferred epithet, as well as appropriately suggesting Miranda's 'brave new world'. Despite the foetal overtones in the stanza (an embryo 'sucks with dumb mouth' at the 'root' of the umbilical cord), the human situation which best fits the terms of the cicada analogy is that of the writer, lonely and introverted, who draws from some unspecified source the ability to convert the 'rasping darkness' of his life into a 'mortared Babel' (tunnel as literary tower) up which he may climb to emerge, like the larva, into a warmer world. It is not clear whether the 'lover' of stanza 1 is meant to parallel, or stand for, the girl of stanza 2 onwards, but this seems unlikely in view of the hermaphrodite attributes it possesses and the fact that the whole cicada/root metaphor is set off from the rest of the poem and not returned to.

Although stanza 2 embarks on a quite new metaphor, there is a certain amount of carry-over of idea from stanza 1. The sea on which (or as which) the poet now pictures himself is as it were the surface which the cicada has been trying to reach; but this 'Atlantic' is in some ways a worse environment than the cicada's darkness. It is freezing, monotonous, scary (the screaming gulls, the mere word 'claw'), and even more chaotic: 'unpointed' means unpunctuated, hence a featureless expanse, but the previous 'mortared' brings out the sense of 'to point' in brick-laying: to fill in the joints of brickwork smoothly with mortar or cement. The troughs between 'hanging, flapping' waves cannot be so smoothed out and made to 'cohere from chaos'. The phrase 'wave-shutter' suggests claustrophobia, limited horizons, and perhaps the click of a camera photographing its immobile victim. The reference to 'a Roman feather' (that used by gormandizing Romans to induce vomiting between courses) hardly fits into the sea image as such, any more than the casual mention of 'nape and jaw', both presumably 'hanging' and 'flapping' like the 'wave-shutter'; but as all these notations seem meant, in the curious inert syntax of lines 10–12, as impressionistic hints at the poet's unenviable all-at-sea state, one may, taking them loosely, conjecture him to be surfeited with his cold and meaningless existence. In view of the earlier 'Babel', and of the fact that napes and jaws operate like shutters when they open and close and when they nod back and forth, one may feel that the poet is sick of empty socialising, pointless conversation, and possibly the obscurer aspects of his own work. Help, however, is at hand: 'on my unpointed Atlantic. . .you lay your sunbeam.' The poem originally read 'You lay your breadth of sunbeam and I soar', but even this cautiously amended version ('a part can soar') makes clear the girl's warmth, towards which the poet rises like vapour drawn up by the sun – if he is 'tear-clouds', the tears are surely those of relief. The airship image functions in a number of ways. The poet, a fat 'tear-cloud', moves with the steady pace, the 'gross security' of an airship; he is like the gondola tucked underneath the airship's enormous belly; and thus, he is like a foetus, safe inside his mother 'maker'. This was the heyday of the *Graf Zeppelin's* commercial voyages from Germany to South America, and the girl's influence carries the poet south from his Atlantic into what seems to be the Caribbean, where he discovers the warm world over which *she* presides – 'fertile lands' instead of floating bergs, the Spanish Main (stolen by or from Spain) of a contemporary 'Virgin Queen'.

Prompted perhaps by the divine implications of 'maker', stanza 3 contrasts the aspirations and nature of earthly love with those of religious, in terms of the two gases used to fill airships, hydrogen and helium. The first four lines are a précis of Jacob's wrestling bout with God, at the conclusion of which he was given the name Israel. (*Genesis* xxxii, 24–30).

Jacob's striving to understand and hold on to God (here called Helium) is given an amusingly irreverent twist, though. He is 'determined to digest' something that does not agree with him, as the later 'bitter in the belly' implies; and one can picture him both flatulently swollen with helium and as carried aloft by a balloon, filled with it, that he will not let go of. For helium, as line 20 states, is 'unvalenced', unable to combine with anything, and thus an exclusive, 'self-enclosing air'. It seems that, for Empson, the ride to such a 'Heaven' is better avoided. By comparison (in the words of the original version), 'We rise with a more earth-born gas as leaven': the hydrogen of human love costs less than helium, and is easily assimilated by the body, like the necessary leaven in dough. The quoted phrase "bitter in the belly" was used by H.J.C. Grierson, in his 1929 edition of *The Poems of John Donne,* to describe Donne's savouring of 'life and experience' – 'sweet in the mouth but bitter in the belly'. (p. xxii.) In its turn, Grierson's phrase derived from *Revelation* x, 10, which refers to the effect on St. John the Divine of the 'little book' given him to eat by an angel. Empson may thus be asserting that human love is less bitter than Donne found it, as well as less bitter than religious experience as described in lines 17-20. Nevertheless, his way of presenting hydrogen's potentialities (greater than those of helium, safe but alien) is equivocal. Hydrogen combines with oxygen to form water, but such 'rain' (disappointed lovers' tears, presumably) can 'make but little in the sea'; conversely, hydrogen exploding and burning (as the airship R.101 was to do in 1930) makes an 'empyry' which is 'too fierce', rather than just fierce. 'Empyry', which means the highest heaven, realm of fire, or abode of God, suggestively embodies the word 'pyre'. Human love, though preferred by Empson, seems a thing of extremes, making only an insignificant splash if it collapses, but also too combustible, either over-incandescent in success or burning up destructively in failure.

As if dissatisfied with this picture (or the metaphor which has led to it), Empson switches in the concluding stanzas to an analogy, taken from Eddington (*The Nature of the Physical World,* Everyman edn., pp. 174-75), which presents a more viable and even relationship: that of binary stars, themselves the result of excessive rotation in a single star, which revolve around each other. That such, at any rate, was his intention, is announced by his 1959 record-notes: 'The lovers form a binary stellar system, but only the rest of the universe decides how it rotates.' Unfortunately, Empson's poetic embodiment is by no means clear, since he overlaps the old image of 'car' (gondola) and airship on to the new one of 'Rotational Phenomena' (why the capital letters?) by suggesting that the gondola (himself or the desired relationship?) be attached to a 'larger ball' which puts its 'eggs' in a larger basket ('wickerwork skywide'). Such a thing is difficult to visualise; taking it schematically, one may conjecture that the 'larger ball' is a star, not the sun implied by stanza two's 'sunbeam', and that it has split in two. Thus, instead of there being a girl-deity and a poet who monogamously clings to her, there are now two people in a relationship of equality. Yet the beginning of the stanza concedes 'all' to the girl (either that she has all to give, or that the poet is willing to give all to her), and the end of the stanza has the poet as 'satellite' to her 'true centre' – which is hardly the binary system of which the distant stars furnish examples.

The last stanza is no less perplexing. Partly this is a matter of syntax, since the referent of 'who' in line 33 may equally be the 'stars' of line 29, the girl ('true centre') of line 32, or both girl *and* poet, the one 'fixed', the other 'far', as in Donne's 'A Valediction: Forbidding Mourning'. What broadly emerges is that this new relationship is somehow reassuring: there is enough distance between the parties to create both 'calm' and 'surprise', and the universe in which they live is 'rounded' – finite but unbounded, a comfortably large womb and airship. ('Shutter' harks back, in pleasant contrast, to the 'wave-shutter' of stanza 2). The last four lines seem to depict the lovers (poet as planet, watching the generous girl 'glow in growth' as she rises in his sky and assists his crops) as a 'free' microcosm existing within the determining macrocosm of the aloof but beneficent heavens, who 'call the tune' to which it dances. The original version of the poem, though clumsy, makes clearer the necessary interdependence of lovers and circumambient universe: 'And as your sun, by yielding beauty, grows/In growth upon the planet, they, as strong,/Resound, by being held aloof, their song,/Compose earth's nature, are his laws, consist his throng.'

Impressively grand in spirit as these lines are, the idea comes as too much of a surprise, indeed as an irrelevance, for them to end the poem satisfactorily. Though 'Letter IV' is full of suggestive possibilities (and, in Stanza 2, demonstrates a witty buoyancy), there are too many of them for even Empson's dexterity to profit from. One suspects, in fact, that he was basically undecided about what he wanted his letter to convey. In his broadcast-talk 'Argufying in Poetry' (*The Listener*, 22 August 1963, pp. 277/290), he maintained that: 'Saying "therefore" is like giving the reader a bang on the nose.' It is a pity that the 'therefore' of stanza 4, while making the reader see stars, does not enable him to understand the 'stars less monogamously deified' which he sees.

DOCTRINAL POINT

First published in *The Year's Poetry 1935,* ed. Denys Kilham Roberts, Gerald Gould and John Lehmann, p. 90.

The doctrinal matters touched on in this engaging poem are both religious (free will and predestination) and scientific (the extent and nature of man's knowledge of the world); but they are, indeed, touched on rather than explored, in keeping with the implications of line one. The uncapitalised 'god' may be a cherished belief, whether in Christian God, some power beyond man, or the claims of science; or it may be an admired beauty like that of the magnolia; but too close an approach causes it to 'dissolve into the air' – a phrase which ambiguously suggests numinous recession and the vanishing of a mirage. In view of the mention of Eddington later on, the first line may be intended as a version of a passage in *The Nature of the Physical World*: 'Our conception of substance is only vivid so long as we do not face it. It begins to fade when we analyse it.' (Everyman Edn., p. 264). The feeling of the poem is indicated by Empson's record-note: '"Doctrinal Point" yearns to be always sure what to do.' But man's position is ironic: he simultaneously wishes, as an intellectual, to understand himself and 'approach' his 'god', and is unable to do so. Thus his self-conscious, uncertain mind may end up envying the assurance of unselfconscious matter, epitomised here by the magnolia. Given the latter's juxtaposition to Solomon, it seems likely that the 'doctrinal point' of the poem is that made in the Sermon on the Mount: 'Consider the lilies of the field, how they grow; they toil not, neither do they spin: And yet I say unto you, That even Solomon in all his glory was not arrayed like one of these.' (Matthew vi, 28–29). The contrast between thinking man and unthinking magnolia is captured, with a mixture of wistfulness and humour, in the poem's structure: loose, prosy, abstract comment alternating with virtuoso passages – the same rhyme sound used fourteen times – conveying the mindless perfection of the tree.

The 'for instance' of line two not only offers the magnolia as an illustration of the sermon-text of line one, as an example of the 'god' whose nature eludes man; it also reaches forward to line three to define the characteristic which differentiates godliness from humanity: whatever they do, gods are always right. Since magnolias cannot properly be said to think, the rightness of 'anything they can think of' means the rightness of their instinctive urges. For them, thought and instinct are identical, as are free will and pre-destination: unconscious, they are 'free' to be what it is 'in the blood' to be, a sinless and efficient part of the natural order, requiring no divine redemption (their sap is 'shed for themselves', unlike Christ's saving blood, shed for man) and no externally imposed 'architecture' of theology or philosophy. Instead, they have the organic form determined by their 'texture' (live skin or tissue), and their sap, punningly 'sapient', always knows what to do next. As the word 'sapient', seeming simply to mean 'wise', carries a strong overtone of would-be wisdom or fancied sagacity, a degree of irritation with the magnolia is suggested. Something of this equivocal attitude creeps into section two's admiration of the magnolia's beauty in all its phases of growth. The felicitous imagery is well-adapted to the look of the blossoming magnolia: 'burgeon' embodies the incipience of its 'plump' maturity, its 'gross prime', and 'sag' gives the process an appropriate conclusion; 'plump spaced-out saints' aptly conveys the posture of the opened blooms, seated on the branches like rows of Buddhas. The religious terminology serves the deeper purpose of presenting the blossoms ('massed wax flames') as taking part in a ritual: they praise creation by existing, and are both worshippers and worshipped – 'magnolia' suggests 'magnificat'. The pun of 'gross prime' is tendentious, however. To associate the fat ripeness of the blossom with the monastic hour of 6 a.m. makes an amusing dissonance, but it also promotes the implication (in 'plump' and 'sag') that the magnolias are well-fed and complacent. 'They know no act that will not make them fair' is a two-edged compliment.

The abrupt jump to section three (whose contrast between man the observer and the nature he observes gradually becomes clear) is assisted by the pivotal word 'insolence', which refers both to the magnolias of line 12 and to the sweeping declaration by Eddington that physics is inadequate to explain them. Men may be outfaced by magnolias, yet Eddington's very honesty in admitting the fact displays a panache ('insolence' is not pejorative here) that is comparable to their self-sufficiency. Like the magnolias, the renowned scientist – 'Professor Eddington' conveys ironic respect – knows no act that will not make him fair. That Eddington 'called all physics one tautology' is not true verbatim, unless Empson had in mind a passage in New Pathways in Science, which seems unlikely since that book appeared in the same year as the poem: 'Does the external world in physics. . .really exist?. . . . For my own part, any notion that I have of existing is derived from my own existence, so that my own existence is a tautological consequence of any definition that I should be willing to adopt.' (p. 25). Presumably, since 'physics' can mean (in Cornfordian fashion) nature, as well as scientific definitions of it, this statement can be inverted to make the definition the tautology. But what Empson is essentially expressing is the limited view of physics indicated by Eddington in, inter alia, the last chapter of Space Time and Gravitation (1920) and Chapter XI of The

Nature of the Physical World (1928). In this view (stated most simply by Sir James Jeans in *The Universe Around Us*, 1929, pp. 328-329), the ultimate truths of nature elude man's 'laws' and systems: 'The mind has by its selective power fitted the processes of Nature into a frame of law of a pattern largely of its own choosing; and in the discovery of this system of law the mind may be regarded as regaining from Nature that which the mind has put into nature.' (*The Nature of the Physical World*, Everyman Edn., p. 238). Lines 15-16 paraphrase this circular process, making use, with a pseudo-scientific 'trendiness', of the difficult new relativity term 'tensor'. Himself simplifying it, Eddington translates the word as 'schedule of pointer readings' (*ibid.*, p. 250); all it really means here is a measuring device chosen for its suitability to a certain type of job. All man can do with nature is describe what his understanding can find terms for; such descriptions leave much out of account, yet are taken as 'law', from convenience or vanity. (The capitalization of 'Assumption', which suggests divine apotheosis – or an attempt to pursue the 'god' 'into the air' – seems to mock the pretentiousness of such a transformation.)

The last two lines of section three draw from Eddington's attitude to physics the implications for human behaviour, and hark back to the mention of free will and predestination in line 4. Empson's formulae (the linking word 'of' is ambiguous) are none too clear, but what he appears to mean is that, if we cannot fully understand the nature outside us (present and future 'existence'), our concepts of 'choice' and 'virtue' (which imply alternatives and require 'effort') are meaningless; we need instead to accept the equal value (moral and existential neutrality?) of all phenomena, and the limitations of our consciousness: if we have 'foreknowledge', we do not know it. Possibly Empson is thinking here of a proposition of Wittgenstein, which seems to abolish any distinction between free will and predestination: 'The freedom of the will consists in the impossibility of knowing actions that still lie in the future.' (*Tractatus*, 1963 translation, proposition 5.1362, p. 79). Such a view of life is not without its attractions, and the other, positive, meaning of 'singularity' carries in it all the pleasure of an unworried

response to the oddity and distinctness of external phenomena, such as the magnolias. To that extent, we may even
become like them.

Yet the very fine, richly-compressed concluding section,
with its references to 'care' and 'despair', re-emphasises the
fact that we are not. Man is a conscious creature, struggling
to comprehend what always escapes him. His mind is both
his 'glory' (the 'cope' worn by wise Solomon, called in
Empson's note a 'priest-king') and his burden; man the
worker and man the scientist both wear an 'over-all', as,
fancifully, does Solomon in his role as temple builder (I
Kings vi). Also, by virtue of his mental powers, man is placed
'over all'; but his supremacy is dubious. His 'care' is both
responsibility and worry, yet the 'lilies of the field' whom he
is in charge of neither share his 'care' nor know of it: they do
not wear his cope (though possessing, in their unconscious
beauty, their own more splendid one) nor can he 'cope with'
them. The gap between man and nature (self and 'other') is
unbridgeable: he gazes at the 'rare calyx', the outer protective cover of the magnolia blossom, in a frustrated wish to
understand its perfection, but the blossoms, crowded together on their branches, can never open a gap in their ranks
into which he may fit. Unlike man, they are unaware of anything other than themselves, and exist in a universe entirely
physical, and devoted to their texture's needs: their defence
is not God's symbolic rainbow but the Heaviside layer (now
called the Ionosphere E-layer) which absorbs the X-rays and
ultra-violet radiation that would harm them. (The Heaviside
layer protects man too, which weakens the image, but perhaps the point of the 'contrast' is that man, a fallen creature,
needs more protection than the sinless magnolias). The
emphatic rhymes (doubled in lines 22–23) build up a sense
of man's inescapable isolation in a universe he observes but
does not control, and almost make the final line sound inevitable. Its last word, which brings the poem full circle,
shows the magnolias, the instance of all that escapes man's
merely descriptive science, leaving man entombed in his
underground 'vault' ('matter includes what must matter
enclose', again) and being themselves 'assumed' into the air.
In a poem which involves religious as well as scientific and

botanical imagery, it seems arbitrary for Empson to deny man this possibility also, and show him only 'pushing up the daisies'.

LETTER V

First published in *The Year's Poetry 1934*, ed. Denys Kilham Roberts, Gerald Gould and John Lehmann, p. 94.

Returning, though with an altered rhyme scheme, to the quatrain form of 'Letter II', Empson's final letter is concerned with the definition of the loved one; its use of mathematical concepts (lines and points), and the human situation conveyed by lines 4 and 8, suggest some influence from Marvell's 'The Definition of Love', with its angles and parallels and its emotion 'begotten by despair/Upon impossibility.' Empson's poem, a string of analogies whose inadequacy to capture the girl's essence is admitted in stanza 3, is a clever but unsatisfactory performance. Without his notes (more extensive than for the other 'Letters'), the initial locus/ envelope contrast and its abandonment at the end would convey little; even with them, it may be claimed that what force the poem has comes not from Empson's intellectual attempts to define the indefinable, but from the reader's sense of an amatory failure for which they are the compensation.

The momentary puzzle created by line one's ambiguous grammar ('but' could mean 'only', 'envelope' could be a verb) is removed by the evolving pattern of the first two stanzas. Lines 1 and 2 of each are chiastic in form, respectively beginning and ending with negative definitions, ending and beginning with positive ones. The phrase 'if you will' can be taken in various ways: as a polite indication to the reader that a hypothesis is being advanced; as a ruminative address by the poet to himself, since lines 3 and 4 of stanza one, proposing tactics, sound like self-communing; and as asking permission of the girl, the 'you' of the rest of the poem, to indulge in speculation about her: 'If I may not, or cannot, define your internal reality, may I try describing you by externals?' Whoever is addressed, what is advanced is that the girl is not a 'locus', a place that can be precisely charted, but an 'envelope', whose contents cannot be penetrated but only guessed at by 'tangent praise', by 'paths of light' that gradually outline a shape. ('Atoms of good form', which would mathematically define a 'locus', also suggest a well-shaped body and a correct and proper manner.) Given the girl's 'humility' (l. 8), an indirect approach to her may have more success than a direct one ('less hope' suggests an earlier failure): it may not fall flat ('crash') nor will it gate-crash (line 3 connects up with line 14). Yet getting 'more for less' seems unlikely, unless 'more' implies merely an extension rather than an increase; and there is surely irony in the word 'intimacy', if what is inside the 'envelope' cannot be known.

What has prompted the image of a mathematical 'envelope' is presumably a real one from the girl, containing a letter ('these lines you grant me') to which 'Letter V' is the reply. Judging from the contrasts of stanza two, the 'enclosed letter' inside the real envelope is unsatisfactory; this allows Empson to bring in the proverbial opposition between letter and spirit – 'enclosed' deadness (the girl's letter, propriety, 'good form') and life-giving 'spirited air'. Little though this means in human terms (since the girl's 'spirited air' leads to nothing of benefit to the poet), there seems even less point in the parallel preference of line 6, for 'detached marble' rather than 'discovered face', the pared-down block from which the head is carved rather than the head itself. Even if the girl's 'discovered face' does not fulfil the promise of her 'spirited air', the phrase 'detached marble' conveys coldness more than the potentiality of a sculpture in the making. The girl is a confusing mixture: graceful, attractive, modest (and perhaps embarrassed by the poet's interest), she is also indifferent and unresponsive. Some clarification is perhaps offered by lines 7 and 8: the poet not only admires the grace of the girl's 'humility that will not hear or care', but stoically accepts it as her true attitude to himself. One is reminded of Donne's sharper response to the girl 'who's therefore true, because her truth kills me.' ('Twicknam Garden'.)

Having furnished metaphors for the girl, Empson asserts in stanza three that she is one herself: as metaphors suggest her, so she, as metaphor, suggests something else. Yet metaphors (since 'they' has nothing else it can be attached to) 'are lies'. Whether this makes the girl a lie seems doubtful; her 'truth' has so recently been referred to, without apparent irony: indeed, line 7 suggests a deliberate contrast with Donne in 'The Indifferent' ('I can love any, so she be not true.'). Empson's intention seems to be to emphasise that metaphor is misleading, and, interestingly enough, most misleading ('true least') when a clear meaning is unravelled from its 'knot chance'. As awkward and artificial as the 'knot-diamond' in 'Sea Voyage', this shorthand phrase expresses the way in which, in metaphor, various implications coincide, according to some hidden logic ('not chance') — implications which, it is claimed, function best when left alone. The connection between this general observation (tinged with special pleading, one feels) and the rest of the stanza may be that, whereas the girl's exterior might be referred to, metaphorically, as 'glanced pearls', she herself (her invisible interior essence) is the 'grit only'. The unusual term 'glanced', meaning 'polished', fits pearls; unfortunately, in suggesting 'glances' and 'glancing blow', it leads Empson to equate the beauty of pearls with the girl's eyes, which thus seem dead (cf. 'those are pearls that were his eyes'). Line 12 is more confused than rich: 'not for me shall melt' may be either Empson's proud claim that he can no longer see the girl in an ordinary way (her eyes are now beautiful pearls for him), or his complaint that she will not take pity on him (opaque as pearls, her eyes cannot 'melt' with emotion). It seems hardly tactful, either way, for him to call her eyes 'small', which would not be complimentary even if the pearls *could* 'melt back' to them. Perhaps the 'small eye' of a needle is meant, through which the rich man cannot pass into the kingdom of heaven (the unknown interior 'locus' of the girl); one wonders whether Empson is debarred from knowing her because he is too rich in intellect or because he belongs to a higher social class than she can respond to. Whatever the point of lines 11–12 (is it possible that the girl is a piece of grit in the poet's eye?), they are obviously themselves metaphorical, and mixed and overloaded at that.

Stanza four, which elaborates line 9 ('You are a metaphor'), is clearer, though ambivalent in its view of the girl. She is a convex mirror which offers a wider but distorted version of reality, into which one can only gaze; in the words of Empson's note, 'you can't imagine yourself inside it.' But since the 'fancy' which cannot enter her looking-glass realm means love as well as imagination, and since the 'wide-grasping glass' distinctly resembles the hall of mirrors in a fairground, the value of what she stands for seems dubious. And if she is a 'map only of the divine states' (one notes the echo of line 11), without herself being an inhabitant of them – '[nor] made, nor known, nor knowing in' – it would seem that, far from having an unknowable interior, the girl only exists as the stimulus to romantic dreams in the poet.

In the original version of the poem, three stars were printed between stanzas four and five, as if to mark an important division. Stanza five's sudden use of couplets indicates a change of thought strongly enough. If, despite the considerable lack of clarity of detail in stanzas one to four, one were to sum up their 'argument', it would appear to run like this: the girl's essential nature can only be apprehended by what is outside it (by tangents not points), and perhaps she is only a clue to things beyond herself. Stanza five appears to dissolve these distinctions, whose theoretical thinness has certainly involved the poet in uncertainties of concept and metaphor. If the girl is loved as a 'Cause unknown' (specified as 'grit' in line 11), her effects are visible (her 'Form' is partly her behaviour, partly her physical appearance, 'your curve'): as causes produce effects, effects imply causes. Similarly, the things outside herself ('envelope', 'divine states') suggest, and are suggested by, what she herself is: an outline gives the shape of what is on both sides of it. Since this sounds complimentary, it is a pity not to be certain whether 'vacuum' is used here only in a technical sense, and not as implying that the girl is vacuous, no more than an 'edge' or 'attitude'.

Line 22, essentially, is a piece of conceptual juggling, in which 'lines' (the tangents of stanza one) are turned into the 'points' which define a locus, and thus the preferences of the beginning are reversed. Having in stanza two dismissed the 'enclosed letter', Empson feels now that it may offer him some clues to pinpoint the girl's inner nature, and that his poem, prompted by 'these lines you grant me', may be able to turn her words against her. The final image fuses points and lines into 'painless' verbal 'arrows', fired in pairs, one to each side of the girl's limbs; these, though not transfixing her ('poor grazing misses' aimed at a poor miss now with her back to the wall), will hold her and register her shape. Empson's image may recall one of Wittgenstein's propositions in the *Tractatus*: 'Situations can be described but not *given names*. (Names are like points; propositions like arrows – they have sense.)' (1963 translation, proposition 3.144, p. 23).

The conclusion of 'Letter V' is a curious amalgam. 'Painless arrows' conveys both gentlemanly reassurance and erotic suggestion; a comic quality in 'joints' (particularly as the word is so near 'grazing') vies with voyeuristic sadism, the picture of the apparently helpless girl recalling paintings of the martyrdom of Saint Sebastian; and there is a degree of pleasure in sheer cleverness, as if the poet were a skilful knife-thrower in a circus outlining the spreadeagled limbs of his attractive girl 'assistant'. Yet all the poem's intellectuality boils down to very little. Distinctions are made only to be discarded, metaphors confuse, whether unfurled or not, and the girl of the poem, and of reality, escapes the bloodless approximations of her suitor.

BACCHUS

Complete poem (ll. 1–92) first published in *The Gathering Storm* (1940). Sections of it previously appeared as follows: lines 1–17, as 'Bacchus One', in *New Verse* (March, 1933), and as 'Bacchus', in *Poems* (1935); lines 18–41, as 'Bacchus Two', in *The Criterion,* Vol. 14, No. 57 (July, 1935); lines 73–92 (plus ten more lines after present line 78), as 'Bacchus Four', in *Poetry* (Chicago), Vol. 49 (Jan., 1937); lines 42–57, as 'Bacchus Three', in *Poetry* (Chicago), Vol. 50 (Apr. 1940). [Lines 58–72 were reprinted, as 'Bacchus Four', in *Poetry* (Chicago), (Feb. 1942.)]

The composition of 'Bacchus', Empson's second-longest and most difficult poem, stretched over a period of seven years: begun in Japan in 1933, it was not finished until 1939, in China. The poem is unique in Empson's work in having been published in instalments; this, as well as its dense, punning texture and the cross-referenced structure, gives it a distinct resemblance to that other large 'Work in Progress', Joyce's *Finnegans Wake*, also completed in 1939. The sections were not composed in sequence, but the title – 'Bacchus Four' – under which Empson published his 1937 episode indicates that he had a clear conception of the poem's total pattern well before he was able to write the actual lines (42–72) which filled in its large central hiatus. Judging from Empson's comments on the poem in the anthology *Poet's Choice* (1962), section three (lines 42–57) was the last to be finished. Its material came to him while he was under gas, having a dislocated arm set during a vacation in northern Indo-China; the sonorous line 'Pasturing the stallions in the standing corn' (its image suggested by the Japanese invaders' habit of 'turning their horses into the ricefields'; they also stabled their horses in the student gymnasium of Tsinghua University) was scrawled down after he emerged from the anaesthetic in a state of 'exaltation'. The dislocated arm had resulted from Empson's falling into a pit 'after a certain amount of celebration'; it is most appropriate that a poem called 'Bacchus', which explores man's situation in terms of drink, should have been assisted to its conclusion by a process which began in drink and ended in subliminal inspiration.

That Empson worked so long on this complex poem – and at a time when elsewhere he was trying to simplify, or at any rate alter, his 'clotted kind of poetry' – indicates its importance to him. In *Poets' Choice* he stated his feeling quite clearly, if apologetically: 'I am afraid I like *Bacchus* best of my own poems, maybe as the traditional mother dotes on the imbecile.' It is rather the 'put-upon reader' confronted by it who feels the imbecile: certainly, few of his critics have shared Empson's predilection. Nevertheless, it is impossible to miss the fierce passion with which Empson reads the poem on his record, particularly the latter part of section two, the last three lines of section four, and the final twenty lines, whose incantatory sestina-like permutations have the effect of change-ringing. Against the intellectual ramifications created by the many puns, which, like the many intrusive brackets, tend to fragment one's response to the four sections of exposition, needs to be set the simpler forward thrust generated by the predominant heroic couplets, and the sheer splendour of many individual lines, from the clashing 'cymbal' of the beginning to the ringing bells of the end: lines like 'Groyned the white stallion arches of the main'; 'He still is dumb, illimitably wined'; and 'Paste for the backs of mirrors, there he lies'.

The extreme taxingness of 'Bacchus' is the product of its local density (the multiple implications of single words, lines and allusions) and its length. One looks at the poem as it were through a pair of binoculars of which one lens is microscopic, the other telescopic: it is possible, with many readings, to grasp individual pieces of the puzzle, closely seen; it is also possible to discern some kind of over-all structure – images of the human predicament, followed by 'tragic exultation in it'. What one cannot do is bring the two lenses to a common focus, since there is too much to keep in mind for too great a space. One reads the poem for meaning (in small units) or for sound and general impression (in rather larger ones), and in practice the nearest one comes to total illumination is the random flash where two separated passages suddenly touch, suggesting yet another possibility; as for instance the 'trophies' of line 34, the many-eyed beasts of *Revelation* (iv, 6), who stand for outward and inward sight and (as animal-skin rugs) form the basis for the 'golden throne' of God and the human mind, and the 'cups' (of suffering and liquor) not only drunk by Prometheus but won by him as the champion of the human right to knowledge and 'acclaimed' even by the tyrant (Jupiter or God) who tortures him. Similarly, the 'wheal' of line 41, which in addition to conflating 'wheel' and 'weal' (cf. 'Plenum and Vacuum') means a Cornish tin-mine, illuminates the 'miner deeps' of the human mind in line 20; thus, what is 'going round' is not only Ixion's wheel of punishment, the human earth, but the inside of man's head, 'fooled' and 'clouded' by drink and divine deception but containing treasures.

153

It seems doubtful whether a whole comprehension of 'Bacchus', even if attainable, could be satisfactorily communicated by means of prose commentary such as we have attempted to provide for Empson's other poems: it would be both exhaustively complex in texture and exhaustingly long. It would also be in some measure otiose. Hilary Corke once suggested that Empson's ' "unit of creation" is not the poem alone, but the poem *plus* the note upon it'. This piece of kindly special pleading better describes the frequent response of the reader, glad to accept Empson's help, than it does Empson's creative intentions: his 'Note on Notes' (1935) makes his own view clear enough. Nevertheless, though the note on 'Bacchus' is no more an integral part of its poem than Empson's other notes are, its amount of detail (nearly six pages of comment on phrasing, reference and structure) makes it not just helpful but invaluable; Richard Eberhart even declared that, in providing it, Empson 'does the critic's job for him'. This is not true – as Empson said in *Some Versions of Pastoral* (p. 277), 'the question for criticism is what is done with the machine', and one cannot feel that this 'jacketed turbine' (as *Time* magazine called it in 1949) functions perfectly; but the note offers the analyst a more generous 'peep at machinery' than usual, suggesting the poem's essentially associative and imaginative logic while explaining many of its local components. This is not to say that the note provides an easy route into a difficult poem, still less a substitute for it; rather that acclimatisation to both poem and note, and a frequent commerce between them in the reader's mind gradually lead to a steadier sense of what is going on. Our few concluding remarks are offered in the hope of assisting this necessarily slow process.

'Bacchus' takes up and draws together a number of threads from earlier poems: the pride and punishment of Arachne (line 83); the fate of Ixion ('Invitation to Juno'); the rainbow ('Iris' arch' in line 21); the 'plumbing' of 'The World's End'; Noah, 'focus' and incestuous inbreeding ('Dissatisfaction with Metaphysics'); and most of all the birth of Bacchus himself, as a result of the fire which was Jupiter's startling 'retort' to the rash request of Semele ('Note on Local Flora'). What links these motifs is Empson's interest in the precarious state of man, a creature of pride, daring and folly who lives mid-way between god and beast, and for all its mention of 'gods', in the title and in the similarly-worded periphrases which begin each of the five sections, it is man and his fate with which 'Bacchus' is concerned. Indeed, only Mercury, the 'herm' of section 4, and Jupiter, who vaporises Semele in section 5, are really gods, and even Mercury is a messenger and pictured in relation to man. Bacchus, the 'laughing god' of intoxication and inspiration, is a demigod, 'cymbal of clash' because so dramatically born; 'the god arkitect' is the human Noah, controlling the Flood by riding it like a bucking bronco; 'the god who fled down with a standard yard' is the human hero Prometheus, whose fennel stalk is wittily represented as containing not glowing charcoal but rum, 'the fire on which these works depend' and the measure of human achievement.

The controlling image of sections 1-4 is the distillation of alcohol ('spirit'), which enables man to transcend his earthly limitations (as in St. John's detailed vision of 'the new Jeru-salem'), but requires careful handling and can have unpleasant consequences: presumptuous Ixion bound to his wheel, revolving like the inside of his head; Prometheus chained to Mount Caucasus, first seen as suffering cirrhosis of the liver, and a fiery nose like Bardolph's, then as Eliot's 'patient etherized upon a table', imprisoned in a nightmare of war's destruction, from Tartar horsemen to poison gas ('the chlorine in the chloroform') to Japanese troops in China. In section 1 Jupiter's 'retort', subliming the earthly nature of Semele 'by fire' and precipitating the birth of Bacchus, imme-diately becomes a boiling chemical retort out of which the spirit condenses and drips into the round 'dimmed flask' of man. Line 7 is a terse description of human 'sublimation': man is 'fitted both to earth and sky', and any rising upward, and losing of 'earth' he achieves is only the fulfilment of an earth-bound creature's aspiration. The distillation of spirit is seen in lines 14-17 as the formation of the primal sea of all life – 'brine' to 'living blood', blood to human 'tears of wine' and to the sacrificial blood/wine of Christ, himself a species of demigod and, like Bacchus and Prometheus, a teaching intermediary between God and man. Sections 2

155

and 3, taken generally, show man as an ingenious and trail-blazing explorer – Noah, Columbus, Ixion and Prometheus – whose risks (calculated in the case of 'Columbus' egg') lead to good and bad results: Ixion, 'helled to earth's centre' by Jupiter for attempting to seduce his wife, at least produced from the false 'inwheeling serene cloud' 'her centaur', the learned Cheiron who instructed heroes.

Humpty-Dumpty's balancing act on 'earth's garden wall' (line 24) leads in Section 4 to a picture of man's Fall out of 'the mortal Eden'. This 'smash resounding in its constancy' – a hangover from which man still suffers – is seen as the bursting of the retort into small pieces (just as 'the planet Bacchus' burst long ago into 'dry lone asteroids') as a result of the frivolous meddling of Mercury. (Since a 'herm' is a small phallic statue of the god, his stirring thermometer which 'measured degrees of heat' suggests a penis; the sexual element here allows Empson to turn Mercury's snake-entwined caduceus into Satan, raising his flickering head to see what was going on in Eden and bringing knowledge of good and evil – a version of relativity, making 'space ends meet'). Man's 'plumbing' is his consequent fall, like a lead weight, and the mental maze of pipes (an image of self-consciousness, like 'paste for the backs of mirrors') running all over the house of the spirit which he now inhabits, as a 'flaked slough' of intellectual despond. ('The sovereigns' is baffling; but 'given with it free', perhaps an ironic view of the Fortunate Fall, repeats a joke about modern American houses which Empson first made in a review in *Granta*, 8 June 1928).

The last twenty lines of the poem, with their rich and con-stantly-shaken mixture of Semele, Arachne, Ixion, King Lear, arches, copes, despair and fire, yield little to analysis, but convey Empson's exultant yet despairing admiration for the human passion which reaches hopelessly for what it cannot grasp. Though Empson rightly described 'Bacchus', as a whole, as 'not meant to be just Imagist', its final section, with its many separate end-stopped lines, can reasonably be described in such terms, though its sharpness – to which sound and heat contribute – communicates visionary rather than merely visual intensity. 'Vatic', Empson's word for it in 1962, is an apt if uncharacteristic description.

YOUR TEETH ARE IVORY TOWERS

First published in *The Gathering Storm* (1940).

The witty title of Empson's poem grafts on to a not-yet-forgotten toothpaste advertising slogan – 'Your Teeth are Ivory Castles' – the denigratory, 'ivory tower' view of literature. The effect of this, at its simplest, is to blow a raspberry at hostile criticism; but it can be taken, more seriously, to suggest that the wariness and self-protection of the writer are no less necessary and natural than the activity of guarding one's teeth from decay – indeed, that the ability of both teeth and poetry to relate sharply to experience depends on the maintenance and polishing of their ivory. Yet though this attitude is reflected in stanzas 10 and 11, it is not the total, and certainly not the final, view of a poem which combines liveliness with uneasiness, and moves from colloquial sly humour to dignified, even sombre, eloquence.

Empson's note presents the poem as a defence of 'my clotted kind of poetry', but the poem itself tells a rather different story, being concerned not so much with clottedness (and consequent obscurity) as with 'Escapism', a charge against literature so new that the term is not recorded in the Oxford Dictionary of 1933. (Thus the statement that 'Escape Verse has grown mortal sin' is really an ellipsis for 'Something nobody used to worry about is now given a disparaging name and thought a betrayal of true literature'.) 'Escapism' (linked by Empson in his note with sentimentality) roughly involves turning one's back on 'real' (often contemporary) problems and setting up a comforting imaginary world in their place; clottedness and obscurity are not the usual tools of this popular enterprise. Such escapism is hardly something Empson's poetry could accurately be charged with, nor in fact does the term ever seem to have been used in connection with it. Which 'critics' objected to Empson's verse on the precise grounds indicated at the start of the poem is not clear from reviews of *Poems* (1935) or from reference to the essays of F.R. Leavis and others in *Scrutiny* during the later 'thirties. The dangers to the writer of the 'ivory tower' attitude are referred to in a symposium article called 'Writers and Politics' contributed to *Scrutiny* in September, 1939 (pp. 151-56); its author, Olaf Stapledon, also wrote in *Scrutiny* on 'Escapism in Literature' in December, 1939; but neither piece mentions Empson, and their appearance preceded that of *The Gathering Storm* by only a small margin. In view of Empson's cartoon of Leavis in stanza 4, it is conceivable that some remarks Leavis made in 1933 may have rankled and later been exaggerated into the 'Piaget's babies' analogy of lines 2-4: 'The uneasiness that qualified the interest one took in Mr. Empson's work long before he became a New Signature is settling into sad recognition that he is becoming less and less likely to develop. He seems no nearer than before to finding a more radical incitement to the writing of poetry (or of criticism) than pleasure in a strenuous intellectual game.' (*For Continuity*, p. 193). In this connection Empson's un-reprinted 'Note on Notes' in *The Gathering Storm* is suggest-ive, mentioning the presence in 'my small output here' of 'an obscure moral worry about whether there was too much puzzle interest going on'.

Whatever the provocation, Empson's response is witty, resourceful and concerned, even if it does not entirely con-vince either the reader or its author. The poem is in two parts, divided by the portentous pause of line twenty-one's alexandrine; the first deals with the literary squabble, the second with the larger problem of belief of which it is a part or symptom. Shifts in the direction of the argument are marked by three summarising phrases of similar pattern: 'This gives just one advantage' (l. 9); 'This leads to anarchy' (l. 21); and 'This gives no scope for trickwork' (l. 37).

Perhaps on the principle that attack is the best form of defence, Empson begins by dressing critical objections to 'Escape Verse' in a hyperbolical analogy from the observa-tions of Jean Piaget, the Professor of Child Psychology at the University of Geneva, which were recorded in *The Language and Thought of the Child* (1926) and *The Child's Conception of the World* (1929). Piaget had discovered (though not exactly 'proved by interview', as Empson declares as if to mock the certainties of scientific method) that children are more egocentric and private than adults. This 'affection' is allegedly equated, to produce a kind of guilt-by-association,

158

with the 'mortal sin' of escapist poets – it is both 'love' (or rather, self-love) and an illness. Such a tendency, in adults, might be clinical madness, but Empson's use of 'mad' in connection with the children has the slang sense 'crazy', and his ironic tactics are made clear by the 'reason' given in line 4: how odd of them to prefer to talk to themselves rather than to Professor Piaget! The reader is thus left to feel that the escapist poets are no more perverse or culpable in not talking to the reader. Nevertheless, having slyly laughed at critical hostility, Empson makes a parenthetical concession in lines 4–7: the 'frank protection' of child and poet (a notion whose plain sense is amusingly played off against its quasi-paradoxical form) need not be so extreme – it is possible both to please oneself and the listener ('Pa') by the experimental noises ('Ba') which one makes. 'Cordial' conveniently means both 'friendly' and 'effective'. (Could 'frank' anticipate – it being his first name – the entry of Dr. Leavis in stanza 4?)

Returning to the attack on line 8, Empson notes the 'advantage' of 'Escape Verse' not for its practitioners but for its critics: it gives them something to criticise and feel morally superior about. The 'Ha' retorted in response to the poet/child's innocent 'Ba' suggests 'Got you!', and enlists the reader's sympathy for the poet as victim. The lines following (10–13) are a far from unfair commentary on the tone of Leavis and *Scrutiny* in the 1930s: that of a consciously-embattled minority, so convinced of its own perception of excellence that its response to anything less was grudging and hard-to-please. 'Gnawing his bone' well conveys literary asceticism, fault-finding ('I have a bone to pick with you'), and even that species of self-destruction that may ensue when 'the best' drives out the good. Such responses, for Empson, are themselves an 'Escape' from confronting what many people are actually writing, and thus the critic is no better than the 'escapist' writers he criticises. Moreover, as lines 13–16 tersely indicate, the very insults ('brickbats') of Leavis, the high standards by which he condemns many modern writers, are bits of brick derived from the ruins of an older, bigger, and more generous-minded critical view (the 'larger building'). Empson's drift here can only be inferred

159

from his metaphor, but he may be referring to the neo-Arnoldian element in Leavis, or to his indebtedness to the neo-Arnoldian Eliot. The use of brickbats as a foundation ('basis') for one's values recalls Eliot's 'These fragments I have shored against my ruins.'

Wherever Empson locates his past 'larger building', he defines its characteristics in lines 18–20: it allowed the writer to function as the safety valve for his society, letting the steam of its driving fantasies escape harmlessly in his art, and/or as the Wordsworthian 'innocent eye' of the child, not yet 'misled' by the corrupt currents of the 'adult' world. Those who see no need for such functions are welcome to their view, if they have wisdom (the reverse face of innocence) or are too 'mild' to require a safety valve; but Empson's tendentious description of their criticism as 'hate' (which is neither wise nor mild) suggests that such people do not exist. The disagreement leads to impasse and 'anarchy': for Empson the 'escapist' poet (essentially, he who goes his own way) has a purpose, for contemporary critics he has none. There is no 'final judge' (a supreme literary court of appeal? God?) who can arbitrate – 'the truth between you' suggests that neither side is completely right. The force of Empson's interim conclusion is unfortunately weakened by the unattributed phrase 'The claim is' (*who* says that there is no final judge?).

What is clear, however, is that for Empson the anarchy of the present has an unhealthy effect on literature; mere dissension between writer and critic, not without cattiness on both sides, must give place to more sober and open-minded consideration of the problem. In a world without ultimate authorities, no one but they can solve it. Stanzas 8 and 9 contrast this position with that of past society, with its belief in either or both Christianity and worldliness, a splendid and generous aristocratic hierarchy. Empson's phrasing – 'ran' presents them as candidates for office, 'rival pets' as attractions in a zoo or circus – avoids serious self-commitment, but at least the society that did admire them above all else could 'carry' anarchy, as a 'passenger' whose weight was not heavy enough to break up the essential system of shared beliefs. Similarly Marlowe's Faustus (before he made his pact with the devil) could safely wish to embrace all worldly knowledge and possibilities, since all were predictably comprised within such a fixed world-view, and would not sink the ship of discovery on which he was embarked (*Doctor Faustus,* Sc. I, lines 51–55).

Stanzas 10 and 11 take up the motif of global exploration provided by Marlowe's 'quiet poles' and Empson's 'on board', and develop it into a fine extended metaphor which culminates in the 'raft' image of stanza 14. They also contrast the simple earlier world, whose two-dimensional 'surface' rolled (stretched and was rocked) between the co-existing polar opposites of 'Christ and the magnificent milord', with the complex modern universe of post-relativity physics, with its four-dimensional 'uncommunicable spacetimes'. In the first world (the present tense suggests it still exists, which Empson may feel is true for some people, though not himself), the 'spry arts' (energetic, cunning, quick on their feet) can still steer a meaningful course, and even exert influence, though appearing not to do so: *'seeming* to evade' functions here as a defence of 'escapism', though 'while' would be more modest than 'by'. (The accuracy of the navigational metaphor here is not clear, nor, in literary terms, what is evaded or seems to be). The world of modern science, however ('if it parts' may imply that, unlike Empson, not all come to terms with it) poses problems for all poets alike: the strict meaning of 'uncommunicable spacetimes' is 'a complex concept which cannot be communicated' (as Empson may have felt he had failed to do in his earlier poems), but it also suggests an enormous area across which communication cannot take place. In this situation the 'direct yell' of (presumably) the 'committed' poet is no more use than the oblique 'hint or ogle' of the 'escapist' one: 'ogle' and 'yell' play with equal irony on both types, and there is a further degree of ambivalence in 'stoutest heart', whose negative element may be intended to mock the more 'scout-masterish' exhortations of Auden and Day Lewis. Lines 34–36 tip the balance, theoretically, in favour of the 'escapist' poet; but even he, sometimes managing to see through the corner of his eyes what a direct look misses (the optical basis of this idea is stated in Empson's note), cannot see any metaphorical 'star behind the blue'. The absent 'star' seems to stand for some ultimate belief or reality: both a guide for celestial navigation, without which there is no 'scope' (telescope?) even for the 'trickwork' of a zig-zag course, and a worshipped idol – the 'rival pets' image of divine or worldly authority replaced by that of a film 'star', ogled amorously but in vain.

The final stanzas (akin in spirit to those of 'This Last Pain') attempt to define a stance in face of the poem's two related problems – the variation of literary opinion and the absence of agreed systems of belief which gives rise to it – and resonantly bring together its various motifs: self-communing babies and poets, the 'larger building' of the past, the need for a 'star', and the precarious voyage of existence. Unlike Empson's old lady, who 'reads a compass certain of her pole', modern man must 'plot' his course without benefit of one, and stick to it; in literary terms, the writer, having devised his characteristic plots (strategies or fables), must have the courage to remain true to himself while trying to 'sustain' the reader's interest. This effort may seem no more than talking to himself, like Piaget's babies, yet his faith (in himself, his work, or the object of his belief) may be re-warded by some revelation. But even if he despairs of a reply (one sense of 'speak again'), or feels that the age of replies is past, he should not therefore conclude that other people's answers to the problems of life (whether given to them or offered by them) are irrelevant or of short-lived usefulness.

There is an obvious narrative sense in which lines 37-41 may be taken as describing two sorts of writer, and thus as a modest request (made apparently by a third party) for the understanding of the second by the first: the answers of the 'escapist' poet are not, merely because of his or their elegant dress, 'uneventful' (unexciting, or unrelated to contemporary issues) or quickly obliterated by time. But one feels that, in a deeper sense, the two are the same, and that both are Empson's attempt to describe himself and his oblique but nonetheless serious endeavour to make what sense he can of a world whose meaning is not apparent. The image of 'wits . . ./In evening dress on rafts upon the main', which summons up visions of aristocratic survivors of the *Titanic*, facing their hazards with courage, wit and style, is one of the finest and most haunting in Empson's work. The 'larger building' of past belief (whether country house, church, or ship) has disappeared; lacking its stability of common ground, not only the writer but modern man is set adrift on an uncertain present. The political problems of the day, and the literary preferences of any one group, are only aspects of a larger existential situation in which mutual tolerance is better, and safer, than anarchy: we are all at sea (calling it 'the main' brings gallantry and dignity to our plight) and all in the same boat.

AUBADE

First published, eight lines longer, in *Life and Letters Today*, Vol. 17, No. 10 (Winter, 1937), pp. 68–69.

A curious and powerful mixture of circumstantial detail and cryptic evasiveness (as though habitual reticence struggled with an intense wish to preserve something of special value), 'Aubade' relates its personal experience – the truncated relationship of 'two aliens' – to the larger uncertainties of the 1930s which provide a context and, in a sense, an explanation for its failure. The initial incident of the earthquake – an ironic, premature and unwelcome 'dawn song' – occasions a hurried parting which seems only temporary but is revealed obliquely to have become permanent (so the earthquake is both literal and a metaphor for the unsteady ground beneath this particular love affair); the angry regret and questioning which ensue are accompanied by a feeling, partly genuine and partly self-justificatory, that there was little hope for two lovers of different races in a decade marked by natural calamity, economic collapse and the spread of war. As the poem progresses and its individual story merges into the historical situation, the alternating refrains come to stand for the unsatisfactory choice by which man is constantly confronted: between the wish 'to be up and go', which may be an act of sensible determination or convenient cowardice, and the need to stay, which may be courageous defiance or submission to the unavoidable.

As Empson made clear in conversation with Christopher Ricks in 1963, the origin of his poem lay in his Japan experience, at a time when 'it was usual for the old hand in the English colony to warn the young man: don't you go and marry a Japanese because we're going to be at war with Japan within ten years'. This attitude is summed up in stanza 9, and the reader is left to infer that such undisclosed private factors as contributed to the relationship's decline were conditioned by an enveloping, and inhibiting, awareness of the worsening international situation. In his record-notes (1959) Empson stated that the poem 'was written in Tokyo during the Manchurian Incident, probably in 1933'; but in view of its publication as late as the end of 1937 it seems possible that it was also worked on in England after his return there in 1934. The 'Manchurian Incident' (strictly, the engineered Japanese takeover of Manchuria in September, 1931, but loosely used for the state of tension between China and Japan which followed it and led to the Sino-Japanese war in 1937) was hardly 'the same war' in 1933, except in a metaphorical sense; there was no literal war to compare it with until the outbreak of the Spanish Civil War in July, 1936.

In the present version of the poem, the large jump between its two parts — from the slightly ominous casualness of the incident recorded in lines 1–22 to the almost strangulated post-mortem expostulations of lines 25–42 — disorientates the reader and may even leave him puzzled about quite what has happened: what is being regretted, why, and from what perspective? The lines which originally followed stanza 8 provided a helpful bridge for readers in 1937:

> *This is unjust to her without a prose book.*
> *A lyric from a fact is bound to cook.*
> *It was more grinding; it was much more slow,*
> *But still the point's not how much time it took,*
> *It seemed the best thing to be up and go.*
>
> *I do not know what forces made it die.*
> *With what black life it may yet work below.*
> *The heart of standing is you cannot fly.*

It was perhaps the logic of line 4 which led Empson in 1940 to cut this passage out; the omission, however, not only helps to raise the temperature of his lyric but may also betray a wish to conceal any cooking of the books involved in the making of 'a lyric from a fact'.

The earthquake that wakes the lovers (asleep in Empson's small rented villa in the western suburbs of Tokyo; the 'cliff' was an 8 ft. drop) is presented by the poem as both the interruption and the effective end of their affair. J.H. Willis's tying of the event (in his unpublished thesis) to the Tokyo earthquake of 21 September 1931 seems implausible: Empson had arrived in Tokyo only three weeks before and is thus likely to have experienced it, but it is neither easy to believe an affair of such moment started so early nor necessary to assume that a foreigner in Japan needs an earthquake big enough to kill thirteen people in order to feel insecure. And the insecurity itself is oddly presented. It inspires first a normal wish (prudence rather than panic) to 'be up and go', then the equally normal contrary feeling that this is pointless since the holes (rendered perhaps by the lacuna in Empson's elliptical line) would be 'far too large for my feet to step by'; but there seems as much concern for property (books and bottles) as for human life, and the poet has leisure for the mild spite of line 7. One is tempted to suspect that, in the first two stanzas, the poet is mentally savouring the thrill of a phenomenon not encountered at home.

What makes him worried is the reaction of the girl: if she, the local, is afraid, he, the visitor, should be, and she is dressing apparently to go outside – safer, in Japanese opinion, if an earthquake is likely to be serious. This misunderstanding of her purpose, an aspect perhaps of the 'language problem' between them, causes the girl some amusement: it is not the earthquake and its imaginary 'deaths' (being crushed or swallowed up) which bother her, and there is no need for her to show him any literal 'solid ground for lying'. Instead, with typically Japanese solicitude, she recommends 'healthy rest' for her lover, while with typically Japanese female prudence she orders a taxi for herself. The 'death' she fears is discovery or scandal, and she needs to get home ('in earshot' suggests not to a husband but to a father) before the inconvenient

earth tremor, waking him too, reveals all. Lines 18-19,
irritatingly imprecise, could imply that it is already too late,
and that she will have a lot of explaining to do; it is possible
to read 'I tried saying Half an Hour to pay this call' as the
poet's hope against hope that she can prevent total disaster,
but in view of her laughter in line 11 and his sleep on line 22
this seems less likely than that he is trying to persuade her
to cope quickly with the awakened bawler and return as soon
as possible to him. Beneath all this, however, a possible
suspicion lurks in the non-literal meaning of line 15: perhaps
the girl's reason for leaving is a lie which, if questioned, she
could not explain away? The various constructions give an
air of uncertainty and precariousness to the situation, as if,
once she has left, the relationship will never be the same
again. The 'blank' sleep of stanza 6 seems a limbo between
past and present, and incidentally provides a transition between one part of the poem and the other. The 'would' of
line 22 conveys a wish to return to the oblivious or ignorant
peace of love, the sleep before the unsettling earthquake and
before the crumbled relationship. Taken with the two lines
that follow, it also means that such a sleep would have lasted
had not the earthquake and its aftermath revealed the hole
beneath the relationship's surface. And the modification of
the refrain (line 24) by the line which precedes it suggests
that the acceptance of the difficulties of the affair ('the
language problem but you have to try') was abandoned as
they grew greater.

The laconic telling (or hinting) of personal story is followed
in stanza 7 by unmistakably urgent rhythms that convey a
sense of loss and even of self-reproach in terms of the larger
mess of world events. To whom Empson is appealing ('Tell
me again') hardly matters (to the evidence of gloomy letters
from home, perhaps, or to that of recent arrivals with their
'news of fresh disasters'); more important is why he wants
to be reminded of 'Europe and her pains'. The reasons are
complex: to drown his own sorrows in the contemplation of
others' worse ones (though these also provide a dramatic
parallel to his own); to convince himself he was right to leave
chaotic Europe and come to the 'Far' East ('a bedshift flight'
suggests the wish-fulfilment of magic carpets, nomadic

wanderings, and erotic daydreams); and (in view of line 31) to rub his nose in the ironic realisation that his decision only brought him to 'the same war on a stronger toe' – the Manchurian Incident and goose-stepping Japanese militarism. (G.S. Fraser has shrewdly conjectured a reference to Shiva, the god of destruction, who is often depicted balancing on one toe). Thus flight seems both futile and ignoble. Lines 27–28 are particularly rich in overlapping meanings, though the phrase 'let him count his gains' is clumsily stuck on. 'Glut me with floods' is a paradoxical and ironic version of 'Comfort me with apples' for the disappointed lover. The floods themselves are real, perhaps those referred to by Auden in 'A Bride in the 30's' ('. . .sombre the sixteen skies of Europe/And the Danube flood'); being real, they might well have in them pigs swimming for their lives and thus risking (as the folk belief has it) cutting their throats with their scrabbling fore-hooves. But the use of 'swine' indicates that the floods are also metaphorical – the economic depression of the 'thirties from which only the 'bloated capitalist' can escape to 'count his gains'. A final and particularly bitter meaning is that the pressures of the time are such that the frantic effort to escape them costs some people their lives (or simply leads to suicide, as with businessmen ruined by the crash of 1929): nothing is 'gained' but death. In view of stanza 9, one wonders whether Empson is accusing himself here, for having let slide a love affair with no future, in the process of which he has deprived himself of something vital.

Stanza 9 certainly seems to question a decision, or perhaps the value of advice taken, as well as utter a lament. 'Tell me' suggests conversation with a sympathetic friend (though 'more quickly' is puzzling – more quickly than what?), who may either reduce the poet's feeling of desolation to manageable proportions or reinforce his sense of the affair's value. As if this may be embarrassing or beyond the friend's ability, line 34 rephrases the request in terms susceptible of a less dramatic and more general answer: what is missed (and this, in different senses, applies to both givers and takers of prudent advice) by those who feel that a foreigner and a Japanese should avoid entanglement? Line 35, awkwardly compressed, presumably refers to the gambler's habit of flattering 'Lady Luck' in the hope of getting a good score when throwing dice (even when the chances are so small that the die might as well be 'no die'); the 'old Japan hand' would not take a risk with any die. The sexual overtones of 'die', and the homophone 'throe', link the gaming image to the terminated affair, which included more than the pathetically little 'one kiss' shared by the 'two aliens'.

To the (essentially rhetorical) questions of stanza 9 there are no answers, except perhaps Tennyson's ' 'Tis better to have loved and lost/Than never to have loved at all'. A strong sense of frustration is conveyed by the first lines of the envoi, and by the assertive formula 'I can tell you why' (which contrasts with the earlier 'Tell me'), but they reach for too wide an area of reference ('risings' as 'getting up', as 'erections', and as political rebellions') to contribute much in the way of meaning to the poem at this late stage. The last three lines take things more quietly, flatly juxtaposing the apparent masculine decisiveness of 'Up was the heartening and the strong reply' with the equal conviction that what cannot be escaped (memories of love, feelings of responsibility, pain of loss) must be endured – and by everyone, as the change of pronoun emphasises: 'The heart of standing is we cannot fly.'

It is a moving conclusion; but the poem, though of considerable poignancy and, for Empson, self-revealing in an unusual way, is not entirely satisfying. There is a tendency not only for the refrains, but for many of the individual lines (so often end-stopped) to echo impressively in isolation, to suggest as generalisations more than they convey in their contexts. It is not easy to tell and comment on a story (which implies time and forward movement) while being committed to a form which involves the recurrence of a few rhymes and of two refrains, fixed once they have been chosen. These must (but do not always quite) coincide with stages in narrative and emotional statement able to support and illuminate them, and to receive support and illumination in return.

FOUR LEGS, THREE LEGS, TWO LEGS

First published, six lines shorter, as 'Travel Note', in *New Verse* No. 16 (Aug.–Sept. 1935), p. 9.

The idea of this poem – a legend illuminated, or at least put into a new perspective, by a modern instance – has something in common with 'Note on Local Flora'; while its unemphatic rhythms and take-it-or-leave-it manner, particularly at the end, give it a likeness to 'Ignorance of Death'. But whereas both those poems are more or less cumulative, 'Four Legs, Three Legs, Two Legs' is a collage of juxtaposed observations, as if Empson had for once adopted the imagist method normally uncongenial to him. The result is a kind of 'do-it-yourself' poem, a verbal doodle of considerable charm, in which the reader is left to spot the many interconnections, contrasts and parallels, and build up a meaning from them.

The original title, 'Travel Note', had a casual ring appropriate to the poem, and makes clear what prompted it: Empson's encounter, recorded in the central and longest section, with the Sphinx at Gizeh on his way back to England from Japan in 1934. His view of the Egyptian Sphinx as dog-like and 'pathetic' seems to have made him wonder about Oedipus' encounter with the 'ogre-like' woman-faced Sphinx of Thebes, who asked him the riddle of the poem's present title: what being has at different times four legs, three legs and two legs? Judging from the poem's ending, Empson may long have felt sceptical that Oedipus' simple answer, 'Man', could have defeated such a fierce questioner. But if the Theban Sphinx was really like the harmless-looking Egyptian one, it becomes easier to understand his success.

Empson's oblique and punning opening (explanatorily expanded by the later addition of lines 3–6) alludes to Oedipus' killing of his unknown father Laius at the meeting of 'three lines' – the roads from Delphi, Corinth and Thebes. This was both a crucial action, a 'cross-road' of his life shadowed by fate (and in mystery, since its precise details are obscure), and a 'trivial case', since it appeared at the time only a brawl between two strangers. (It also, given the meanings of the Latin 'trivium', occurred at a place where three roads met and was a stage in Oedipus' education). The 'chance' meeting was 'odd' because three roads led to it (strictly speaking, only two lines meet at a point), and because of strange and fateful coincidence: Oedipus had left Corinth to consult the oracle of Delphi, who had warned him of his dark future; having left Delphi, whom should he meet but Laius, on his way there from Thebes to ask advice about the terrorising Sphinx. The idea behind 'the delta zero' is that the area bounded by Corinth, Delphi and Thebes makes a triangle; but Oedipus' life, instead of being as it were fruitfully enclosed within that mathematical 'delta', was excluded, or squeezed inwards to that symbolic zero 'point' between the towns at which he committed his first unwittingly decisive act. To describe his act, Empson with dry functional wit takes over what 'somebody said' about metaphysicians; the 'somebody' was I.A. Richards in *Principles of Literary Criticism*: 'A blind man in a dark room chasing a black cat which is not there would seem to [many people] well employed in comparison with a philosopher apprehending such [metaphysical] 'Concepts'.' (1930 Edn., p. 40). Oedipus' 'black cat', whom it might have been good luck not to kill, was Laius, 'mistaken' for an arrogant road-hog. Equally, given her lion's body, it was the Sphinx, the killing of whom brought Oedipus the delusive reward of the Kingship of Thebes and the hand of Jocasta.

Added after 1935, lines 7-8 are a wearily sardonic comment on the hopeless relationship between mortals of all ages, condemned to be 'in the dark' and to do nothing right, and their remote, inscrutable gods. Both lines are wittily phrased in relation to the post-1935 title, line 7 a modification of Cowper's hymn beginning 'God moves in a mysterious way/His wonders to perform', line 8 a conflation of Psalm 147, x: 'He delighteth not in the strength of the horse; he taketh not pleasure in the legs of a man.' Man may be able to answer the riddles about himself that God (a non-pedestrian like the Sphinx) poses; but God takes no pleasure in his creatures, whether as babies on all fours, grown men standing on their own two feet, or old men supporting themselves on a stick.

Lines 9–15 – line 11 being another post-1935 addition –

attach the Oedipus story to the observed Egyptian Sphinx, patiently waiting at the apex of the Nile Delta (and beside the triangle-faced Pyramids). Though this Sphinx stands for Horus, the male Egyptian god of dawn (and thus is 'orientated' eastward), Empson's delightful description represents her as female, like the Sphinx of Thebes – but 'touching', not savage. While correctly denying (in his note) that Napoleon broke her nose with a cannon-shot, Empson finds it convenient to believe that he painted her face red; 'raddled' suggests 'raddled whore' and thus reinforces 'wrecked girl': she is an Egyptian version of 'one of the ruins that Cromwell knocked about a bit', and though the 'less clear conqueror' of her nose may be time and decay, in terms of the 'wrecked girl' and the 'toy abandoned' it is surely syphilis. (The lack of a comma after 'man' on line 12 allows a quick side-glance at him also as 'a toy abandoned' – by the remote creator of line 8). The wistful final image, of the Sphinx gazing up at her succession of 'average' dawns like a dog hoping to be taken for a walk, is worlds away from the classical legend of a dramatic man-eater. One may even suspect, in view of the numerical order of the legs in the title, an allusion to the song in which 'Four men, three men, two men, one man and his dog/Went to mow a meadow.'

The last section shows Oedipus answering the riddle, as he did after killing Laius. His brief reply ('Man') is implied by Empson's phrase 'placed the riddle' to be a pat answer rather than the product of deep reflection; one may agree, yet still be puzzled as to why Empson thinks the generic 'name' a non-generalised solution. The point is clearer in the light of the meaning of 'generalise' in mathematics and philosophy, which is 'to extend the application of': no metaphysician, Oedipus did not think the riddle anything more than a crossword-puzzle clue capable of a mechanical 'solution', whereas it described *him*, crawling in infancy because of his injured ankles, and destined to walk prematurely with a stick because he had blinded himself. Nevertheless Oedipus' 'commonplace' answer (cf. 'trivial' in line 3) was a 'triumph', at least enough of one to get him by, if not to annihilate the Sphinx. Empson's tone blends intellectual scorn with pragmatic admiration and relief.

If there is any 'conclusion' to a poem as lightweight and loosely structured as this, it is perhaps (leaving aside the rest of the Oedipus story, which Empson chooses not to mention) the wry one that man is luckier in life than he deserves: his sketchy answers satisfy the examiners. But (to draw the Greek and Egyptian parts of the poem together) there may be a reason other than Oedipus' commonplace answer why Empson cannot believe that the Sphinx 'fell and burst', as the Oedipus myth maintains. Legend also has it that the Sphinx flew to Thebes from Ethiopia (Graves, *The Greek Myths II*, p. 10); and the story of the Sphinx is itself said to have originated in Egypt. Can it be that she flew back home, and now sits, a 'wrecked girl' with a broken nose, quietly between the desert and the world of man?

REFLECTION FROM ROCHESTER

First published in *Poetry* (Chicago), Vol. 49, No. 2 (Nov. 1936), p. 68.

The year in which this poem was published saw the outbreak (in July) of the Spanish Civil War; though this is unlikely to have been the spur for Empson's reflections, the poem is clearly a response to the worsening tensions of the decade, particularly those connected with an international 'race of armament'. As well as being topical and public in its application, however, the poem is timeless and personal in its feelings: its relationship to Rochester's 'A Satire against Mankind' (1675) emphasises the weakness and folly of the human race itself, and its conviction that man is 'from birth afraid' is generalised from Empson's own childhood trepidation recalled in *Milton's God*: '. . .when I was a little boy I was very afraid I might not have the courage which I knew life to demand of me' (p. 89). In keeping with the plain but magisterial tone of Rochester's satire, the poem is more sonorous and even than than its companion piece, 'Courage Means Running'; but both poems have ideas in common — each, for instance, starts with the notion of controlling fear by attaching it to recognisable causes – and together they suggest the various ways in which fear governs or modifies human behaviour.

The passage from 'A Satire against Mankind' on which Empson's poem elaborates runs from line 127 to line 144 (with lines 155-56 as a tailpiece). In it Rochester proposes the question: 'Which is the basest creature, Man or beast? (l. 128); his answer is Man, whose killing of his fellows occurs 'Not through necessity but wantonness' (l. 138), and whose driving motive is the negative one of fear. The two lines, contrasting man and the beasts, which Empson quotes as a frame for his own observations, and his epigraph, a general truth appropriate to the particulars of the 'thirties, are deployed thus in Rochester's original:

> For hunger or for love they bite and tear,
> Whilst wretched Man is still in arms for fear.
> For fear he arms, and is of arms afraid,
> From fear to fear successively betrayed; (ll. 139-42).

In the manner of 'Your Teeth are Ivory Towers', the poem is divided into equal parts, the downright phrase on lines 11-12 marking its change of direction. The first four stanzas sum up rather too tersely man's strange psychological 'progress' 'from fear to fear'; the last four assert the large-scale dangers of this in a world of mass movements and more powerful weapons. The working hypothesis of part one is that man is born fearful, and can neither explain nor escape his 'first fear' – perhaps a state of uneasiness resembling original sin; all he can do is 'deceive' it by a succession of rationalisations and substitutions. 'Feeling safe with causes', Man translates his large incomprehensible fear (the mystery of life and its meaning?) into 'risks', smaller problems that he can define and hope to surmount. The reader is left to fill in details, but the general idea seems to be of life as a game of daring and resource, for which Empson himself provides the image of mountain climbing – man pushes higher, and thus risks greater dizziness, from a fear of confronting the dizzy realisation of how far up he already is. Lines 5-6, which sound paradoxical but are perhaps only compressed, show man dubiously moving forward by destroying his 'loved system' (personal, social or political): instead of being taken for granted, it has come to look 'strange' — either (frighteningly) clear or impossibly complex. Empson's abstract shorthand leaves the reader to infer one of those abrupt shifts of perspective by which the familiar ceases to be comforting; but 'mere destruction' hardly suggests approval for what this realisation causes. Lines 8–9 are obscure because ambiguous: one is not sure whether 'a new fear' is consequent on the (avoided) 'great' change, whether it accompanies any needed change, or whether it is the product of being uncertain just how great a change one *has* made. A broad sense does emerge, however, from the threefold process ('making risks', 'climbing higher', 'needing change') suggested by lines 2–8 with their cumulative syntax: that of an apparently inexorable chain-reaction — fear leading to activity, activity generating new fears. Man's claim is that he thus distances himself further from his original fear and gains 'All the advantage of a wider range.' The phrase grows out of the earlier mountaineering image but cuts two ways: man's 'climbing higher' has brought him a splendid view (vantage point), but since the 'wider range' is not only one of mountains and future possibilities but of fears, any 'advantage' seems equivocal. An ironic tension is also set up by the verbal patterns of lines 1 and 10: man 'Successfully has the first fear deceived', but he has only done this by himself being ' "From fear to fear successively betrayed" '.

The suspicion that Empson is speaking, obliquely and with reservations, about 'Progress' is confirmed by the railway image of line 11: man has 'Thought the wheels run on sleepers.' Literally, sleepers support the track and enhance the train's movement, perhaps over the bodies of those not awake to the needs of progress (an attitude which does not 'let sleeping dogs lie'). But one may conjecture that 'sleepers' is meant to stand for 'sleeping fears', those left behind at each stage of man's journey, which yet facilitate his advance to new ones. Whether or not man is correct in thinking he has 'deceived' his 'first fear', left behind later ones, and ridden rough-shod over potential resistance, the final phrase of section one offers a round criticism of man's fear-driven forward urge: 'This is not/The law of nature it has been believed.' Why it is not, technically, a 'law of nature' is made clear by Rochester, for whom 'Nature' is the world of animals. These, if cruel, have positive reasons; Man, in Rochester's view, has no excuses:

> *Pressed by necessity,* they *kill for food;*
> *Man undoes man, to do himself no good. (ll. 131-2).*

The cautionary second part of the poem points out why the human psychology of section one (which may aptly be given the modern label 'escalation') cannot afford to be taken for an unchangeable 'law of nature'. Simply, man has too much to lose when his fears have modern weapons to play with. Empson's illustration of this in stanza 5 is a grimly witty adaptation of the 'wider range' achieved in stanza 3 (one notes 'increased power' and the proximity of line 17's word 'gas'). Fear may not always drive man to suicide (flying to other fears that he knows not of), but the wish for change – and for attention – may make him an ' "attempted suicide" ': one who, as Empson's mocking inverted commas make plain, does not intend to succeed. In the past such a one's 'margin' for error was less narrow and he was likely to be discovered in time; now, with more efficient gas ranges, his imprudent gesture may cost him his life. ('Embarrasses' is a brilliant piece of sardonic understatement). The domestic image lends itself easily to political extension: to such acts as risky territorial claims, to flirtations with Fascism, to Communist fellow-travelling, and to the outdated patriotic 'policies' of lines 15-16, whose view of war as a testing ground for maleness (Empson's slogan sums up such attitudes from *Henry V* to Henley, Brooke and Julian Grenfell) is a wasteful luxury. The 'process' of war (men turned into corpses) and the twisted mental process that leads to it are 'crass' in two senses: both 'extremely stupid' and, because so many people are now likely to be involved in them, uncolloquially 'thick'.

The intervening passage, lines 17-20, unduly compresses a difficult idea. What seems to be a wish to link man's fearful state of mind with the war it can result in causes Empson to compare the two. As war spreads poison gas above ground and digs tunnels beneath it, so the mind operates both consciously — a 'gasbag' demagogue with his chauvinistic rhetoric — and unconsciously. Empson's rhythm and word-order in line 17 places the emphasis on 'mining', thus apparently on the greater danger and complexity of the hidden forces now at work in man. From this assumption Empson seems to reason as follows. It was once possible (as indicated in lines 2–3) for man consciously to channel his fears into self-selected risks (the first of these being the 'root-confusion' from which the others grew), and build up as a result an increasing sense of 'safety' from overcoming the despair created by those risks, an 'irrelevant despair' because it was not the hereditary existential despair which drove him to his strange shifts in the first place. Now, the inference seems to be, things have got out of hand; any 'decision' to take a calculated risk for some attainable object is likely to 'get much besides': the understatement carries sinister weight.

The last stanza leaves it very doubtful whether man *can* control his fears and limit their tortuous and terrible consequences. The eyes that now look for a 'pattern' of behaviour in the 'less involute compulsion' of Rochester's beasts, who fight and kill from the simpler (but still savage) instincts of hunger and sexual rivalry, are unpromisingly 'blank'. They are also 'blanc': the 'whites of their eyes' that men show when frightened and shoot at ('range' again) when aggressive. The doubled rhyme and parallel construction of lines 23–24, turning terza rima into quatrain, add an appropriate gravity to the poem's conclusion.

COURAGE MEANS RUNNING

First published in *Contemporary Poetry & Prose* No. 1 (May, 1936), p. 6.

In order to approach this not very satisfactory poem at all, one must dispel the obfuscation created by Empson's curious 'Corrigenda' to the 1955 *Collected Poems*. There he said that it was written in 1937, and that his choice of the adjective 'wise' to describe England's 'patience' (l. 28) was 'pretty near backing Munich' and repugnant to 'the editor of the literary magazine' (this was Roger Roughton, whose interest at the time was surrealism rather than politics, who left England when war broke out, and who committed suicide in neutral Eire in 1941). Since the Munich agreement (which sacrificed Czechoslovakia to Hitler) was signed in September, 1938, even a poem written in 1937 could hardly be said to have backed it, let alone one actually published in 1936; and even if 'Munich' is loosely intended to mean the attitude of appeasement which led up to the agreement itself, that attitude was not so shameful in 1936 as to require apology in 1955 and the changing of 'wise' (which at least states a view once honestly held) to 'flat' (which does no more than avoid a metrical hiatus). The effect of Empson's disingenuous 'corrections' is to claim for the poem two things it neither had nor needed: involvement with a major issue of morality and *Welt-Politik*, and the 'proper' (viewed by hindsight) response to that issue.

What the poem is about is fear: not fear leading to the over-compensation of risk, dare and aggression, as in 'Reflection from Rochester', but the fear that co-exists with courage (as in Bunyan's two characters), the fear that inspires prudence and restrains foolhardiness, the fear whose existence is implied in the adage 'Discretion is the better part of valour'. If Empson's paradoxical title means anything, it is presumably something like this; it does not seem to recommend cowardice, since running *away* is not insisted on by the poem, but the unrestricted formula it employs (allowing a range of interpretations from 'All courage is synonymous with running' to 'Sometimes it takes more (moral) courage to run') is not very helpful.

The poem has an argumentative air, but the components of its 'argument' are too clipped and oblique, and the transitions between them too abrupt, for it to come over as more than a skittish string of comments. Considerable skill is expended, almost perversely, in counterpointing a casual, prosy manner against the strict form of terza rima in such a way that the units of statement never coincide with the stanzas themselves, and hardly ever finish at the end of a line. The result is an

177

odd mixture of the jerky and the fluent, according as one emphasises sense or rhyme, but there is none of that regularity of rhythm by which Empson involves the reader's feelings as well as his intellectual interest. It may be, of course, that lack of intensity is appropriate to a poem praising caution; certainly there is no image (like the raft of 'Your Teeth are Ivory Towers' or even the range in 'Reflection from Rochester') that possesses richness or bite.

Empson's opening use of Bunyan — Muchafraid and Mr. Fearing (there is no 'Fearful') are conveniently-named characters in Part II of The Pilgrim's Progress — is casual, intended simply to establish the view that fear and courage are closely related. Taken as a gloss on Bunyan's meaning, lines 1-4 are dubious. Muchafraid volunteered to accompany her father Mr. Despondency through the river of Death to meet God, and indeed 'went. . .singing, but none could understand what she said'; there is no indication in Bunyan that her song (l. 10) was ballasted by fear — if anything, the context implies that her fears had been left behind. (1907 Edn., Cambridge University Press, p. 418). Mr. Fearing is described by Honest as 'a Man that had the Root of the matter in him', but not because, as Empson's phrasing suggests, he localised his fears in particular 'things'. It is hard to tell whether 'he read well that ran' is an ironic comment on the hymn that begins 'There is a book who runs may read,/Which heavenly truth imparts'; or a straightforward reference to Habakkuk ii, 2: 'And the Lord answered me and said, Write the vision, and make it plain upon tables, that he may run that readeth it'. Neither view fits the Bunyan context (Mr. Fearing never ran, either away from or towards), though both have a flippant relationship to the poem's title.

After juggling with Bunyan, Empson jumps rather shockingly to venereal disease, the 'clap' which can afflict man's 'two most exquisite surfaces of knowledge' — the sex organs and the eyes. (The effect of literal gonorrhoea on the eyes is indirect, transmitted by infected mother to baby born blind). Since the primary infection causes the sex organs to discharge, the reward of sexual 'courage' may well be 'running'; such a case demonstrates the respectability of fear. The larger metaphorical point is that the organs of sense by which man obtains his greatest knowledge and pleasure are commensurately vulnerable; both courage and fear are required in their use. (The point is made in abstract terms in stanza 6). Lines 7-9 offer a more humorous illustration of the care needed in life, yet there is more at work here than mockery: the negligible dangers of a slip of the toothbrush are increased by association with the sharper ones of a misplaced cut-throat razor. Lines 9-10 (reinforced by lines 19-20) assert the positive contribution of fear: it adds weight — that is, value — to everything man does. (The use of 'ballast' so soon after 'steadily' recalls Donne's 'Air and Angels'.)

Line 11 introduces a rather different point. Fear is ever-renewed; man cannot rely on the precedent of earlier experience and conquest in dealing with it. When the brute fact of fear confronts him, 'it does not' (the image is perhaps from pantomime) 'suggest its transformation': it looks like nothing but its frightening self, it gives man no help in transforming it, and he has no idea what it may be turned into. The wanted transformation is presumably into courage, which helps to identify the fear, and knowledge, to which it is the avenue. Lines 13-16, which seem to describe a mental process by which fear is transmuted into 'cold truth', are darkened by the ambiguity of 'to get/Out by a rival emotion fear': 'to expel fear by means of a rival emotion'; 'to escape emotion by means of a rival "emotion fear"' (i.e. fear of emotion)'. If anything emerges from this peremptory and obscure passage it is the unlikeliness of escaping from emotion, and the low-mindedness of the wish to do so — the 'hope' is a 'common' one in two senses. Lines 16-19 affirm 'truth' as the combined result ('gift of' implies 'we are given' rather than 'we give others') of pleasure and courage and of their necessary counterparts, pain and fear. The phrase 'to put it sanely' is intended, one feels, as a plain man's reminder that truth is not 'cold' or abstract (despite the poem's own schematic presentation here); it also defends fear, and those who feel it, against the sneers of the insensitive and unimaginative. Lines 19-20 state Empson's *credo* with a mixture of diffidence and firmness: a man's 'self-respect' (both courage and maturity) resides not in his lack of fear but in his recognition of its centrality in human character and its importance as a yardstick ('measure' also means, in line 20, 'a policy' and 'a certain amount of'): the degree of fear something provokes in us is what determines the nature of our response to it.

What seems finally to be recommended by means of the last ten lines is a habit of sensible caution and avoidance of extremes. Not all the examples (the 'as' clauses) which Empson adduces as determinants of such an attitude are equally clear and cogent, however; nor are they of the same type – some, like the picture of the economists, are single instances; some, like the example from human psychology which precedes it, contain apparent opposites. The cumulative effect is thus blurred and weakened. 'The operative clue in seeking treasure' is presumably the first one, which leads the seeker on; in adventure stories it is 'normally trivial' – something ordinary whose significance is yet hard to spot. In that 'Fearful' and Muchafraid were in search of 'treasure', Empson may be speaking here of religious or cognate beliefs, with their divergent basic arbitrary assumptions; set against these is the 'urgent creed', the one we need most, which will 'balance enough possibles' (beliefs or clues). Literature too, at its highest and lowest levels ('bard and hack') has to be a sort of compromise, able to communicate with actual readers only by being either more vague or more crudely specific than either type of writer really wishes. I.A. Richards glosses Empson's verbs thus: 'We "blur" when – to avoid irrelevancies – we use a wider word than fits our thought. We "peg" when we adopt a routine word in current use in place of the word which would better let our thought be itself'. (How to Read a Page, pp. 80-81). ('Peg' also suggests both the artificial stabilising of a price – which baffled economists might recommend – and the persistent hammering away at an idea). The theory behind Empson's claim is surely arguable: it sounds like the bad workman not only blaming his tools but his employer as well.

The last six lines give more graspable encouragement to moderation. The first suggestion is personal: extreme emotion, sensitivity leading only to a sense of grievance, is no better than insensitive lack of emotion, stupid hardness. The second relates to the economic situation: not only are the economists baffled by the problems of the decade (though J.M. Keynes's shot at a solution, *The General Theory of Employment, Interest and Money,* appeared early in 1936), they take pride in being so; oddly enough, this is comforting – if the 'experts' aren't worried by not knowing the answers, why should the man in the street be? Empson's phrase in line 27 is clarified by a reference he made in 1937 to the political poetry of Auden and Spender: 'in England there was an obscure safety and bafflement in moving from the poem to consider what the country could possibly do.' ('A London Letter', *Poetry* (Chicago), Vol. 49, Jan. 1937, pp. 219-20). The poem ends with the political alternatives left open to England by a difficult international situation (Italy had taken over Abyssinia by the end of 1935, Hitler re-occupied the demilitarised Rhineland early in 1936). The choice (a pitifully poor one, but in 1936 war seemed neither necessary nor desirable) was between looking over the edge of a precipice – an ironically compelled species of 'wise patience' little distinguishable from suffering – or a risky and laborious climb, 'clinging' to whatever possibilities offered. There is both dry wit and poignancy in the phrase ' "high" policy'. It is the policy of senior statesmen, it is above the heads of ordinary people, it may be 'high-minded'; it is also, as sharply visualised here, very precarious and even undignified. In such a plight, personal, artistic, economic and political, the courage of 'fear' (which, for all the poem's convolutions, seems to boil down to nothing more surprising than prudence) may indeed be the only thing that, with a last spurt of paradox, 'we dare to praise'.

IGNORANCE OF DEATH

First published in *The Gathering Storm* (1940).

Wry, quizzical and detached, this survey of human responses to death is one of Empson's most attractive and accessible poems. Technically, it goes one step further than 'Courage

Means Running' by freeing its discursive manner and irregular rhythms from the restraints of rhyme; in the words of Empson's record-note, it 'is printed as if in *terza rima* . . . but throws away form to feel like rock bottom.' The last three stanzas, however, are far from seeming arbitrary, since they coincide exactly with units of meaning; and the confusion potential in the overlapping of stanzas and sense-units is eliminated in lines 1-12 by the 'list' method of presentation (Buddhists and Christians, Communists, Freudians, Liberals) which makes it clear that sequential argument is not intended. The advantage which 'Ignorance of Death' derives from abandoning rhyme is that its statements can spread themselves and really sound conversational: one of the greatest pleasures of the poem is that of listening to a human voice, its tone varyingly amused, sceptical, puzzled and sympathetic as it passes from point to point. But since these variations are not played against a regular, 'poetic' rhythm, there are occasional places where the precise fall of the stress – and thus the exact nuance of tone and meaning – is not easy to be sure of.

One such place is the first phrase, which is less the beginning of the poem than the point at which the reader is admitted to a catalogue of foibles as it were already begun; according as the main stress falls on 'civilising', 'love' or 'death', one may infer Empson's mind to have been ticking off various attitudes to death, a new species of which (to be followed by others) he now produces, or to have been pondering general human responses, those to death being his present topic. Empson's recording delays the emphasis until the word 'death', and so supports the second view. The effect, like a long run up to bowl followed by a forceful delivery, is to suggest the strangeness of human preoccupation with this subject.

Neither the concept nor the *modus operandi* of a 'love of death' alleged to be 'civilising' is made very clear. (It sounds a little like E.M. Forster's statement in Chapter 41 of *Howards End*: 'Death destroys a man, but the idea of death saves him.'). As 'civilising' relates to social responsibilities as well as to 'culture', the claim may be that an awareness (is it really a love?) of death extends a person's whole range of response to life. Thus 'even' music and painting (let alone, presumably, the verbal medium of literature with its obvious blend of form and content) 'tell you what else to love.' But what 'else' exactly? The dimension of death (as implied especially in religious music and sacred painting), as well as the aesthetic pleasures of the arts themselves – harmony, melody, texture, colour, shape? Or the potentialities of life, as well as the attractions of oblivion or heaven?

Lines 3-7 contrast religious and non-religious views of death. That Buddhists and Christians, for all their differences, 'contrive to agree about death' is partly a joke: members of both groups die, quite apart from their success in managing, by means of the elaborate artifices of theology, to make death their shared perfect gateway to the 'different ideals' of nirvana and personal immortality. The play on 'ideal'/'ideals' conveys a touch of irreverence for 'other-worldly' theorising. For the Communists, death is an irritating interruption to – and thoughts of it a distraction from – the building of paradise on earth. Its only use is 'practical': not just in getting rid of opposition (which Empson can take as read), but in providing corpses as a handy outlet for sexual urges. 'The people' (are there many?) who dig them up for such quasi-necrophiliac purposes are 'not reported' to the police. What evidence Empson had for his gruesomely amusing sidelight on 'Communism' (stories 'reported' in the papers?) is not clear; there is delightful impudence in his well-informed 'I understand'.

From this fortuitous blend of death and lively erotic clamour Empson passes on to the Freudian theory of civilisation as a struggle between death-wish and life force. But though, to Freudians, the death-wish is 'fundamental' (in view of Freudian terms like 'anal', a pun may be intended here), it is 'not their story' whether cases of it are more to be admired than the noisier ones of its equal opposite, ' "the clamour of life" '. (One senses impatience here with psychologists as unwilling to make judgements). The last briefly-stated view of death is that of 'Liberal hopefulness' – that is, the diluted hope of agnostic/atheist intellectuals; for them death is no more than the limiting frame around the really important thing, life's 'improving picture' – a prospect that grows better all the time and a painting which provides moral uplift.

Stanzas 5 and 6 offer two more functions of death – as the 'trigger' of the most powerful literary works aimed at the public, and as the supreme sacrifice made ostensibly for a cause; but they also act as a general summary. Whatever man's view of death, whatever 'conceived calm' – sleep, silence, oblivion, heaven – he is 'happy to equate it to' (whether 'happy to' is a formality or involves real joy), the fact is that he does not *know* what death is like. And, as stanza 6 asserts, a man's readiness to die – not 'because of himself' (from suicidal tendencies, despair or ennui) but for, and because of, 'something' outside himself in which he believes – tells nothing about the truth of his belief or about death. What it tells is something about him, and that only his readiness to die. Empson's awkwardly reduplicating lines suggest the unknowableness of human action, and his old-fashioned exclamation 'Heaven me' a half-admiring, half-ironic throwing up of hands: literally, 'to heaven' means 'to beatify', but the effect here is of 'Bless me' and 'Heaven help me' combined.

Having presented the range of conflicting attitudes to death and committed himself to none, Empson concludes, or rather fades away, with an engaging mixture of modest disclaimer and ironic judiciousness – to concede that death is an 'important' topic and 'proper to bring up' is a nice understatement which balances the Communist 'disapproval' dryly noted on line 5. The last line is slyly deflating: the large category of people who should be willing to admit 'ignorance of death' includes, after all, those whose claims on the subject have been aired in the poem. Perhaps, too, just a touch of chill insinuates itself into the slightly stilted casualness of 'It is one that most people should be prepared to be blank upon.' Whether or not they have opinions on 'the topic' of death, 'most people' should be ready to be 'blank' when the thing itself arrives.

MISSING DATES

First published, as 'Villanelle', in *The Criterion*, Vol. 16, No. 65 (July, 1937), p. 618.

The genesis of this powerful and much-admired poem was reported in 1956 by Robin Skelton in his book *The Poetic Pattern*: 'William Empson did not consciously decide upon writing a villanelle when he began his poem *Missing Dates*. He was intent upon patterning a certain mood or attitude of mind. He wrote several lines before he realized that the poem was taking the form of a villanelle, and then be deliberately allowed this tendency to develop, and within three hours, produced the completed version.' (pp. 52–53). In 1959, a further comment on the poem by Empson was quoted by Elizabeth Drew in *Poetry: A Modern Guide to its Understanding and Enjoyment*: 'The poem, I think, consists of true statements, but I suppose what they add up to is a mood rather than an assertion, anyway not something you can feel all the time.' (Sixth Impression, 1965, p. 139). As a set of statements about life, and particularly as the philosophy of a writer of thirty, 'Missing Dates' is almost too pessimistic to be true. The skill of the poem is such, however, that the reader does not think of it in this way; rather, he is compelled into emotional acceptance by its single-minded intensity. While the poem lasts, its mood of gloom is inescapable, rendered so by the pressurising effect of the form, with its two constricting rhymes and its slow, relentless refrains; by the wide-ranging meanings of 'waste'; and by the Tennysonian insistence of the second refrain, with its echo of 'Tithonus': 'The woods decay, the woods decay and fall.'

The personal key to the poem's mood – a burdensome awareness of physical decline and emotional suffocation – may be the last stanza's reference to 'the poems you have lost' and 'the ills from missing dates': poems that have miscarried (the phrase suggests 'losing a child'), forgotten engagements, missed opportunities, unused time. But if the poem is at root a lament for waning poetic powers, that regret spreads widely: throughout the poem the physical and the emotional are so blended and overlapped that it is not always possible

185

to tell one from the other. The very first line (the poem's first refrain) builds up with its six heavy stresses, the last four juxtaposed, a sense of physical clogging which is felt as the inexorable accompaniment of all earthly processes. Analogous to this 'poison' is the 'waste' of line 3: a sense of desolation which, like the waste products unexpelled by a deteriorating body, gathers in the emotional 'blood stream' and blocks its flow.

The tricky distinction posited in stanza 1 between 'waste' (a totally negative by-product) and 'failure' (the result, however unsuccessful, of positive 'effort') is to some extent renewed in stanza 2, which turns on two meanings of 'consequence'. 'Your system or clear sight' suggests a combination of intellectual acuity, honesty, hard work and ambition, on which a man may pride himself; such a combination may bring about one kind of 'consequence a life requires' – the position of importance he wants and which makes sense of life. It is not, however, this sort of effort which leads to the other kind of 'consequence' – the death logically and sequentially 'required' by any life. What produces *that* is implied by Empson's verb – a process like 'the mills of God', which 'grind slowly. . .but exceeding small'; one may take it to be the process of time itself, during which 'poison' and 'waste' inevitably accumulate. The reader is left to read a human meaning into these concepts – guilty conscience, perhaps, or a sense of inadequacy.

The sad instances of stanzas 3 and 4 show contrasted aspects of waste. The 'old dog' undergoing an experiment in rejuvenation could not profit from the young blood transfused into him (new wine in old bottles, teaching an old dog new tricks) because his body which received it had aged – a natural wasting which was not his fault. The Chinese ancestral tombs, however, which occupy more cultivable land than a crowded country can afford, and the 'slag hills' thrown up as a waste product of mining and smelting, are the results of human choice; here the 'waste land' encroachment of death on life is presumably avoidable. Though these two stanzas increase a general feeling of decay and death, their analogical relationship to the psychologically-subtler human situation hinted at by the outer stanzas is fairly loose – a kind of atmospheric association in which slag heaps may 'stand for' the negative results of human effort (but hardly for the lack of it), and the piety of ancestor worship be seen as a futile obsession with the dead past.

If the first two stanzas have tried to focus on the true cause of human decline – a sense of defeat, apathy or inertia rather than the wearing out of mind and body by necessary effort – and if the last stanza provides a personal source for this feeling in Empson's sense of poetic inadequacy, stanza 5 represents the nadir of general pessimism, not only describing man's untenable hot and cold extremes but the ultimate hopelessness of any middle position. Death is 'the complete fire', a purifying but total and final combustion, whether physical or emotional. Lack of any 'fire', of passion or enthusiasm, makes man cold; schematically, this must be the meaning of 'a skin that shrills' (whistles with cold, thrills with fear, shrinks?), but the suggestion of metaphor in the phrase is too obscure to pin down. Elizabeth Drew's conjecture (*Poetry*, p. 140) that it means a bagpipe is not easy to accept, since a bagpipe 'shrills' with noise and sounds warlike or sorrowful – in both moods it has 'fire'. The rigorous logic of Empson's pattern leaves man in a halfway house of 'partial fires', which warm him for a time but whose embers are gradually choked by the ash which their own burning deposits. How far this 'waste' is useless regret and how far it is simply the expiration of any life, however spent, the image does not say.

SUCCESS

First published, as 'Poem', in *The Criterion*, Vol. 1, No. 5 (May, 1940), p. 315.

Since Empson married in 1941, it seems reasonable to suppose that this grateful love poem was addressed to his wife-to-be, Henrietta Crouse. The basic situation – the removal of 'the torment and the fear' by a praised girl – strongly recalls

'Letter III', with its view of love as a bringer of calm and sanity; but there is an element of ambivalence in 'Success' which the earlier poem does not have. This is registered in the ambiguity of 'should'; in the discrepant responses of 'You should be praised' and 'Blame it upon the beer'; in the subtle obscurities of the Dostoevsky reference and the curiously floating central line; in the occurrence no less than five times of 'doubt'. Placed at the head of such mixed feelings, the title becomes equivocal: though 'success', in love and life, may solve problems and bring stability, it may to an intellectual seem vulgar and smug, and to one unused to it, disquieting. The clue to the disquiet which underlies Empson's gratitude seems to be 'Verse likes despair.' The prevalence of despair, torment and fear in Empson's poetry hitherto is clear enough; in removing them from the man, successful love may deprive his poetry of the painful impulses that benefited it. The strange, and rather beautiful, structure of the poem – a cross between villanelle and terza rima, with more refrains than the one and fewer rhymes than the other – delicately balances free exploration of the differing feelings with awareness that they all belong to the same experience; at the same time, the introduction of a new rhyme sound in line 11 and its strong repetition in line 15 enable the poem to shift its emphasis very noticeably towards acceptance: the girl takes away, but also gives.

G.S. Fraser's distinction (referred to in the Introduction) between 'broad' and 'narrow' semantics is an apt means to describe the double effect of the first three lines. Their 'broad semantics' indicate what the girl has done, show it as praiseworthy, and bestow that praise; the undue clottedness of 'Those that doubt drugs' causes it to be only partly apprehended, and the reader focuses on the large gesture of 'let them doubt', which conveys pride in the girl (whether or not she is a 'drug'), and warm defiance of observers possibly sceptical about Empson's transformation. (The alteration of the original 'Those who doubt drugs' was presumably to allow the reading 'People drugged by doubt', as well as the two other meanings mentioned by Empson in his note). The 'narrow semantics', however, imply tentativeness and reservation. Although from line 8 onwards Empson talks of

'losses', the 'torment and fear' of line 1 are not lost but 'mis-
laid', which suggests two things: that they are more likely to
turn up again, and that (since 'mislay' is often used in the
context of domestic articles like cuff-links and umbrellas)
one may even wish them to. Hence, perhaps, the rather
grudging use in line 2 of the passive voice and the word
'should': the poet is not sure whether to praise the girl or
not, since her cure may be only temporary and/or she may
have taken away a state of mind he feels odd without.
Those inclined to wonder whether drugs (pain-killing and/or
habit forming) have been used, or to doubt their value, are
invited to consider, in the present case, 'which' (if any)
'was here.'

Lines 4–8 prolong the poet's double response by means of
the ambiguity of 'dear' – 'costly' and 'much-loved'. Line 4
may be taken either as rueful: 'People are right to be
suspicious of drugs, because one pays a high price for using
them'; or as devoted: 'Something that has become so dear to
me cannot possibly be mistaken for a drug.' The girl's remarkable effect on him, to which these are the possible
reactions, is suggested by line 5 – a picture, it seems, of a
party (perhaps given by the girl) at which the poet stays later
than anyone else, feeding on 'flatness', an unlikely diet yet
positively relished: 'flat' beer (as the proximity of 'Blame it
upon the beer' suggests), stale cigarette-smoke, yet also the
tranquillity (a 'flat calm') induced by the presence of the
beloved. Though happy, the poet of despair wishes to blame
something for the disappearance of his stock-in-trade (as may
his friends); let it be 'the beer', however, not the girl.

Empson's ambivalent feelings ('All losses' – even of fear –
'haunt us') are given an analogue in the strange experience of
Dostoevsky, who with others was sentenced in 1849 to be
shot for subversive activities. Unknown to the condemned,
the sentences were commuted; nevertheless, to terrify them
with uncertainty, an elaborate mock-execution was staged.
Dostoevsky's ecstatic reaction to his 'reprieve' on that occasion was embodied in an immediate letter to his brother,
but when, in the story told by Prince Myshkin in *The Idiot*
(1866), he later recalled his 'torment and fear' while waiting
for death, the sharp yearning for life was juxtaposed to a

radiant mystical apprehension: 'There was a church not far off, its gilt roof shining in the bright sunshine. He remembered staring with awful intensity at that roof and the sunbeams flashing from it; he could not tear his eyes off those rays of light; those rays seemed to him to be his new nature, and he felt that in three minutes he would somehow merge with them. . .' Both Dostoevsky's reactions were 'queer and clear', and a 'reprieve' made it possible for him to write them down; but it was not only the fear of death he felt but the loss of death he soon experienced which made them so intense and mixed. Like Dostoevsky, Empson is haunted by the 'torment and fear', with its illumination, that he has lost: both relieved and 'deceived' (let down). (Line 10 also suggests the more obvious lover's fear: that of being soon deceived by the girl and unable to forget her).

Isolated in the centre of the poem, line 10 serves to bring to a point Empson's previous doubts. But it is also the poem's pivot, its syntax leading on to the assertion (built on earlier gratitude) which is dominant in the second half. Those losses (of torment and fear, of death) are suddenly 'no loss': they cause no diminution of the 'various zoo', the assortment of lively feelings which comprise social responsibility and human responsiveness ('public spirits' – with perhaps a play on the earlier 'beer'), and such 'private play' as personal memories, amatory romps, verbal games, allusive poetry. As a poet now less worried about a possible loss of métier, Empson may intend 'various zoo' to recall the concern of Yeats in 'The Circus Animals' Desertion'; but the use of 'zoo' as an image for human emotions resembles the wording of Lord Peter Wimsey's apology to his beloved Harriet after a passionate kiss: 'I didn't mean to wake the whole zoo.' (Dorothy Sayers, *Busman's Honeymoon*, 1937, Ch. 1). Having achieved the praiseworthy removal of 'the torment and the fear' (the 'these' of line 13), the girl's large powers ('such a thing') may be capable of much else.

If line fourteen's question-formula is technically non-committal, its tone is more positive, and the girl's possibilities are bravely declared in the splendid volte-face of 'Lose is find': not a mere will-o'-the-wisp who leads travellers from their true course, she is rather a 'great marsh light' (appropriate to a poet born near the 'fructuant marsh' of 'Flighting for Duck') guiding in a direction unwonted and unforeseen but of great promise. The doubters of line 3 may defer their doubts until a 'green afterlight' – not a sinister, but a rare and beautiful, ending to a perfect day – confounds them. That the girl will bring this about Empson seems now confidently to expect, despite his admission in line 18 that no one – doubters or hopers – can foretell the future. Meanwhile, gratitude for the removal of 'the torment and the fear' surely predominates over a sense of loss, and the emphasis on the final 'should' has a far more whole-hearted ring than it had in line 2.

JUST A SMACK AT AUDEN

First published, with a further stanza after stanza 4, in *The Year's Poetry 1938* (ed. Denys Kilham Roberts and Geoffrey Grigson), pp. 48-50.

In his 'London Letter' published in *Poetry* (Chicago) in January, 1937, Empson mentioned in passing '. . .the comparatively large (and well-deserved) sale in England of poems by Auden and Spender, who were viewed as young Communist uplift'. (Vol. 49, pp. 219-20). In 1963, writing on 'Early Auden' in *The Review* (No. 5, pp. 32-34), he professed always to have felt admiration for Auden's early poetry, with its 'curious curl of the tongue', and approval for the remedies proposed by the 'pylon poets' for the problems of the 'thirties. None of these feelings is supported by the title of 'Just a Smack at Auden', nor by its content, which postulates a view of Auden and the 'boys' (presumably Spender and Day Lewis, and perhaps Isherwood too) as a mutual congratulation society not merely failing to propose viable remedies but seeming to relish its sense of helplessness and approaching disaster. Whatever the element of recantation in the article, the poem displays all the swingeing unfairness of a young poet's irritation with clever and better-known contemporaries.

Empson's objection to Auden *et al.* is directed not at their matter (as contained, for instance, in *The Orators, The Dog Beneath the Skin,* and *The Magnetic Mountain*); he had registered his own sense of the mounting dangers of the times in 'Reflection from Rochester.' It is aimed, rather, at their manner, which Empson's mocking (even jeering) hyperbole implies to be cliquish, self-satisfied (one meaning of 'knowing we are able'), alarmist (stanza 4), fashionably Marxist (stanzas 5 and 9), and irresponsible (stanzas 6 and 8).

But if one feels that the victims, 'sitting two and two', are sitting ducks, or that they are burnt in large-scale effigy rather than as life-size people, this in no way decreases enjoyment of the poem as a brilliant performance. Its hammering lines (the phrase 'Waiting for the end' is repeated twenty-three times) may have as their intention the parodying of 'public address' verse, but they quickly develop a real nihilistic gusto of their own, and one can only admire the characteristically Empsonian virtuosity which is brought to them. From stanza 2 onwards, there are eighteen rhymes on 'end' (suitably placed at the end of each line); in addition, stanzas 2-9 have their individual sets of four rhymes in the middle of each line, with some of these sets (tower/wire/clear; cable/bubble) even related to each other by half-rhyme. To add a final flourish, the hesitant first stanza, with its introductory question 'What is there to be or do?' (to which the next seven stanzas propose and reject various answers), is balanced by the densely purposeful last one, which doubles the number of 'end' sounds. Empson's resourcefulness is such that he manages all the rhymes without strained or unlikely meanings: stanza three's 'pyre', for instance, adds a suitably Wagnerian quality to the end of Western civilisation (the title sounds like, and the poem is an ironic version of, 'Just a Song at Twilight'); stanza five's 'Tower of Babel' suggests the chaos of international politics, together with, perhaps, such polyglot assemblies as the International Brigade and the International Writers' Congress (Auden, Spender and Isherwood were nothing if not Europe-minded); stanza ten's 'not a chance of blend' conveys the impossibility of compromise between conflicting ambitions and ideologies, and 'those who vend' is a sharp reminder of the Depression, with its shabby destitutes selling matches and pencils (in America, apples) in the street.

Lexically, there is little in the poem that needs glossing, though it is worth pointing out the Poker overtones of 'bluff' in stanza 7, which are activated by the Bridge image of 'Double and re-double' in the stanza before. Nor is the broad range of literary attitudes which Empson criticises difficult to label – the ivory tower, the grim warning (which enjoys the 'cold fear' of its audience), the false hearty and hopeful, the frivolous and escapist (whose shining swollen 'bubble' also suggests an inflated reputation). To the criticism of attitudes, however, phrases like 'sitting two and two, boys', 'shall I choose a friend?' (particularly in view of what it stands next to), and 'Shall I pluck a flower, boys?' (equivocal Wildean aestheticism) add a sly *ad hominem* bias, increased by the sexual connotations of 'spend' (line 8). But as well as being a physical 'smack' delivered to an individual or group, the poem also shows Empson trying out – 'having a smack at' – the 'Auden style', or at certain trademarks of it. The 'wire' and the 'cable' (in one sense, a cable is made of many wires) are surely references to Auden's early 'telegraphese' – 'sparks' in stanza 9 can thus be a radio-operator, as well as 'bright sparks' (wits or gallants) – and to the idea of the poet as reporter in, say 'Spain' and *Letters from Iceland*: 'It has all been filed, boys', as stanza 8 proclaims. That stanza also features the key word of the 'Auden group': 'history', with its definite and sized-up trend, as declared in Auden's 'Birthday Poem' for Christopher Isherwood ('. . .history, that never sleeps or dies/And, held one moment, burns the hand'), and in 'Spain' ('History to the defeated/May say Alas but cannot help or pardon').

But for all the poem's enjoyable display of technical skill, and lively appeal to an unfocused sense of the ridiculous, it is hard to feel it is much more than shadow-boxing: it is too vague in reference, and too unlike Auden's manner, to be deadly parody, and too elusive in its 'point of view' to come over as serious criticism. 'Auden' is accused of too many different things (did he both over-insist on doom *and* try to deny its inevitability?) – and one is not even sure that 'accused' is the right word for what Empson is doing. Where exactly is Empson? Is the speaker throughout (both questioner and answerer) Empson himself, masquerading first as Auden, then as one of the 'boys', and putting exaggerations of their attitudes into their mouths? (On this reading the Auden group must be assumed to know some of the answers to their questions and to the attitudes they strike, and therefore to be not entirely silly.) Or is the questioner Auden (or a pseudo-Auden created by Empson), and the answerer Empson, so much wiser and sounder? (Stanza 7 suggests such a division, and its third and fourth lines seem nearer to measured hostility than anything else in the poem.) Are the references of stanza 9, to Marx and to Julien Benda's *La Trahison des Clercs* (1927), intended to suggest a frame of reference assumed by Auden and company (in which 'Treason of the clerks' might imply the guilt of middle-class intellectuals at not entering fully into the class struggle)? Or do they constitute a double warning issued by Empson: the first a Marxist one, to writers of bourgeois origins who (as John Cornford, for instance, believed) were only playing at revolution; the second – a reminder of what Benda's phrase originally meant – to writers who had betrayed their art in favour of politics and social commitment?

The reader is left to discern the possible interweavings and alternations of voices, attitudes and tones. If one may hazard basic motives behind Empson's wish to take 'just a smack at Auden, two seem likely: in professional terms, a touch of sour grapes; and in terms of character, an aversion from undue fuss, of whatever kind, about 'curtains that descend', and a preference for decent reticence and a dignified stoicism.

THE BEAUTIFUL TRAIN

First published in *The Gathering Storm* (1940).

Empson's journey in the late summer/autumn of 1937 to his university post in Peking took him first via the Trans-Siberian railway, then via the Russian-owned Chinese Eastern Railway which diverged (to end at Vladivostok) south-eastwards across Japanese-controlled Manchuria. At Harbin he changed to the Japanese-owned South Manchuria Railway which ran south-westwards to Mukden and Peking. Since Peking had fallen to the Japanese at the end of July, Empson found himself sharing his train with Japanese troops, and thus with divided emotions: admiration for the graceful train, 'a surprised pleasure in being among Japanese again', but dislike of Japan's imperialist expansion. This last feeling – intruding on sensuous enjoyment like a pang of conscience – gives an effective mental tightening to the end of a poem which, unusually for Empson, otherwise works by juxtaposition of images: that of the train's movement, and that of the Spanish dancer of whom it so strongly reminds him that she is described first.

'La Argentina', so called because she came from there, was born Antonia Mercé in 1888. She established Spanish dancing as a theatrical form, and was highly praised for her performance in Paris, in 1929, of Falla's 'Ritual Fire Dance'; she made her London début in 1924. Empson's memories of her prowess had perhaps already been awakened by the fact of her death in 1936. At any rate, they were crystallised by the sight (did its metal appear silvery?) and movement of his train into a vision of her 'shunting' a curtain call – moving with tense rapid stamping steps from one side of the stage to the other, her feet hidden beneath her bell-like skirt just as the front wheels of Empson's train were perhaps (since the South Manchuria Railway had some American locomotives) obscured behind a 'cowcatcher' grille.

The progress of the train is rendered in the next four lines first as the performance of a sort of super-Argentina, then as the rangy stride of an animal making for home. Since 'all art aspires to the condition of music', the 'last art' which the train 'laughs' (the phrase seems needlessly awkward) may be the music of its wheels (ha-ha-ha-ha, ha-ha-ha-ha) – a rhythmic chattering perceived by the ear not as monotonous but as a constantly-varied accompaniment ('syncopate/or counterpoint') to a wide range of different dances: 'in their turns' gives both the idea of sequence and that of dance-steps. This medley of sound and movement is linked by the apposition of line 6 to the attractive scenes glimpsed, like an ever-changing stage backcloth, through the train window.

With great rhythmic felicity, and with apparent verbal appropriateness, the description of the train journey comes to rest on a short phrase ending in 'home'. The ensuing metrical silence, however, gives time for the irony of that word to sink in: this Japanese train is steaming towards China, 'so firm' on the rails because 'so burdened' — with a load of Japanese soldiers and territorial ambition. Empson's love for the train is intertwined with his abhorrence of what it represents; equally, he feels a swindler for being able to love in such circumstances. While asserting that love and recalling Argentina for a final appearance, the last phrase — 'such light gay feet' — cannot avoid having, after 'burdened', a bittersweet quality.

MANCHOULI

First published in *The Gathering Storm* (1940).

A small frontier town lying just inside Manchuria and very near the border with Mongolia, Manchouli was Empson's point of entry into the Far East from Siberian Russia. Graham Peck, who left Manchuria by the Chinese Eastern Railway in November, 1937, only a couple of months after Empson entered it, described the frontier area itself as 'a mile-wide no-man's land, striped with barbed-wire entanglements and guarded as grimly as if war here were also a fact.' (*Through China's Wall*, 1941, Ch. 19). The start of the Sino-Japanese war must have heightened for Empson the interest of Manchouli as a line of demarcation not only between countries ('these great frontiers', a piece of sophisticated world-travellership, reminds the reader that Empson had crossed plenty of national boundaries already on his long journey), but between large racial groups, the European and the Asiatic.

Different in its plain-spoken manner from 'The Beautiful

Train', 'Manchouli' nevertheless has in common with that poem (to which it is closely related in time) the use of one contrastingly short, pregnantly-worded line, which turns casual exposition into more sombre conclusion. In 'Manchouli', since the particular word 'normal' is repeated from earlier on and in a rather altered sense, the final effect is also epigrammatic. In line 1 the word simply means 'usual': the habitual gaze at new faces outside the window when one crosses a frontier. Empson's clever placing of words in the first phrase of lines 1-2 enables them to do double duty for himself and the 'crowds in rags': he watches them 'eagerly' and 'with awe'; in the same spirit they gather round. (In addition, 'each side' serves for each side of the train and each side of the frontier). A salutary sense of mutual interest, examination and respect is thus given, before Empson passes to more general reflections of his own. Seen close up, 'the nations seem real' – people, not large political abstractions; 'their ambitions. . .seem sane', one would guess, because they appear as the varying personal ambitions of individual men, not as the group ambitions of the 'type' to which they happen to belong.

The occurrence of the word 'sane', however, gives a sinister edge to the repetition of 'I find it normal', which fills a whole line and seems to proceed from a wish for verbal reassurance. Looking at frontier faces is a usual thing to do, and thinking these tolerant thoughts about them seems 'not mad', since they look as real and reasonable as oneself, for all the difference of 'type'. But, as the last line bleakly comments, the comfort given by 'that word' – 'normal' meaning 'usual' or 'sane' – is 'false': 'extract' sounds like getting blood out of a stone. In a world dominated by the large mad ambitions of 'nations' (Japan and others) the 'normality' of people counts for very little.

REFLECTION FROM ANITA LOOS

First published in *The Gathering Storm* (1940).

Anita Loos's frothy but acute *Gentlemen Prefer Blondes*, subtitled 'The Illuminating Diary of a Professional Lady', became a best-seller immediately on publication in 1925. Empson's 'Simple but Quite True Story', published in the 'Highbrow Number' of *Granta* (3 Feb. 1928) seems to be an exercise in the style of Lorelei Lee ('So I asked mamma afterwards what was all that. Well, of course, it wasn't true, she said, probably she was just off her head.'). The line Empson 'quotes' as the basis for his reflection is spoken by Lorelei's friend Dorothy in Chapter Four. She has agreed to go to 'Fountainblo' provided 'Louis' will take off his absurd 'spats. . .made out of yellow shammy skin with pink pearl buttons'. 'Fun is fun', she states, 'but no girl wants to laugh all of the time.' Unfortunately, Louie's socks – 'Scotch plaid with small size rainbows running through them' – prove no more sober than his spats, which a 'discouraged' Dorothy tells him to put back on. In context, all Dorothy's statement does is lightly suggest a (momentary) wish for seriousness even in frivolous people – a wish that is not gratified. Out of it, and by coupling with it a refrain of his own that well conveys man's uncertainty, ambition and aspiration, Empson elaborates a view of civilisation (the 'social system' of stanza 6) as a peculiar mixture of good and bad impulses, not amenable to the categoric simplifications of 'right and crime' (right and wrong). Despite the linking of the refrains, in stanzas 3, 4 and 5, to statements primarily related to one or other of 'man' and 'girl', the poem seems not to be concerned with sexual differences but with men and women as together making up humanity. Lines 4–5 are equally true of both, and the final stanza's 'It' refers to the two refrains as if they are a single unit of meaning.

Although it has two particularly striking and well-balanced lines ('Wrecked by their games and jeering at their prime' and 'Christ stinks of torture who was caught in lime'), and although a certain range of nuance is perceptible in its refrains as they recur, this is the least resonant and emotionally involving of Empson's three villanelles, moving briskly from one laconic end-stopped statement to the next with just enough coherence to maintain a mild intellectual interest. The first stanza, whose negative forms ('No man. . .'/'It is not human. . .') imply that only gods feel safe where they are, establishes a broadly approving attitude to the human wish for self-betterment, even if the wish springs from a sense of precariousness: a good ambition may have a dubious root. The approval is reinforced by lines 4-6, with their fastidious contempt for those who can 'go on laughing all the time': as 'prime' suggests both the innocent liveliness of youth and the responsibilities of maturity, such people are made to appear at once frivolous and corrupt, disgusting and pitiable – monsters rather than men.

It may be the erotic overtones of 'Wrecked by their games', and perhaps thoughts of the amatory/economic manoeuvres of Anita Loos's girls, that prompt the questioning of 'Love' in stanza 3; but the jump is still an abrupt one, and this stanza the hardest to get into clear focus. Love may inspire in everyone ambition of various kinds, and a sort of love certainly makes the world of *Gentlemen Prefer Blondes* go round; but love as questioned here seems a doubtful commodity since any positive element in it appears at first to be left out of the terms in which the question is put. 'Rude' and 'slime' seem to exhaust its possibilities, and in the colloquial sense in which Lorelei and Dorothy would use them these words are virtual synonyms. Such a shallow, shop-girl view fits them better than the poet, as does the genteel optimism of 'All nasty things' (the rude and the slimy) 'are sure to be disgraced'. It is possible, however, to think of the question as Empson's own, by taking 'rude' and 'slime' as contrasting terms: love can be 'rude' in the sense of natural, artless, vigorous and hearty, as opposed to the purely pejorative 'slime' – the sophisticatedly depraved, the furtive, the unhealthy.

Human love, whether pleasant or unpleasant, as an incentive for climbing, leads in stanza 4 to the other kind of love that 'rules the world', that of, and for, God. The refrain implicitly contrasts man's aspirations with God himself, who is 'safely placed' and 'does not need to climb', but because the stanza concentrates on Christ (God as man), one is also reminded of His need to 'climb' the cross: man is enabled to aspire heavenward (himself aiming at a star) because of Christ's human sacrifice. Empson's equivocal view of sacrifice is expressed in line 10. Christ 'stinks of torture' because he himself was tortured; 'caught in lime' pictures him both as a captured bird – thus ironically resembling, as Empson's note points out, the sacrificial Temple doves which he freed (Matthew xxi, 12) – and as a common criminal, buried after execution in quicklime. What Christ's death has led to, however, is (in Empson's often-stated view) a religion founded on the notion of blood-sacrifice and given to cruelty: Christianity itself 'stinks of torture', and divine love is accompanied by repressions and persecution. Nevertheless, the ambiguity of line 11 seems to tip to the side of positive assertion: Christ's efforts have borne some fruit – they are not 'wasted' and earth is not entirely a waste land.

If man's secular and religious impulses are such a mixture (a necessary confusion, it would seem), there is little point in simple moral protest: speaking of 'right and crime' is 'too weak' to express the realities of the situation and one's tense emotions about it. The whole of 'culture' is shot through with the anomalous and often perverse tastes instanced by line 14, which carries on the 'torture' motif of stanza 4. The 'gentlemen' who 'prefer blondes', and offer them something worth serious effort, may also prefer (if Chinese) the prettiness of 'bound feet' and (if Western) the alluring hour-glass figure. Both fashions involve distortion, subjection and enough physical pain to make laughing difficult (pointedly so with the 'wasp waist'); yet, the flat manner of presentation suggests, such are the unpleasant side-effects of the good thing called civilisation: anyone who feels the need to climb must accept them.

Empson's childhood reaction to tightlacing is described in *Milton's God*: 'I crept away sweating with horror, but feeling I had learned an important truth about the way people behave'. (p. 111). It is some such version of this 'truth' (presumably that people, being people, do the strangest things) with which the poem closes, in terms too vague to give it much of an impact. The two refrains are conflated into 'It', their common denominator being the human wish for seriousness and improvement. The forms this wish takes – gold-digging, 'social climbing', love, worship – involve a vast range of 'gambits': opening moves which make a sacrifice in the hope of getting something valuable later. These create a 'mime' which either is, or is the basis for, life's 'social system'. Whether the word 'mime' is used for purposes of rhyme, or whether its ingredients are offered as an ironic parting shot, is not easy to say; dumb show and farce may apply to the world of Anita Loos's heroines, but they seem less appropriate to the wider world of Empson's reflection.

THE TEASERS

First published, without stanza 3, in *Furioso* Vol. 1, No. 2 (1940), p. 13.

During his conversation with Christopher Ricks, published in 1963, Empson indicated that these cryptic stanzas were originally part of a longer poem which 'started grousing and grumbling about the conditions of the modern world'. Not liking what he was saying, Empson 'cut [the poem] down to rags so that it doesn't make sense, you can't find out what it's about'. These 'rags' are referred to in his record-notes (1959) as the 'general verses' of the poem; the further one (stanza 3) printed in *The Gathering Storm* supplies an element of contrast, placing 'Our claims to act' against 'the teasers and the dreams' described in the others. But as it is impossible to say whether these stanzas belonged together in the parent poem or were scattered about – and in either case to know their context and thus, perhaps, the precise limits of their generalised phrasing – any interpretation is necessarily tentative, however many elements in the present structure it manages to explain. (G.S. Fraser's painstaking 1955 reading tacitly assumes the poem to be a unified whole, however difficult). There is a wry appropriateness in Empson's calling his four stanzas 'The Teasers'; whatever the phrase means in line 1, a 'teaser' is a conundrum. One may agree, however, with Empson's claim that the poem, with its hermaphrodite form, musing repetitions, mid-stanza pauses and slightly wayward rhymes, is 'a beautiful metrical invention'.

Though at one point the poem seems to assume a reader

(the 'you' of stanza 2), most of the time it suggests self-communing, its concern being the impulses and yearnings in the individual which lead, in the gloomier sense of that phrase in 'Missing Dates', to 'the consequence a life requires.' The poem begins by conceding, both sadly and grudgingly (as if their loss did not diminish their importance) the death of 'the teasers and the dreams'. These may simply be our emotions, set in stanza 3 against reason and will ('our claims to act'), but a little more specifically they may be our aspirations, enticing daydreams, erotic urges and fantasies – everything, in fact, that we want but rarely obtain. These wishes, the poem Freudianly suggests ('clamour' recalls ' "the clamour of life" ' in 'Ignorance of Death'), not only die but *ask* for death and oblivion: the 'why' of this is not only disappointment but the underlying death-wish itself. One explains 'the careful flood' as death and oblivion because nothing else seems to fit the context: a 'flood' is a river and an inevitably in-coming tide, and this is 'careful' because it controls our lively wishes and because it receives the pains and worries that we willingly empty into it. Lethe seems meant or, even better, 'Sad Acheron of sorrow, black and deep' (*Paradise Lost* ii, 578). But though our 'dreams' seek death, their force – and their basically libidinous nature – is made clear in stanza 2. 'You could not fancy' (whether addressed by Empson to himself or to the reader) seems hyperbolic nonsense on one level: people can imagine, indeed know, the sharpness of their desires, raging within or directed outwards, perfectly well. 'Fancy', with its amorous overtones, is better taken to mean 'like': we can imagine the effects of our desires, but not approve of them where they take a sadistic form and 'rip to blood'. No more could one like the ever-viscous 'mud' of animal instincts in fantasies or the subconscious. 'Fancy' as 'imagine' has some point here, however. No commentator has identified 'that mud' other than metaphorically, but there is a quite literal mud that Empson could 'have heard speak' in Japan: the celebrated pools of boiling mud (called 'Hells') at the seaside spa of Beppu in Kyushu, which constantly heave and bubble. (The story is that an extremely greedy monk was transformed into one as a punishment.) It is thus possible to read the stanza: 'You could not imagine the destructive force of my "teasers and dreams" any more than you could imagine the existence of these hellish mud-ponds.'

Stanza 3 contrasts our mad – hopeless and dangerous – passions with the 'colder lunacies' of 'Our claims to act'. These – presumably our attempts at conscious control of our lives, and the illusion that we have such control – not only seem small 'in relation to' our passions, but are viewed as small *by* them: our emotional side despises our rational side because it cheats 'the love, the moment, the small fact.' There is an irritating degree of vagueness and paradox here, but a preference seems to be implied for the lunacy of emotion over that of reason: the 'small fact' – small but real – brings more pleasure than our 'small-minded' but large-sounding 'claims to act'.

The last stanza reiterates, however, the fate of our 'teasers and dreams' (which, if fulfilled, might bring us such loves, moments and small facts). Like shooting stars, fireworks, or orgasms, they 'flash and die'. Nevertheless, we are to 'make no escape': one may conjecture here the 'escape' of suicide, or that of undervaluing dreams because of their transience. But if dreams and emotions die, it is puzzling to know what kind of 'love' can be built up, and how, other than by conscious, rational effort. (One wonders, at this point, whether 'The Teasers' is tangentially related to 'Success'.) Such a love, whatever it is, may make a man 'safe to die', having had some degree of happiness in life; but the last line sounds more grimly stoical than that, recalling the disguised Duke's advice to Claudio: 'Be absolute for death'. (*Measure for Measure* III, i, 5). If a man is told to abandon what he 'dies for' – a cherished ambition or ideal worthy of self-sacrifice, or a longed-for pleasure, sexual or otherwise – he is being told to abandon illusions, the 'teasers and dreams' which themselves seek oblivion. What he is then left with seems no more than the ultimate safety, and certainty, of death itself. Such, at any rate, is the bleak and possibly misleading conclusion made available by Empson's edited version.

ADVICE

First published in *The Gathering Storm* (1940).

The advice offered by this intriguing but excessively oblique poem is contained in its last two lines, which allude to Edgar's speech in *King Lear* IV, i, 25–28. Having begun the scene with a modicum of hope ('The lamentable change is from the best;/The worst returns to laughter'), Edgar is then shaken by the entry of his blinded father Gloucester into the realisation that, however hellish 'Now' seems to be, life always has something worse in store:

> *O Gods! Who is't can say 'I am at the worst'?*
> *I am worse than e'er I was. [. . . . .]*
> *And worse I may be yet; the worst is not,*
> *So long as we can say, 'This is the worst'.*

Here, and in Empson's last line, there seems to be an emphasis on 'say': the worst, when it comes, will leave us speechless. Since the word 'policy' in line 9 most naturally suggests politics, the unpleasant 'Now' which we are with grim politeness 'disadvised' to call 'Hell' seems likely to be the outbreak of war, viewed by the poem as a visiting on the children of the sins (taken metaphorically) of their fathers, and of their own, indicated in lines 1–4. Like 'To an Old Lady', which also quotes Edgar, 'Advice' is concerned with parents and children, but in a very ironical spirit: both generations have mis-spent their youth, though in different ways, and both are paying the price. This general view, however, is drawn with difficulty from a poem whose structure is uncharacteristically random and whose thought moves in abrupt zig-zags.

Lines 1–3 show Empson regretting his youth: he would not, given the chance again, 'murder' his teenage years in the way mentioned – by getting up hastily from the table before the fish course. As Empson's 'teens' were spent at a school whose motto is 'Manners makyth Man' there is a nice irony in his picture of adolescent rudeness; but it is also a metaphor of youth itself – a nourishing meal of which his own restlessness largely deprived him. The placing of 'away' emphasises *pointless* departure, which line 3 confirms:

'the first of May' suggests both the spring pleasure of sowing wild oats and the declaration of left-wing political commitment. As Empson indulged in neither, his dramatic-sounding 'murders of my teens' were no more than killing time; though he may have been adolescent enough to exaggerate his griefs ('teen') and 'cry blue murder'. Line 4 is confusing because its balanced form sets up expectations of logic that are not fulfilled: 'crash' and 'poisons' can be ways of killing oneself, but what is the equivalent link between 'cloth' and 'greens'? In one sense the line relates to the earlier 'busting. . .away': firstly by means of the pun explained in Empson's note – his crashing away from the table (like jumping through a window to land in a sheet – cloth – stretched out by firemen?) proved harmless; secondly, because 'greens' are the vegetables he 'hated like poison' and wanted to avoid. (Was the fish – 'poisson' – also a poison?) The line may therefore be saying no more than that to leave one's dinner (youth) seemed safer at the time than to eat it.

Green – the colour of poisons, youth and grass – assists the transition to lines 5-9, though these are both obscure in meaning and ambivalent in attitude. Since Empson has already expressed regret, line 5 at first seems a lament for wasted youth – the grass, once 'lovely' because green, is now dry and faded. If, though, 'all greens' really are 'poisons', grass *is* lovely when dry and faded: early middle age (Empson was only about 33) is preferable to youth. Yet the real and metaphorical 'sheep' that 'safely graze' on that faded colour of grass are docile and 'useful' – a quietly bitter word which gains force from line 9. Lines 7-9 suggest, however, that it would still be possible for the sheep to 'rush' youthfully and eat the 'green one' (the green shade of grass) if they were protected from the dangerous indigestion that might result. The 'stabbing' Empson refers to (it does not kill, since the sheep can 'go munching on' afterwards) is presumably the skilful therapeutic kind practised by Gabriel Oak on sheep swollen from eating young clover. (*Far from the Madding Crowd*, Ch. 21.) The attitude suggested here – that it is better to live riskily than to 'feed safely' – is understandable, but what process analogous to Gabriel Oak's will save the human 'sheep' from the consequences of their actions is not clear.

The claim is simply that they will survive them, and so not need to 'ask a policy to drown a smell' – the smell their bursting and putrefaction would have produced. By implication, the 'useful sheep' do ask for such a 'policy', and at this point Empson's drift seems only explicable in historico-political terms – certainly line 9, isolated despite its syntax from what precedes it, conveys a shift of focus. One thing that had begun to 'smell' by the end of the 'thirties was appeasement, and the policy that would drown it was warlike defiance of Fascism – a policy as likely, now, to slaughter sheep as appeasement had kept them quiet and apparently safe. Sheep are 'useful' because they can be easily led, 'fleeced', and turned into mutton.

Against the plight of Empson and his generation, men of military age but placid and with no youthful extravagances to remember, lines 10-13 set the predicament of their elders, who 'looked wiser than we stayed'. Since they 'looked wiser', they are now presumably senile or dead; but the important (and exaggerated) point is that beneath their bland appearance of wisdom they were 'more murderously scabbed' by the ravages of syphilis. 'Murderously' recalls line 2 (these old men really did 'make murders' of their teens), and to be 'scabbed' – a lasting mark – is more murderous than to be 'stabbed' in the sense of line 7. (The verbal link may mean that repression is worse than letting something out; given Empson's note, 'stabbed' may also be meant to suggest that syphilis can now be operated on.) Calling these elders, immobilised in their bath-chairs by general paralysis – the tertiary stage of syphilis – 'the great and good' is distinctly mocking (the phrase, Stendhal's description of Corneille, was the title of an article published in *Scrutiny* in December, 1938, in which Corneille was called 'the champion of youth in revolt against the corruption and pretence of an older generation'). Yet they had the advantage of being, in an appropriately old-fashioned phrase, 'not known to shame', because they were unaware of the reason for their state – hence 'cosy'. ('G.P. came late' may refer not only to their 'general paralysis' but to a 'general practitioner' who could have told them its cause. J.B.S. Haldane had spoken of the connection in 1927 in *Possible Worlds*, p. 201).

Looking wise, but not 'wise to' the cause and effect of their lives (sins leading to paralysis and, one is left to assume, analogous political mistakes leading first to one world war, then to the brink of another), perhaps these elders were better off than those who came after them, whose wisdom (youthful prudence and middle-aged docility) has got them nowhere. Juxtaposing lines 10-13 with lines 1-4 suggests that, though vice is punished, virtue is not necessarily rewarded. But if it is now too late to relive one's youth in the at least temporarily enjoyable style of one's forebears, one thing can still be learned from 'their long experience who all were first': the worst, like the paralysis that finally overtook them, is yet to come.

Arbitrary in its movement between literal and metaphorical, and in its apparent linkage of personal error with political failure, 'Advice' is as problematic as anything in *Poems* (1935) and at the same time lacks the memorableness of texture that could make up for this. Throughout there is a sense of momentary patterns and suggestions not realised in terms of the whole poem, like the echoes of Marvell (the 'green shade' of the grass) and of 'Lycidas' (the sheep which may or may not 'rot inwardly'); or individual passages – such as line 11, its ambiguities of meaning and association ('dugout', 'spoil', 'game') compounded by an awkward double negative – offer too many possibilities and elbow each other aside. Most simply, 'Advice' is a poem whose parts do not hang together.

ANECDOTE FROM TALK

First published in *The Gathering Storm* (1940).

During his period with the 'National Southwest University' in Yunnan, Empson spent a vacation, some time in 1938 or 1939, visiting Singapore and Malaya. It was presumably at some point in his visit that he heard the ironic, Maughamesque tale recounted here, of the whisky-drinking 'tin-mine man' of northern Malaya whose hasty and repented death-wish finally caught up with him when he was posted to a shaky, back-seat job.

There is nothing to explain in the story itself, whose enigmatic inconsequence is its point. What is really puzzling is why Empson should have wanted to tell it, particularly in such an odd, mixed form as this: three stanzas (the last falling flat on the pointless 'point' of its extra phrase) that seem clumsily modelled on the five-line stanza used by Housman in 'Bredon Hill', the other two an awkwardly-rhymed version of the stanza used by Auden in such ballads as 'Victor' and 'Miss Gee'. Too wide of any conceivable literary mark to be parody, and too inconsistent and low-key in presentation to be memorable as poetry, 'Anecdote from Talk' nevertheless has a degree of rhythmic vigour and colloquial verisimilitude that is attractive.

CHINA

First published in *The Gathering Storm* (1940).

For its length, 'China' has more annotation than 'Bacchus', which makes it seem more difficult than it is. In fact, its notes are not so much the explanation of inherent complexities (dense texture and multiple meanings) as an attempt to fill in for non-Sinologues the context of knowledge which the poem's rapid manner needs to be able to assume. They do not clarify everything in the poem, nor always confine themselves to what can reasonably be inferred from it, but on the whole their general information (which amounts to a miniature essay on China) is genuinely helpful to the reader.

Though the poem is printed before 'Autumn on Nan-Yueh' (to which it is technically related by its use of octosyllabics and its economy of rhymes – the first and third lines of each stanza have the same rhyme-sound throughout), the reference to 'spring and rawness' in line 4 suggests that it was written later and that its physical observations – the Great Wall apart – derive from Empson's 800-mile journey, early in 1938, from Nan-Yueh to Kunming. Certainly the short, un-punctuated lines give the impression of sketches and thoughts jotted down while on the move. Nevertheless, for all its casual tone, the poem is not without a structure. The opening and closing stanzas, made graver by their pentameter second and fourth lines, present the wartime relationship of China and Japan first in terms of 'allied fabulous creatures', senior and junior, then in terms of host and parasite. Framed within these contrasting yet related metaphors (as between the rollers of a scroll-painting), the five central stanzas offer more literal contrasts of various kinds – between China and other countries (stanza 2), between China and Japan again (stanza 4), and between aspects of China itself (stanzas 3, 5, 6). In addition, in a compressed version of the alternating-stanza method used in 'Part of Mandevil's Travels', the even-numbered lines of each stanza comment on the odd-numbered ones, and to some extent each carries a contrasting strand of thought, though it is only in the last three stanzas that these strands take the form of syntactic sequence in alternating pairs of lines.

Throughout the poem China is viewed as a country of con-trasts and anomalies, with splendour and decay, the real and the ideal, existing side by side. In stanza 1 China is both the traditional majestic 'dragon', the ancient civilisation which has fostered and hatched out the 'cockatrice' Japan, and a piece of crumbling cheese inhabited by cheese mites. There is irony in the two meanings of 'repair': plenty of 'mites' (the image allows apt allusion to the small stature of Chinese and Japanese) 'frequent' or 'repair to' China, but few of them help to 'mend' the country. Since the mythical 'cockatrice' is hatched by a serpent from a cock's egg, one is reminded of the greedy cuckoo which outgrows its foster-parents; the word also suggests 'cocky' and (as J.H. Willis has pointed out) suits the inhabitants of the 'Land of the Rising Sun'. 'Cockatrice', of course, is the synonym for 'basilisk', which blasts whatever it looks or breathes on; but line 4, responding to the raw spring weather in which the struggle of the two countries is taking place, leaves open, in 'tantalise', a slim possibility that the outcome may not be altogether destructive:

there is 'a Nature' (an equivocal naturalness) about their relationship, even though this 'Nature' is called in Empson's note 'a repulsive deity' and thus suggests not only Tennyson's 'nature red in tooth and claw' but the 'Nature' who is 'goddess' to the bastard Edmund in *King Lear* (I, ii, 1), that story of ungrateful children.

Stanza 2 describes China as loose and relaxed, and 'the nations' (essentially, the European ones) as stiff and awkward; but the terms allow much ambiguity. What the Chinese are 'most proud' of is being the most 'at ease' country in the world, but though there may be 'comfort' for them in being 'on hands and knees', this attitude (bowing deeply from a sitting position) might strike a Westerner as slavish – surviving by yielding. The 'solid ground' on which they rely is paradoxically 'the sea', a constant shifting in response to circumstance (literally, the Chinese live on boats as well as in houses); but this could seem mere untrustworthiness – Empson's phrasing recalls his line in 'Aubade': 'Some solid ground for lying could she show?' And though 'perch' does suggest discomfort in the contrasting Western posture – sitting on a 'high moral tone' as on the top of a pole – it also gives a hint of vultures and of the European trade concessions scattered profusely 'about around' China.

Stanza 3, developed by stanza 4, contrasts the real disorder of China (the only trees not cut down are 'holy trees', preserved – presumably by Buddhists – for non-physical reasons) with the theoretical system of education supposed to produce efficient government: the Confucian 'classics', a 'single school' perhaps because unlike the wider-ranging universities of the West. Such a system may have taught the Chinese something, but it can hardly be thought, from its visible results, to be much use to 'the nations', and will teach no lesson to the Japanese, whatever their close physical resemblance ('as like them as two peas'). Ruling 'by music and by rites' sounds admirably calm, pious and orderly, but it is hardly practical, does not win wars, and leaves nation and country looking an 'untidy sight'. (Empson's 'All' in line 16 may be an attempt to extend sympathy here: the unworldly Confucian method leads to confusion, but perhaps no method is perfect.)

The mention of music and ritual leads in stanzas 5 and 6 to a comparison between 'official' China and the greater vitality of its peasant life, Empson's images being provided by his refugee 'flight', by bus and plane, into the hinterland. China's 'serious' (i.e. 'classical') music – whose sound, costive slowness, and unfamiliarity are all wittily conveyed by 'strains' – exacts such high-flown proper responses as 'duties' and 'literature' (how it squeezes 'fees' is less clear, unless the handing over of taxes was once done to music). All this seems remote compared to the down-to-earth folk-music chanting ('like us' because in a recognisable style, and because the passengers no doubt lent a hand) of coolies getting a stuck bus out of the mud; they are 'angel coolies' because they help, and perhaps because their carrying-poles when set across their shoulders look like wings. The paddy-fields of stanza 6 are also the result of useful labour: 'wings of bees' conveys not only a sharp visual impression (whether that of someone actually looking down from an aeroplane or of someone simply in flight and thus seeing things clearly) but also the idea that peasants resemble bees in their assiduity. The internal contrast of stanza 6 permits the reflection that a bee, though less majestic than a dragon, is real, and that a paddy-field, though less celebrated as a symbol of China than the Great Wall, may do better the job for which it is created ('crawls' seems a loaded verb here). Empson's syntax, however (line 24 completes not line 22 but line 23), also implies a similarity – enlarged on by his note – between the retaining-walls of hillside rice-fields and the convolutions of the Great Wall: the strength and defence of China lies in its people as much as in its rulers.

The last stanza, returning to the current war-situation, implies that China's salvation may lie in her ability to 'absorb' the Japanese invaders, who are not (as stanza 4 has indicated) very different from her own people. China's pride in her 'complacencies' (self-satisfaction, tranquil pleasures, and – since the word is linked to 'complaisance' – her polite deference) is at this point praised more resoundingly ('Most rightly proud') than the associated qualities in stanza 2; her ability, despite repeated disasters, to survive for thousands of years argues its reasonableness. Nevertheless, the host/

parasite relationship which Empson envisages as the form this invasion/assimilation will take (the rhyme-pairs are as barely distinguishable from each other as the liver-fluke and the snail) is distinctly disturbing. Empson's analogy, taken from *The Science of Life* (1931) by H.G. Wells, Julian Huxley and G.P. Wells, mixes up two different kinds of liver-fluke (his note incorrectly indicates a single fluke cycle, as well as confuses the book from which it comes with Wells's *The Outline of History*). The first (*Fasciola hepatica*, pp. 140–42) is his 'liver fluke of sheep', whose cyclical progress is from pond-snail to sheep's liver through sheep droppings back to pond-snail; the second (*Distomum macrostomum*, p. 572) moves from passerine birds to land-snail and back to birds again via a coloured growth on the snail's horns. It is this latter fluke which, in a peculiarly repellent way, 'agrees/With snail so well they make one piece', growing inside the snail to become 'a shapeless radiating web of living tissue. . .which becomes so mixed up with [the snail's] tissues that it is difficult or impossible for a dissector to separate it completely away.'

Whether this kind of biological take-over bid, which the snail can hardly be said in any meaningful sense to survive, is an accurate image for the Sino-Japanese struggle seems open to question; even more doubtful is whether such a consummation could be viewed with the apparent equanimity of Empson's lines here. It is not surprising that his note of 1940 expressed reservations about the image, and about the belief – related perhaps to a wish, by one who had taught in both countries, not to take sides – in Japanese-Chinese cultural similarity that underlay it. In spite, however, of its final error – whether of tact, taste or emphasis – 'China' is a lively, intelligent and stimulating tribute.

AUTUMN ON NAN-YUEH

First published in *The Gathering Storm* (1940).

At once Empson's longest and most relaxed poem – 'a flow/

Of personal chat', as he calls it in stanza 8 – 'Autumn on Nan-Yueh' has been unaccountably neglected by his critics. Richard Eberhart, a notable exception, justly spoke of it in 1944 as displaying 'an ease and brilliancy unparalleled in his other work'; in it, Empson 'writes with the sheerest pleasure, making perfect strokes [and] with rapid energy forming the most readable verse. . .' The relaxation of manner does not preclude an increasing seriousness as the poem proceeds, nor is it accompanied by looseness of versification; it is typical of Empson's enjoyment of rigorous technical challenge that the poem's conversational octosyllabics are poured into alternating twelve- and fourteen-line stanzas whose rhyme-scheme – *abcb abcb abcb (ab)* – demands the utmost verbal dexterity. (In stanzas 5 and 17 Empson reduces his option of rhymes by one, and rhymes *ab* throughout). Despite occasional awkwardness – such as stanza ten's 'all we/Can't hope for' instead of 'none of us can hope for' – Empson handles his strict form with masterly ease: the rhymes provide satisfying echoes while the argument, often compressed and allusive but rarely obscure, ranges at will over the immediate situation and the broader reflections – personal, literary and political – which it stimulates. Empson's Chinese experience, from his entry at Manchouli to his arrival in Yunnan, was particularly valuable in that it led to poems which combine liveliness of thought with a vivid sense of place and person. 'Nan-Yueh', with its many different tones of voice (the bracketed passage in stanza 4 is delightfully dry), is the best of them, and one of its most likeable elements is its direct presentation of the poet himself, courageous and modest, fair-minded and wry.

The poem dates from the late autumn of 1937, when the universities retreating from Peking had come to a temporary halt in the small mountain village of Nan-Yueh, some 80 miles south-south-west of Changsha, the capital of Hunan province. Han Suyin, who stayed there briefly in the late October and early November of 1938 (by which time there were even more Kuomintang 'Ministers upon the spot', including Chiang Kai-Shek himself, and soldiers were using one of the temples as a training camp), described it in her third volume of autobiography, *Birdless Summer* (1968, pp. 43-64).

Deep in the sacred Heng-shan mountains (Empson's department was isolated on one of the foothills), surrounded
by 'red-walled, golden-roofed' Buddhist temples, its river,
fed by 'sparkling torrents', spanned by a Sung dynasty
bridge, Nan-Yueh was a very beautiful place; Empson's
regret at leaving it, expressed sharply in stanza 18, is
understandable. Renewed flight clearly came as a surprise,
and had the effect of deciding Empson to bring his stanzas
to a premature and poignant end; structural calculation,
however, could not have contrived a more appropriate conclusion than circumstances gave the poem, whose long medi-
tation on all kinds of 'flight' is thus framed between arrival
and departure.

Empson's description of that departure ('With convolutions for a brain,/Man moves, and we have got to go') presents change and uncertainty as the inevitable human condition. This is in keeping with the epigraph from Yeats
which, as stanza 8 indicates, was 'pushed. . .up to the top' of
the poem in order to keep it from getting out of hand by
providing 'one root' for its meditations to 'grow' from. 'The
Yeats' is a quotation from 'The Phases of the Moon', published in 1919 in *The Wild Swans at Coole*. Since, as stanzas
4-5 make plain, the refugee universities had left their libraries
behind and lectures were given largely from memory, it is not
surprising that Yeats is slightly misquoted: 'within' should be
'upon', 'soldier' should be 'dutiful husband'. (The latter mis-
quotation allows Empson's conclusion to suggest that, at
Nan-Yueh, the cycle of the professor is succeeded by that of
the soldier.) Much is made of Yeats's lines, at first irreverently
('cradles' as crowded beds; 'deformed' temple beggars who,
though possibly 'saved from a dream' themselves, would give
bad dreams to anyone who saw them and do give a bad time
to the pilgrims who, ascending the stone steps to the monas-
tery on top of the 'holy mountain' Tu Yun Feng, are shaken
in the 'sieve' of their demands); later more seriously, as
Yeats's 'Dream' is examined in stanzas 8 and 10. Most rele-
vant to Empson's poem, of course, is their picture of man 'in
flight', which is documented throughout by various means:
the insistent repetition of the words 'flight'/'fly'/'flee' (aerial

and refugee flight; the quasi-holiday flight of the 'plodding' pilgrims; flying by drinking 'Tiger Bone', which Empson stoutly defends against its detractors; the flight of poetic styles); references to 'soaring' (eagles, 'balanced on a rising column of air' as Haldane described them in *Possible Worlds*, p. 23; Japanese pilots in stanza 11; the Red Queen and Alice, running to stay in the same place in *Through the Looking Glass*, Ch. II); the 'Pegasi' or professorial hobby-horses in stanza 4; and even the 'topmost abbot' of stanza 3, who, if he could theoretically qualify for an Oxford degree in Classics, must be something of a 'flier'.

The poem falls into three roughly equal sections, the first (stanzas 1-6) dealing jauntily with Empson's immediate circumstances as a 'footless' (and footloose) 'bird' involved in the 'general flight' deeper into China (Han Suyin estimated that twenty million people were 'then walking on the roads of the central provinces'). The vicissitudes of those fleeing are suggested by Empson's twisting of Francis Thompson's lines in 'The Kingdom of God': 'The angels keep their ancient places;–/Turn but a stone, and start a wing!' The wings here belong not to angels but to stinging insects and, perhaps, marauding Japanese planes ('movement' and 'wing' also anticipate the politics of later stanzas). Travelling partly by air, Empson and his teaching colleagues may resemble Shelley's skylark ('Thou scorner of the ground'), but are also 'Eagles by hypothesis' – an eagle flies high and a hypothesis is a 'groundless assumption'. Empson's resilient enjoyment of his experience is conveyed partly by verbal jokes like these ('rust' in stanza 2 allies gathered 'moss' to corrupting 'moth'), partly directly: being in China represents an escape from an unspecified 'They/Who sat on pedestals and fussed.' (The image resembles stanza 2 of 'China', but it is not clear whether 'This timid flap', which Empson discounts, was made by their fussing wings, or refers to the present panic.) Stanza 5, giving an example of the problems of teaching from memory (what one remembers isn't always much use as 'classroom patter'), identifies 'Them' in terms of a quotation from Peter Walsh in *Mrs. Dalloway*. Reading, like him, the 'yatter' of magazines from 'home', Empson is equally grateful to have exchanged the snobbish 'hubble-bubble' of London, and

215

perhaps Cambridge, even for the noise of coolies and baboons. Empson feels 'a brother' to Peter Walsh, yet his warmth towards his Chinese colleagues is very evident. The drinking described in stanza 6 is no fearful flight into solitary remoteness ('the blue'), but the conviviality of people 'getting near' each other, as well as to truth.

The idea of 'plain beer' as a possible 'broomstick' (denied at the end of stanza 6) turns Empson's thoughts in the next four stanzas to various poetic styles. His defence of 'Escape Verse' in stanza 7 is along the same lines as 'Your Teeth are Ivory Towers': its critics, finding it 'blah' (the word, meaning 'nonsense', dates from only 1927), are more off the point than its practitioners, who know that only by 'soaring' can one hope even to keep abreast of events. The last four lines are obscure in detail (World War I zeppelins had a 'car' or 'spy-basket' which could be lowered beneath the clouds while the airship remained hidden, but the connection with Phoebus' 'chariot' is baffling), but their cautionary note suggests that the results of 'soaring' are not always praiseworthy. The 'Blimp' image carries over to stanza eight's discussion of Yeats, whose grandeur of language is admirable, despite his detachment from the current world of poetry and politics: he is both a reactionary ('just scolding all') and an airship (sending no 'advice so far below'). Even if 'all the latest people' (a dismissive reference, presumably to critics of Escape Verse) think his poetic emphasis on 'Dream' a 'flop', Empson disagrees: far from being a 'leak' needing mending, or a dangerous 'gas-escape', it is rather the measure of 'truth' by which others are found wanting.

Such lesser poets, uncongenial to Empson, are indicated in stanza 9: the self-congratulating Auden clique, whose game of revolution is no more than a 'sit-down. . .strike' avoiding true literary responsibility; and the surrealists (Empson's use of Herbert Read's term 'superrealistic' mocks by inflation), who ride their mechanical 'nightmares' – 'Pegasi' again – as easily as bicycles. 'Comp.' suggests schoolboy essays, and the 'student' sounds very like Dylan Thomas, 23 at the time and the literally 'curly-headed' pet of Edith Sitwell and Herbert Read; the cloying 'cluster' – of surrealists and their compositions – recalls his description of his own work as a build-up of conflicting images. At this point, however, Empson suddenly loses his polemical confidence and concedes that no literary 'convention' (style or group) is perfect, his own by implication included, and Yeats's too — 'pomp' relates well to 'organ stop'. Stanza 10 completes this uneasy *volte-face*. The 'Escapist' label may be 'crude' but cannot entirely be dismissed, and Yeats — still the yardstick for other poets — has acknowledged by his later work a different application for 'his old word Dream': to the subconscious charted by Freud and, perhaps, to the 'desolation of reality' spoken of in 'Meru' and the acknowledgement of 'where all the ladders start' in 'The Circus Animals' Desertion'.

Stanza 11, referring with casual but angry disdain to the inaccurate Japanese bombing of the 'next town' (probably Heng-yang, an important railway junction), and perhaps implying in its bracketed line, with its ambiguous 'driven', a degree of contempt for Kuomintang high-ups, leads properly to stanza twelve's assertion of the rightness for the poet of a response to political realities. Together, the two stanzas occupy a pivotal position, serving equally to round out section two — with its literary focus — or begin the last section, which is concerned with the large pattern of current events and Empson's relation to them as a human being. Empson's purpose in stanza 12 is to show that, as a poet, his heart is in the right place ('Had I speeches they were song' alludes to a phrase from 'The Phases of the Moon' not quoted in the epigraph: 'True song, though speech', line 30); and to claim that he too, though far away in China, 'belongs' 'at home' — in England. In fact, his doubts and 'heat-mists' — emotions that do not make for intellectual clarity but yet permit, within the narrow limits of circumstance, a sound instinctive response — are so much like those of the British public that no real purpose would be served by writing them down. Thus the poet's diffidence about political *verse* is nicely balanced by the patriotic compliment of a plain man.

Stanzas 13-17 are a kind of interior dialogue, the 'passive style' of politico-economic rumination (which, Empson self-deridingly decides, would suit an intellectual 'squatting in England with the beer') being countered by the paradoxical hopefulness of the man who is, in both senses, 'on the spot' —

in physical danger, but at least free of the fear caused by rumour and the evasiveness of politicians. Both states of mind, one may feel, are creditable, though the first is perhaps of its nature not easy to fathom, being concerned not with visible 'excuses, consequences, signs' but 'the large thing' (stanza fifteen's Minotaur-like 'monster') that lies behind them and would, if seen clearly (or faced up to) cause 'entire', rather than partial, 'despair'. What this is does not emerge (even the divine and divining economists will need 'twenty years' to unravel its secret), only that it causes a deeper disunity than 'nationalism' or 'race'. But since China's new heir seemed likely even in 1937 to be Mao Tse-tung, one infers the underlying problem to be the working out in the 'thirties of the ideological (and economic) class-struggle posited by Marx and given a sharper edge, in forward-looking theory, by Stalin. ('Saul' is the pre-Christian, persecuting Paul, seen as a right-wing leader, his followers not inspired by 'fire' but destined for it.) Though Empson shows some sympathy for Communism as a possibly efficient, if not a merciful, system, and sees that people might well wish to act rapidly if ignorantly ('It seems unpleasantly refined. . .'), the beginning and end of stanza 15 seem nevertheless to warn that progress and victory (the 'destiny' that has to be made 'absurd' being that of Germany and Japan, as indicated in stanza 16) do require 'the tedious triumphs of the mind', even though time for thinking is running out.

After these rather confused thoughts (through which the motif of 'flight' is hinted at in 'larks', 'got the bird' and 'high repose' – a version of the eagle's 'soaring'), stanzas 16 and 17 return to China and justify Empson's presence there in terms that implicitly suggest the courage to put genuine 'sympathy' to work for small financial reward in hazardous circumstances. Though not involved in the fighting, he is no 'good for nowt' hanger-on (the modesty is complemented by Yorkshire downrightness): he usefully takes the place of 'men who must get out' – presumably Chinese professors who have joined the army. With a return to the polemical tone of stanza 9 Empson is quick to distinguish his wish to be 'where the important things occur' (in China no less than in fashionable Spain) from that of those queer, cat-like 'trout' who gain vicarious pleasure – sexual and literary – from watching others get killed. Auden's 'Spain', whose phrase 'they clung like birds' is recalled by Empson's 'clinging wholly as a burr', was published in May, 1937; in the spring of 1938, as if to justify Empson's malice retrospectively, Auden and Isherwood made the tour of the Chinese war theatre recorded in *Journey to a War*.

By that time Empson was in Kunming, as a result of the move announced in stanza 18. 'Winnow' brings the poem round to the 'eagle flight' of its beginning: man's life is a flapping of wings, a scattering of himself, as well as a separation of wheat from chaff and an attempt at sowing. Having to wind up his reflections causes Empson no great regret; having to leave the place – the literal and metaphorical 'balcony' – that gave rise to them does, and his sense of loss produces one of the most beautiful 'bits of verse' in his entire work, both plain-spoken and sharply lyrical. The 'flow/Of personal chat' breaks off; instead, but no longer to be heard, 'the streams will chatter as they flow.'

LET IT GO

First published in *Collected Poems* (U.S.A., 1949).

One of Empson's three poems written between 1940 and the end of the war, 'Let it go' seems likely to date from about the time of 'Thanks for a Wedding Present', with which it shares its neat and unusual form – two tercets rhyming *abc abc*. Given the poetic doubts voiced in 'Success' – with its suggestive phrase 'I feed on flatness' – and the rapid decline thereafter in Empson's output, it is not surprising to find that his record-notes (1959) call 'Let it go' a poem 'about stopping writing poetry'. Given also the nature of so much of Empson's poetry, which attempts to wrestle with the conflicts, anomalies and 'contradictions' of life, it is possible to reconcile with Empson's description the view of critics like G.S. Fraser, who see the poem as about the mind's escape

THE POEMS OF WILLIAM EMPSON

from madness ('madhouse' as lunatic asylum) by means of a
protective 'deep blankness'. Blankness figures in 'Aubade'
and in 'Ignorance of Death'; in the former as soothing sleep,
in the latter as sensible refusal to speculate about the unknown. Here it may plausibly be taken as both the in-
explicable resignation of the creative powers *per se*, and as a
necessary defence against the increase in tension brought
about by the war.

The first stanza, though simpler than the second, is very
closely knit, lines 2-3 not only explaining the nature of the
'deep blankness' in line 1 but also accounting for the peculiar
emphasis which that blankness is given by Empson's characteristic 'it is. . .' construction and by the inversion and heavy
stresses of 'real thing strange'. More and more things happen
to one; these things, it is implied, are strange; but what is
really strange is one's failure to respond to them – indeed,
the greater the pressure of events, the greater the lack of
response, a surprising situation for an intellectual poet. Instead, there is a 'deep blankness' – virtually an amnesia –
which prevents him from even remembering, let alone
'telling' (deciding, distinguishing, relating in words), what
they were.

The three laconic, end-stopped lines of stanza two, however appropriate stylistically to stanza one's state of mind,
are teasing in themselves, in their interconnections, and in
their relationship to stanza one. It is hard to be sure whether
the wide-ranging 'contradictions' of line 4 stem from the
basic anomaly of 'blank' mind and things happening, or
whether they represent the stock-in-trade of Empson's
earlier poetry (as summed up, for instance, in his note to
'Bacchus'), which his present 'blankness' does not deal with.
Similarly, the 'would' of line 5 may indicate the futility of
trying to comment further on this situation, or (as 'used to')
imply that the former intellectual poetry, which thought itself useful, was in fact no more than 'talk', and way off the
mark.

The two possible viewpoints (stanza 2 as comment on
and/or contrast with stanza 1) are perhaps pulled together in
the final line, by means of the word 'madhouse'. This, while
seriously suggesting 'madness', has in its slang sense the virtue

220

of connecting up 'contradictions' (opposite views, conflict, people *talking against* each other) with 'The talk would talk' – noise for its own sake. To discuss the conflicting implications of anything, especially a situation such as that of stanza 1 which is too 'deep' for analysis, would lead to a 'madhouse' – a mad babble solving nothing. And if 'there' means anything, it is surely the state of 'blankness' itself: in it, one willingly lets the confusion of events fade away, and the poetry which once seemed a means of coping with it. 'The whole thing', to judge from a passage in *Milton's God*, is life in all its co-existent contradictoriness: 'Recent studies have made it clear that Blake meant the whole thing by such utterances [saying that 'Milton. . .was of the Devil's party without knowing it'], not merely that Milton's Satan was good but that his God was bad'. (pp. 17-18). Life's complexities are more than poetry can solve; if the deep well dries up, one can thus 'let it go' without regret, though with a degree of wonder at the strange passivity that succeeds it.

THANKS FOR A WEDDING PRESENT

First published in *Collected Poems* (U.S.A., 1949).

Empson married in 1941, so this thank-you poem is unlikely to date from much later. The verses on which it comments are neatly turned: their light Augustan pastiche manages to incorporate topicality (the 'dark nights' of the blackout), allusion to the unsteadying consolations of the pub ('the uncharted track' home from 'the *Load of Hay*'), and Empsonian science ('de-Gauss', meaning 'insulate from unwanted and dangerous magnetic fields'). Empson's elegant reply, its stately sentences syncopated across the stanza division, does rather more than return wit for wit (the *Load of Hay* becomes a haystack in which the compass 'needle' gets lost); it carries a hint of reproof – 'bears' can mean 'tolerates' – in its reminder that there is more to life than journeys between home and pub.

Choosing to misinterpret 'With me drink deep', Empson contrasts that short journey, which is all the 'poor needle. . . needs heart to learn' (its 'heart' being its magnetic power and the bravery it gains from drink's 'fuel') with the 'longer journeys' — man's adventures and tribulations of mind and spirit — which require greater sense of direction, and more courage, than a compass needs or can provide. Such journeys (Hetta Empson had already, in 1938, undertaken the long journey from home in South Africa to England) she is equal to and 'safe to return from'; like Empson's mother in 'To an Old Lady', she too, metaphorically, 'reads a compass certain of her pole.'

Line 4, whose construction parallels that of line 1, makes explicit the way in which she, being such a person, 'bears your gift': not needing it as help, she accepts it as adornment, a 'jewel' and a 'flower', compass 'rose' not compass. Both thanks to the giver and a greater compliment to the wearer are conveyed by the splendid terms in which magnet and compass are described: the lodestone, used from ancient times in navigation and in alchemy, could be said to have given rise to modern physics and to all the far-flung 'maritime empires'. This warm conclusion has the grandeur of a metaphysical conceit: the 'compass on a necklace' is worn by someone who in her own right is so much more wonderful than anything in the scope of human achievement which it represents.

SONNET

First published in *The War Poets,* ed. Oscar Williams (New York, The John Day Co., 1945), p. 337.

Although it first appeared in an anthology of 'War Poetry of the 20th Century', Empson's last original poem seems not to be about war but about the 'dismaying' prospect of machine-like uniformity in the post-war world, against which Empson sets 'a more heartening fact': the stubborn endurance of human diversity. Such a reading of the poem is supported by the evident contrast, in the octave and in the sestet, between 'one' and 'all'; and by the contrasting connotations of, on the one hand, 'organising', 'machine' and 'nations' (one recalls the slightly pejorative tone of this word in 'Manchouli), and, on the other, 'circus', 'earth' and 'man'. Lines 1-4, however, dense and impressive in sound but open in syntax and lacking in punctuation, may cause some momentary confusion.

The splendidly Johnsonian opening line – sombre, restrained, magisterial – has such an air of self-sufficiency that one does not immediately notice that its feeling (of being 'Not wrongly moved') is unattributed and that no main verb follows it. It is possible to take 'the thinkers' as its subject and 'joined' as its verb, but the aspect of tense suggested by '*this* dismaying scene' and a growing sense of the poem's drift effectively rule out this possibility. The thinkers do not react to the scene; they cause it. It is Empson who is 'Not wrongly moved', and the meaning of line 1 is clearly seen if one supplies the tacit 'I am' at the beginning and a colon at the end. The remaining three lines describe the 'dismaying scene': one in which not only the Allied 'nations' (a group mentality) but their intellectuals, instead of continuing to fight the destructive totalitarianism of the Fascist 'machine', get caught up in the wish to impose their own mechanical rigidities instead. Empson's judicial phrasing of his reaction leaves it too non-committal: 'not wrongly moved' may mean only that he thinks it right to be moved rather than indifferent; or that he is moved in the right way (anger? dismay? dignified disapproval?) rather than in the wrong one (enthusiasm? despair?).

A sharper sarcastic edge is felt in the colloquialism to which Empson turns in lines 5-8 as an aid to defining the 'brave new world' of post-war reconstruction. 'The thinkers' are now 'these hopers' (cf. the 'hopeful chaps' in stanza 16 of 'Autumn on Nan-Yueh') who feel sure that they can 'swing' whatever they want. The 'loony hooters' are not, now, demagogues like Hitler and Mussolini (hooter as siren); they have been defeated. Instead, they are any of their own people – including derisive, mad poets – who disagree with their so sensible plans. Such opponents, mere 'loonies' on an earth shrunk by 'improved' communications, can be bought off. That done, the reformers can get on with their task of bringing earth's masses back to a way of life which is 'kind and clean' — simple and uncomplicated perhaps, but utterly dull for those leading it and offering no challenge to those in control. What Empson has in mind, no doubt, is the societies envisaged alike by Communist theoreticians, Welfare State Socialism, and consumer Capitalism, all postulating an unquestioning acceptance of values dictated, however benevolently, from above.

If men are capable of such 'dismaying' Utopias they are also, however, capable of resisting them. The froth of change may ruffle the surface of life, but deeper down (only 'three fathoms' in the original version) 'the sea/Is always calm'. The 'cultures of man' (not organisations of machines) may really appal the planners, but for Empson their 'stubbornness' is only colloquially 'appalling' – a 'heartening' and admirable sign of sanity. The jump from 'calm' sea to 'riotous' circus is metaphorically abrupt, yet both images only celebrate aspects of the same thing – the depth and diversity (lawless and joyous) of real human life, an 'open' not a closed society. 'Booths' means all the sideshows of the 'gigantic' circus, but suggests polling booths and thus what people (as distinct from 'thinkers' and 'nations') really want. Against this, the 'pygmy plan' has little to offer: its collective 'tune' (demonstrated in the travel film referred to by Empson's note) may sound as 'free' as an improvisation, but those singing it contribute only 'one note each' – like soldiers 'numbering from the left' in the army. Empson's juxtaposition of the two kinds of life, in octave and sestet and in his two final sentences, leaves the actual shape of the future to make itself known, yet states clearly enough his own enjoyment of the 'anthropological circus'. He repeated it in *Milton's God* (p. 276), when describing a visit ten years or so later to a Sheffield museum: depressed by 'a sheer hall containing nothing but Sheffield plate', his spirits were 'raised. . .no end' by the contrasting spectacle of 'two huge ivory tusks, carved all over for the appalling and splendid court of Benin'. For him the reaction demonstrated the human need to feel that 'whatever we do with our own small lives, the rest of the world is still going on and exercising the variety of its forces'.

SELECTED BIBLIOGRAPHY

1. Poetry by William Empson (excluding poems in magazines)

Songs for Sixpence, No. 1. ed. J. Bronowski and J. Reeves. Cambridge, Heffer's, 1929.

(*Songs for Sixpence* was a series of six separately-printed poems, in cardboard covers. No. 1 was 'Letter IV'.)

Cambridge Poetry, 1929 ed. Christopher Saltmarshe, John Davenport and Basil Wright. London, The Hogarth Press, 1929.

(This was No. 8 in the *Hogarth Living Poets* series. It reprinted six poems by Empson: 'Part of Mandevil's Travels', 'To an Old Lady', 'Villanelle', 'Letter' [later entitled 'Letter II'], 'Legal Fiction', 'Arachne'.)

New Signatures: Poems by Several Hands. Collected by Michael Roberts. London, The Hogarth Press, 1932.

(This was No. 24 in the *Hogarth Living Poets* series. It reprinted five poems by Empson: 'Letter' [the first three stanzas of 'Letter I'], 'Poem' [later entitled 'The Scales'], 'Note on Local Flora', 'Camping Out', 'Invitation to Juno'; together with 'This Last Pain' [minus the present stanza 5].)

Poems. Printed for private circulation by The Fox & Daffodil Press, Tokyo, 1934.

(Contains the six poems printed in *Cambridge Poetry, 1929*; the six poems printed in *New Signatures*; together with 'Homage to the British Museum' and 'Bacchus' [the first 17 lines].)

Poems. London, Chatto and Windus, 1935.

The Gathering Storm. London, Faber & Faber, 1940.

Collected Poems. New York, Harcourt, Brace, 1949.

Collected Poems. London, Chatto & Windus, 1955. Reprinted 1956, 1962, 1969, 1977.

2. Studies/comments on Empson's poetry

A. Alvarez: *The Shaping Spirit.* Chatto & Windus, 1958, pp. 73–86.

Alan Brownjohn: Review of *Collected Poems. Departure* (Oxford), Vol. 3, No. 9 (Spring 1956), pp. 20–21.

Hilary Corke: Review of *Collected Poems, The Listener* (6 Oct. 1955), p. 565.

John Danby: 'William Empson'. *Critical Quarterly*, Vol. 1, No. 2 (Summer 1959), pp. 99–104.

Denis Donoghue: 'Reading a Poem: Empson's 'Arachne'.' *Studies* XLV (Summer 1956), pp. 219–26.

Elizabeth Drew: *Poetry: A Modern Guide to its Understanding and Enjoyment.* Dell Books, 1959, pp. 139–40. (On 'Missing Dates'.)

Lawrence Durrell: *A Key to Modern Poetry.* University of Oklahoma Press, 1952.

Richard Eberhart: 'Empson's Poetry'. *Accent* IV (Summer 1944). Reprinted in *Accent Anthology,* ed. Quinn and Shattuck. New York, Harcourt, Brace, 1946.

William Empson: Notes printed in *Poems* (1935), *The Gathering Storm* (1940), *Collected Poems* (1955); 'Mr. Empson and the Fire Sermon'. *Essays in Criticism,* Vol. 6, No. 4 (Oct. 1956), pp. 481–82; Note on 'Bacchus', as reprinted in *Poet's Choice,* ed. Paul Engle and Joseph Langland. New York, Dial Press, 1962, pp. 85–86; Sleeve notes for record of *Selected Poems* (The Marvell Press).

Colin Falck: 'William Empson'. *The Modern Poet: Essays from The Review,* ed. Ian Hamilton. MacDonald, 1968, pp. 50–63.

G.S. Fraser: 'On the Interpretation of the Difficult Poem'. *Interpretations,* ed. John Wain. Routledge & Kegan Paul, 1955. (Second Edition, 1972, pp. 225–34.) (On 'The Teasers'.) *Vision and Rhetoric.* Faber & Faber, 1959, pp. 193–201.

THE POEMS OF WILLIAM EMPSON

John Fuller: 'An Edifice of Meaning'. *Encounter* (Nov. 1974), pp. 75-79.

Philip Gardner: '"Meaning" in the Poetry of William Empson'. *Humanities Association Bulletin* (Canada), XVIII, No. 1. (Spring 1967), pp. 75-86. (Includes an analysis of 'Part of Mandevil's Travels'.)

Roma Gill (ed.): *William Empson: The Man and His Work*. Routledge & Kegan Paul, 1974.

Thom Gunn: Review of *Collected Poems*. *The London Magazine* III, No. 2 (Feb. 1956), pp. 70-75.

Ian Hamilton: 'William Empson'. *A Poetry Chronicle*. Faber 1973, pp. 37-44. (Reprinted from *The Review*, 1963.)

William L. Hedges: 'The Empson Treatment'. *Accent* XVII (Winter 1957), pp. 231-41. (On 'Four Legs, Three Legs, Two Legs'.)

Philip Hobsbaum: Review of *Collected Poems*. Delta (Cambridge), No. 8 (Spring 1956), pp. 31-37.

Hugh Kenner: 'The Son of Spiders'. Review of *Collected Poems* (1949). *Poetry* (Chicago), LXXVI (June 1950), pp. 150-55.

F.R. Leavis: Review of *Cambridge Poetry, 1929*. *Cambridge Review* (1 March 1929); *New Bearings in English Poetry*. Chatto & Windus, 1932.

L.M. (Louis MacNeice?): Review of *Poems* (1935). *New Verse* No. 16 (Aug.-Sept. 1935), pp. 17-18.

H.A. Mason: 'William Empson's Verse'. Review of *Poems* (1935). *Scrutiny* IV, No. 3 (Dec. 1935), pp. 302-04.

W.H. Mellers: 'Cats in Air-Pumps'. *Scrutiny* IX, No. 3 (Dec. 1940), pp. 289-300. (Includes a review of *The Gathering Storm*.)

Angelo Morelli: *La Poesia di William Empson*. Niccolò Giannotta, Catania, 1959.

David Ormerod: 'Empson's "Invitation to Juno"'. *The Explicator* XXV, No. 2 (Oct. 1966), item 13.

The Review Nos. 6 & 7 (June 1963). Special number: William Empson. (See especially Martin Dodsworth, 'Empson at Cambridge', pp. 3-13; Saul Touster, 'Empson's Legal Fiction', pp. 45-48; 'William Empson in Conversation with Christopher Ricks', pp. 26-35.)

I.A. Richards: 'The Poetry of William Empson'. Review of *Poems* (1935), *Cambridge Review*, 14 Feb. 1936; *How to Read a Page*. Kegan Paul, Trench, Trubner & Co., 1943, pp. 79-81. (On 'Courage Means Running'.); *Poetries and Sciences* (New York, 1970). (This revised version of *Science and Poetry* (1926) contains a note, pp. 115-17, on 'Legal Fiction'.)

Christopher Ricks: 'Empson's Poetry'. *William Empson: The Man and His Work,* ed. Roma Gill. Routledge & Kegan Paul, 1974, pp. 145-207.

A.E. Rodway: Review of *Collected Poems*. *Essays in Criticism* VI, No. 2 (1956) pp. 232-40.

Geoffrey Thurley: 'Partial Fires: Empson's Poetry'. Ch. 3 of *The Ironic Harvest: English Poetry in the Twentieth Century*. Edward Arnold, 1974, pp. 38-53.

Anthony Thwaite: *Essays on Contemporary British Poetry*. Tokyo, Kenkyusha, 1957, pp. 147-51.

William Troy: Review of *Collected Poems* (1949). *Poetry* (Chicago), July 1949, pp. 234-36.

John Wain: 'Ambiguous Gifts'. *Penguin New Writing*, No. 40 (1950), pp. 118-28; 'The Poetic Mind of William Empson'. *Lugano Review* (Autumn, 1976), pp. 95-118.

John Howard Willis, Jr. *William Empson*. (Columbia Essays on Modern Writers, No. 39), Columbia University Press, 1969.